EMANCIPATING SPACE

Geography, Architecture, and Urban Design

ROSS KING

THE GUILFORD PRESS
New York   London

© 1996 The Guilford Press
A Division of Guilford Publications, Inc.
72 Spring Street, New York, NY 10012
Marketed and distributed outside North America by Longman Group Limited.

Printed in the United States of America

This book is printed on acid-free paper.

Last digit is print number: 9 8 7 6 5 4 3 2 1

Library of Congress Cataloging-in-Publication Data

King, Ross.
    Emancipating space : geography, architecture, and urban design /
Ross King.
        p.   cm.—(Mappings)
    Includes bibliographical references and index.
    ISBN 1-57230-045-0 (hc.)—ISBN 1-57230-046-9 (pbk.)
    1. Architecture—Environmental aspects.   2. Human geography.
I. Title. II. Series.
NA2542.35.K56 1996
720'.47—dc20   95-51109
                                                                        CIP

For Julie, Clare, Brigid, and Louisa

Preface

Speech is the medium in which we commonly seek to represent our experience and dreams of time. To capture those moments of intensest memory and thereby hope—to escape from the prison of multifarious social languages—we seize poetry and music, returning to speech's metaphoric and affective origins. Architecture, the built world and the constructions each of us would place upon it, equally clearly would seem to be the medium in which we represent experiences of space, and hopes of a better space in which our lives might soar and, in time, erode. This is an abstraction, no doubt; for we also experience time through the medium of architecture (visit Chartres!); and space is also represented in the languages of speech (James Joyce on Dublin!). But the generalization, in the main, holds. The *lingua franca* of architecture is also our prison—the "architecture as prison" of both Georges Bataille and Michel Foucault: the monuments that are our masters, the celebrations of possession ("the commodity as Hell"), suburbia (the world of self-surveillance, and conformity as virtue). It is from space that we strive to break our chains and to fly; and architecture for its part, in its too-rare moments of poetry and music, has sought to rise above the *lingua franca* and to offer visions, however incomplete, of an emancipatory space where we might redeem both the promise of the past (unrealized, half-remembered dreams of a reconciled world) *and* Walter Benjamin's "new nature"—the now-possible relations to each other and to the external world. We are variously presented with visions of a space of the rule of reason (emancipation from superstition, "enchantment," the arbitrary), spaces of power (oppressions vanquished—or is it replaced?), of the commodity (the cornucopia of modernity, equality at last—but at what a price!), spaces of revolution, of the erosion of delusions and self-repression, space that unmasks space itself and its chains and our assumptions about it, deconstructive space, heterogeneous space, the space of reenchantment (of reimmersion in the natural world and its magic). . . .

If our experience of space is the proper study of human geography, it must seem mildly risible that the geographers choose the language of speech, in its most abstracted, metaphoric voice, as the medium of their inquiry. The affective voice (musical, of the emotions and dreams—Jacques Derrida's "originary melody") only occasionally flashes through; and the languages of space itself (as against those of time), whether of the prison or of the dream, are in the main left unengaged. If, to go further, we are to see the focus of *critical* geography as the place of space in the endeavor of human emancipation—freedom, fulfillment—then the neglect of the emancipatory voices, of the billowing poetry as of the dreamed-of architecture for a better world, must seem extraordinary. The intersections of these ways of representing space—the geographical and the architectural and, crosscutting each, the obfuscating and the emancipatory—constitute the focus of the present book. The concern is with the interplay of languages and of texts—to break open the constricted discourses of the geographers and critical social theorists, *and* of the architects and urban designers.

Much of the text that follows will be words and phrases torn from other (con)texts, evoking images and ideas special to each reader. No one reading, of this as of any other text, can ever be privileged over any other. Already the words above, to account for the emancipatory endeavor—dreams, new nature, redemption, power, revolution, the commodity, erosion and reenchantment, architecture and language—have themselves this "freedom" of instability and the ambiguous. It is this transparency of words that enables any translation, from language to language or from one context to another, to preside over the birth of new language—new worlds. "For if the sentence is the wall before the language of the original, literalness is the arcade," writes Walter Benjamin. There is however one border at which both wall and arcade must be negotiated—the argument (context) as much as the intonation of voice and value (text) will be inescapable as we face that labyrinth where the languages of both speech and space constitute the prison of gender and its segmentation of the human.

For here one cannot just present narratives, quotations, and aphorisms (all writing is aphoristic, declared Derrida!), but instead go for the metanarrative. It would seem that everywhere the male construction of space has become *the* construction of space; that there is no feminine urban space, or architecture; and that the social production of this state of affairs is scarcely reflected upon. There is, in fairness, a "feminist geography" (for want of a better name) that attempts to understand women's entrapment in the city; and there is a movement which concerns itself with women's place in the professions of architecture and urban planning. But the intersections of voices—the male and the female, the geographical imagination and the architectural, rational explication of the world (the metanarratives) and the poetic evocations of the dream of emancipation and redemption—are unexplored. This is the unemphasized subplot that runs through the present, otherwise intentionally fragmented perspective on the place of space in the emancipatory project.

The book is intended for students of the disciplines under attack— geography, social theory, urban planning and urban design, and architecture. If, to its readers, it seems initially simple and inconsequential, then ask why architecture and urban design still enslave, and why we still fail to question; if it seems obtuse, and incomprehensible, then its argument is proven.

Acknowledgments

... most especially to my editors, Michael Dear and Peter Wissoker; to Ted Relph, Nigel Thrift, and Derek Gregory for critiques and comments during the course of the project; to various colleagues at the University of Melbourne for patient ears and encouraging voices, most notably Laurie Cosgrove, Brian Nettleton, and the late Brian McLoughlin; to Matt Spinaze and Clare King for help with illustrations; and to Alison Temperley for endless patience with word processing of numerous drafts.

Contents

CHAPTER 1

Introduction: The Design of the City, the Progress of Modernity, and the Crisis of Postmodernity

This said, it is pointless trying to decide whether Zenobia is to be classified among happy cities or among the unhappy. It makes no sense to divide cities into these two species, but rather into another two: those that through the years and changes continue to give their forms to desires, and those in which desires either erase the city or are erased by it.

—Italo Calvino, *Invisible Cities* (1979)

In the advanced, capitalist societies of the so-called West, the promise of human perfectibility and fulfillment through material progress, that sustaining myth of the past four centuries, seems now revealed as supreme delusion. The idea of the welfare state and the cozy cohabitation of big business, big unions, and big government (infelicitously dubbed Fordism) appears in retrospect a bureaucratic nightmare; the deliverances promised by Thatcher and Reagan failed, emancipating only the entrepreneurs and paper-shuffling sharks in yet another round of violence on labor and on each other; and the god of material progress has long since descended into the fetishism of mere commodities. As if this were not enough, we now have the further fetishism of the media and images alone; we are in a world of unending communication without messages. The myth has lost its motivating magic. Meanwhile the loss of faith in the promise of communism in Eastern Europe, the erstwhile Soviet empire, China, and their once aspiring clones, has been even more dramatic: As the better world envisioned in the Russian Revolution and those that followed it is shown to have come to less than nothing, destroyed by the contradictions seemingly embedded in all human behavior, its onetime protagonists turn toward capitalist "market economics" at precisely the moment of capitalism's own seemingly immanent collapse, undermined by those same contradictions. With the promise of a material paradise as presented in both capitalism and socialism revealed to be chimerical, many people are turning (back, or is it forward?) to spiritual values and to a wider understanding of the human condition and experience. Nowhere is this stronger than in the Islamic world. Elsewhere they turn to the Nation, or the *volk*, or to other older ideas.

The problem of the times is the problem of human motivation.[1] What are we to make of ourselves? For more than a thousand years until around the sixteenth century, in the world centered on the Mediterranean, human perfectibility was thought to be attainable only in the next life, and the meaning of this life was in the preparation for the next. But throughout the Middle Ages there was that rising skepticism: How can the promise of another world justify my acceptance of oppression, violence, humiliation, suffering, and ignorance in the *present*? From that crisis of faith and of human motivation sprang "the project of the Enlightenment"—to secure perfection and fulfillment in the present life as well as in the next (or, in some minds, *instead of* in the next). The new motivating myth came to be that of *human reason*: the new age, the Modern Age; and the new idea, Modernity. The Enlightenment project became the project of modernity, rational science was mobilized as technology, and the rational ordering of social interaction as the efficient and bureaucratically regulated organization of social life. But modern technology has, in many eyes, all but wrecked the planet, and we face the greenhouse effect, ozone depletion, rain forest destruction, soil degradation, and mountains of nuclear and toxic waste defying all ingenuity. And modern bureaucratic organization and the liberal–democratic state seem merely to support and perpetuate inequities across space (my resource use is only possible because that of another is so much less), across time (how, finally, can we tolerate a world where the resource depletion of this generation beggars all those to follow?), and within the institutional structure of society (to the disadvantage of women and of all those able to be labeled as "others"— ethnic minorities, the handicapped, the unsmart).

The profound disruption that marked the end of the feudal age in Europe and the coming of the Enlightenment, on the one hand, and that arguably comparable disruption of the present, on the other, are to be seen as shifts in the way that people experience and understand time, space, nature, and themselves. Architecture and urban design, like other forms of artistic production, have been actively mobilized to represent the trauma, maelstrom, and excitement of these forms of shift in human experience. So the secular time of material progress, we shall see in the following chapters, was actively represented in the rapid successions of styles, institutions, and investment cycles of the modern city, in such marked contrast to the expression of eternal time in the medieval city.

Today, in yet further contrast, the representations of time are much more ambiguous and circumspect—not that palpable, unequivocal expression of progress of, say, the 1960s "Western" city. The same is true of the representation of new experiences of space: from the space of material defense but heavenly aspiration of the feudal world, to the expression of universal reason, to an international politics and global economy in modernity, but now the uncertain turning—inward!—not only to a national politics and local culture and its representation in fragmentation and "local place" but also to the self as isolated.

The new experience of nature as controllable, that came with the Scientific Revolution, found expression successively in baroque vistas, ordered parks, the highway grid, and nature subjugated as resources; the skepticism of the present has (a few!) architects and landscape designers seeking ways of representing ecological interdependence, sustainability, and a new consciousness of the natural world.

Finally, there are those shifts in the understanding of the self and of "difference." Michel Foucault, Anthony Vidler, and others have shown us how the Age of Reason had to confront the new problem of its own antithesis—unreason—the criminal, the insane, the handicapped, and others judged "different," and how the City of Reason had to represent, not just the appropriate realm of the new and enlightened self, but also the institutions for the control of unreason and the irrational. Today, the problem is how to represent not only a new tolerance of difference and diversity but also a skepticism toward "agreed" norms and to deconstruct the cult and expression of the "Great Man" in human progress—and of the "great man" in the unsafe home, in the unsafe street, and in the economic and political relations of society itself.

The proper study of architecture and urban design is the way in which these shifts in the experience of time, space, nature, and ourselves are represented. But it is also more than that. For architecture and urban design, far more than the other areas of artistic production, are intimately and inextricably involved in the human emancipatory endeavor—the search for a space of everyday life that is liberating and capable of motivating us to human fulfillment and the attainment of our real potential; they are equally involved in the repression of that endeavor, and both the pursuit and the repression are central to that proper study.

Yet a further claim must be made here. For it is the "self-clarification of the struggles and wishes of the age" that is the focus of critical social theory, as Marx has insisted. And, I would add, the question of space as the expression of wishes and as the medium of power in those struggles is the proper focus of a critical social geography. Hence, the cultural, purposive production of space and of the motivating (and demotivating) meanings that it conveys are central to critical social theory and a critical geography; and that production arises most notably in architecture and urban design.

What follows is a history to tease out these intermingled stories of *the representation of the experience of the times*, in architecture and urban design, and *the spatial expression of the emancipatory endeavor in the context of that experience*. The aim is to establish the ground on which the proper study of architecture and urban design can be built, and on which critical social theory and critical geography can be reconstructed to address the question of the cultural production of space and of its meaning, and its role in both human emancipation and repression. This intention may well be objected to as arrogance, implying, as it does, dismissal of previous traditions in these disciplines. The present stories and arguments do, however, build on those traditions; and I need at the outset to indicate my main debts—some of the voices that "ventriloquate through the present text," as Mikhail Bakhtin would have it—as well as some of my differences with various "mainstreams."

| ANTECEDENT ACCOUNTS

There is a tradition of what might be called "philosophy of postmodernism," from Heidegger of half a century and more ago, to Derrida, Lyotard, Vattimo, Baudrillard, and others of the present. From this tradition one can derive a variety of accounts of the experience of the times, to link the idea of loss of faith in human fulfillment (emancipation) through modernist material progress and universalism, on the one hand, to the ephemerality—even immateriality—of a world where the media image supplants the message and where life is reduced to mere appearances and the city, in Baudrillard's analysis, to mere spectacle, on the other. Thus, Gianni Vattimo explores the seeming dissolution of the nineteenth-century conception of history as a single unitary process. With the speeding up of technological change, ever-newer products, and the continual replacement of commodities as a "necessary" condition for survival of the system, we find that "novelty has nothing 'revolutionary' or striking about it, it merely permits things to go on in the same way" (Vattimo, 1985, p. 15). Similarly, new technology for the collecting, transmitting, and global diffusion of information vastly expands the locations where a picture (history) of human activity can be constructed. At the same time, the multiplicity of images of such activity, at the very moment of its occurrence, shifts attention from a past-to-present linear progression to a multifaceted, ever-changing, ungeneralizable present. The effect of these processes is a "dehistoricizing of experience." So the new era is characterized by the experience of the "end of history"—a new experience of time itself (Vattimo, 1985).

What occurs as experience is paralleled in the development—or, more appropriately, the "deconstruction"—of theory. Vattimo argues that, with modernity, the idea of progress moved away from its Christian roots in "salvation" and became increasingly secularized, meaning little more than the unending creation of new opportunities for material development and serving history's winners rather than the losers. Ultimately, the idea of infinite progress is vacuous, undermined by its own logic. Any account of history is essentially a story—a *narrative*. But for that to be related to an idea of progress, there needs to be an overarching *metanarrative* about the progressive unfolding of some fundamental subject—salvation, Reason, universal prosperity, the workers' paradise, etc. Once the metanarratives are revealed as empty, and ultimately arbitrary, we are left with the narratives that reflect the position of the narrator rather than metaphysical ideas or else that reflect the positions of those dominant groups whose interests prosper with such progress. Thus we get Jean-François Lyotard's (1984) argument: Once the search for metanarratives is abandoned—and we have achieved the "end of philosophy" as well as the "end of history"—then a genuine heterogeneity of discourse can prevail, and we can achieve ease in the presence of otherness and difference.[2]

Certainly, it is something of this shift in the experience of the times that is represented in much of the cultural production of the present—in architecture and the design of the city, as in music, cinema, the graphic arts, theater, literature. A single example will suffice.

Le Corbusier's *Ville contemporaine* of 1922, a city for three million people, remains one of the icons of modernity, a vision of a postbourgeois world freed from the baggage of the past, universally applicable, and forcing the dream of technological efficiency and progress to some logically conclusive apotheosis. It is also totalizing and nightmarish—how could you be a dissenting minority in a world like that! More recent representations of an ideal space of (post)modern life, in architecture and urban design, tend to be vastly different and vastly more diverse: fragmented, incremental rather than draconian; sometimes attempting references to local and vernacular culture rather than to universal themes, seeking heterogeneity and "difference" rather than universality and thereby signifying a tolerant more than a totalizing vision of society; often incorporating historical references randomly and even chaotically, as if to deny the idea of historical sequence and a linear experience of time.

These representations have the value of illuminating for us something of the variety of the experiences of space, time, and the self (otherness, difference) and of shifts in those experiences; they are windows to the study of society and space. But there is another dimension. Michel Foucault, in focusing on the microspaces of power, incarceration, and repression, has compelled us to "deconstruct" the links between institutions, space, language, and self-delusion. Aspects of this enterprise are translated into architectural analysis, specifically of late Enlightenment design, in the writing of Anthony Vidler (1987). Far more significantly, deconstruction in the hands of Jacques Derrida becomes a method for the pulling apart—laying bare—of all forms of text, including all of architecture, spatial programs, and the city itself. Various architects and urban designers expressly take up this method, to pull apart the conventional images and spaces of modernity and to reassemble them in ways that challenge our sustaining assumptions (myths!) about how things should seem and about how society should work. The method is emancipatory, at least in its intent—it tries to free us from self-delusion and to expand the ways in which space can be socially constructed. The attempts and their failure are, again, windows to a critical study of society and space in the present era.

Although insights from this "philosophy of postmodernism" run through every aspect of this book, the judgment is that these accounts remain unsatisfactory. Their failure is in what they generally omit: a further linking of these shifts in the experience of space and time to shifts in human political and economic behavior and to the new experience of nature that is represented in the environmental movement, the debates on sustainability and ecological responsibility, and the question of fair shares of resources. The first omission is supplied in part in various writings of Edward Soja and David Harvey, among others. Soja's *Postmodern Geographies* (1989) is motivated by an insistence on reintegrating *space* into a social theory that has become preoccupied with the exploration of history (time). There are two main keys to this enterprise. The first is Foucault's notion of the spatialization of power—the deconstruction of language and institutions, largely through a *historical* analysis, to lay bare the linkages between space, knowledge, and power. He quotes Berger's extraordinary provocation that "it is space not time that hides consequences from us" (p. 22). The second is Henri Lefebvre's spatialization of Marx's *historical* materialism, to yield a Marxist critique of the phenomenon whereby power in the present age seems increasingly mediated through space rather than class. The Industrial Revolution seems paralleled today in an "Urban Revolution."

This reassertion of the explanatory power of a Marxist critique also informs the work of David Harvey. In *The Condition of Postmodernity* (1989), he takes up that preoccupation of Vattimo, Rorty, Lyotard, and others with shifts in the ways in which space and time have been experienced since the Enlightenment (the contraction of space and the speeding up of time through new technologies of communication); these he links to the long evolution stretching from the Commercial Revolution and early mercantile capitalism, to the Scientific and Industrial Revolutions, to that so-called Fordist consensus between big government, big corporations, and big labor that has marked the greater part of the twentieth century, then to the collapse of the consensus and its apparent replacement by more "flexible" ways of organizing the creation and appropriation of wealth. Ephemerality in the representation of wealth (credit cards, junk bonds, funny money, the commodification of images) parallels ephemerality in cultural production. Each reinforces the other.

Harvey's argument goes further than this perceptive linking, however. For the whole progress of modernity has been characterized by a tension, a wavering to and fro, between the fleeting and the ephemeral, on one hand, and the eternal and immutable, on the other. In cultural production as in philosophy there has been that restless darting for the brilliant insight or novel provocation, yet simultaneously an attempt to deal with fragmentation and chaos—to make sense of it all. Similarly, innovation and constant change have characterized all economic success—capitalism, asserts Harvey, is essentially *revolutionary*. Thus postmodernity has been immanent in modernity from the start. This is not an especially original insight. Jean-François Lyotard (1984), for example, also asserts that postmodernity is unquestionably part of the modern, but it seems to lead Harvey into something of a denial of any real change in the experience of time, space, nature, and the self—and hence of new ways to analysis and action. In his central project—linking specific aspects of that experience of the age to economic and political change, via a Marxist critique—Harvey's success is considerable. Yet ultimately his account of the times sits uneasily alongside the insights of Foucault, Derrida, Lyotard, Rorty, and their ilk—insights that Harvey simply explains away or else dismisses out of hand.

Much of what follows owes some debt to Harvey's project, though his work, like that of the postmodernists, also ultimately falls through its omissions. Most notable of these omissions is an almost extraordinary inattention to the environmental question, either as the empirically observable effect of the evolution that he describes or as the context that accounts in large part for the apparent collapse of the project of modernity and for the contemporary disorientation and "experience of postmodernity." (This is also an omission from Soja's work.) Second, and of a kind with Harvey's unease over the postmodernist heterogeneity, is an inattention to "differences" and the "experiences of others" that so much preoccupy the postmodernist philosophers—despite Harvey's protestations to the contrary. Simply, one's experience of space, time, nature, and self will be different with levels of repression or liberation in family, work, education, religion, and the like, but Harvey writes as if this is unitary. (We will especially draw on critiques of these arguments by Deutsche, 1991, and Massey, 1991.) Third, and probably because of this inadequacy in addressing the various dimensions of the experience of the times—the experience of others, of nature, and of the self, as well as of space and time—Harvey is unable to specify where we are headed as a society or what we can do to facilitate the passage. There is some vague suggestion of a rekindling of the Enlightenment project (human reason was a good idea, but it somehow got suborned by aberrations like capitalism, global conflict, the nuclear arms race, and the Holocaust, so let's have another try!); but we are not shown how, in an age of fragmentation and plurality, this might be pursued. There is no convincing theory of action.

Clues to understanding how scientific and economic "progress" is linked to transformations in the experience of nature are developed in the writings of Morris Berman. Notably, in *The Reenchantment of the World* (1984) there is an account of the uneven and chaotic shift from an experience of oneness with nature, where observable phenomena and our attitudes toward them were inseparable, to a distancing of ourselves from nature that culminated in the Scientific Revolution and the "disenchantment" of the Enlightenment, to the idea of nature as a limitless resource to enable material progress, and to the collapse of that delusion in the present day.[3] Earlier, the central ideas of Berman's argument are found in the work of Gregory Bateson. The key to human history is understanding the processes of human learning.[4] Just as the Scientific Revolution involved an entirely new, *learned* experience of nature (only achievable, furthermore, through a *learned* suppression of that older, immersed experience), so a new "ecological revolution" of the present time will only come about through a further fundamental shift in the way we see ourselves and the world—that is, through new learning. Fundamental change involves "paradigm shifts"—shifts in "worldviews."

This insight immediately opens up the whole question of action in effecting a new understanding of oneself and of the world. We *can* take some command of human evolution. The most sophisticated development of this theme is presently to be found in the writings of Jürgen Habermas, and it is to those writings that I must acknowledge my greatest debt for the various lines of argument in the pages that follow. New learning must embrace a new experience and understanding of nature and our place in it, as Berman insists; from Habermas there is the insistence that new learning must also address the very nature of human interaction and argumentation. The shift to a sustainable, ecologically restorative way of life in city and countryside, guaranteeing fair shares of resources and opportunities across space and time, will involve the bitterest struggles over material interests, and thereby over questions of empirical truth (what is sustainable, what is restorative?), moral right (what is fair?), and aesthetic judgment (what is an appropriate and "authentic" representation of that new way of life—what might ultimately be judged a remotivating vision of a fulfilling and reconciled world?).[5] Those questions however arise in the context of a tension between the tolerance of difference and diversity, on the one hand, and, on the other, the suppression of individual behavior that is either destructive or repressive. The resolution of this conflict calls for a new, consensual effort at rationally grounding the claims of validity that are implied in the arguments of the opposing protagonists—which represent *opposed material interests*. Rationality needs to be restored, though it will be a rationality *different* from that with which we have become familiar in the age of modernity.

The basis for this difference lies in Habermas's insistent distinction between *instrumental* rationality (that form of rationality manifested in the choice of efficient means to achieve predefined ends) and *communicative* rationality (implicated in the structure of human speech as such, when two or more speakers raise "intersubjective validity claims" that a statement is true or false, normatively right or wrong, an aesthetically sincere or otherwise representation of human experience—involving ends rather than means). With modernity, the explosive advance of instrumental rationality has been at the expense of communicative rationality and, accordingly, at the expense of the potential richness of everyday life, or what Habermas calls the "life-world." So he speaks of the *colonization* of the life-world by the imperatives of instrumental rationality, in the creation and maintenance of a capitalist economy and nation-state. It is what Max Weber referred to as the "iron cage" of modernity—expanding, invasive capitalist economy, bureaucratic organization, and professionalized empirical science. Habermas ultimately insists, however, that this suppression of communicative rationality by instrumental rationality was never logically necessary—never inevitable. It could have been, and still could be, otherwise: Everyday life *can* fight back. For Habermas, the path to human emancipation lies in a reinvestment in communicative rationality and action.

The prescription has scarcely been met with universal rejoicing. A variety of critics, generally gathering under the philosophical banner of postmodernism, have slammed the residual modernism of Habermas's faith in historical progress and the emancipatory potential of rationalization. It is a faith similar to Harvey's; but since it is far more rigorously based and defended than Harvey's nostalgic wish, it deserves and has received far more critical attention—most stridently in Lyotard (1984). In the pages that follow, I will argue that no postmodernist rejection of metanarratives and acceptance of the experience and discourses of others can absolve us from the responsibility of articulating and defending motives and consequences for our acts. The task is precisely to reconcile a heterogeneity of discourses with the imperatives of communicative rationality and action.

There is, however, a more substantial criticism of Habermas's theory, insisted upon by Nancy Fraser (1991). Societies must reproduce themselves materially (regulating their exchange with a nonhuman, physical environment and with other social systems) as well as symbolically (maintaining, and transmitting to the young, the socially regulating norms and socially motivating meanings that ensure the integration of society). Modern societies, argues Habermas, have "uncoupled" these two spheres of social reproduction, with material reproductive functions being handed over to the (official) economy and the state, while the symbolic go to the "life-world" institutions of nuclear family ("private sphere") and the space of political deliberation ("public sphere"). Fraser employs a feminist critique, however, to object that this model is at best mistaken and at worst "ideological"—reinforcing existing structures of meaning, power, and repression by portraying those structures as "normal." Rather, both family and the public sphere of everyday life are permeated by the money economy and state bureaucratic power; and the relations of economy and power, for their part, are prestructured in gender relations arising in the sphere of symbolic reproduction. This insight of Fraser's challenges a central tenet of modern social theory: that economic relations, "in the last instance," determine the direction of social evolution. Despite any uncoupling of economy and state from the world of everyday life in modernity (and postmodernity!), I will eventually be arguing that economic relations, on the one hand, and the realm of beliefs and motivating meanings, on the other, are two sides of the same coin.

THE PRESENT ACCOUNT

Habermas's argument and the critiques thrown against it bring into focus the two questions that preoccupy this book. First, does the prison from which emancipation is sought arise in the economic realm (Marx, Althusser, in part Habermas) or in the realm of culture and meaning? My eventual answer will be, emphatically, the latter—though, to repeat, each stands only upon the support of the other, and the relationship between them is yet to be adequately theorized. This answer brings into focus the purposive production of environmental meaning in architecture and urban design and the centrality of meaning to the understanding of human enslavement and emancipation.

Second, is human emancipation—fulfillment, enrichment, the finding of motivating meaning—to be sought through the completion of the project of modernity (Habermas's fight back of everyday life through a reinvestment in communicative rationality), or through a postmodernist freeing from metanarratives, from the search for universal norms, and through acceptance of the experience of others? The answer, already hinted at, is to be that any path to human fulfillment must negotiate *both* experiences of enslavement—unreason and intolerance—to which those visions (the Habermasian and the Derridean, one could call them) variously refer. Thus the tolerance of otherness does not absolve us from the defense of *our own* statements as being true rather than false, normatively right rather than wrong, or as being aesthetically sincere (or sublime, or revealing?) expressions of the human condition rather than otherwise. And the only permitted intolerance is to be directed toward those who refuse to communicatively ground the truth, rightness, or expressive truthfulness of their own statements. Since those "statements" may be carried in the "text" of a building, a streetscape, the broader city or countryside, the role of the designer must be respecified at a new level of communicative rationality and action.

The first of these questions—the nature of the prison, the success or failure of the emancipatory endeavor, and the place of the built environment in that endeavor ("to give their forms to desires")—is explored through something of a history. It is a history designed to trace the intertwining stories of *the representation of the shifting experience of the times through architecture and urban design* and *the representation of the emancipatory dream in the context of that experience*. It will begin, in the next chapter, with the beginning of modernity itself, in the profound dislocation of the European Enlightenment—roughly the century and a half to the French Revolution. Human emancipation is foreseen in the seemingly imminent triumph of reason, new architecture will usher it into being, and the space of the city is to represent the banishing of its opposite in unreason. The nineteenth century—the high age of modernity—replaces reason with progress, gives the dream of abundance, the cornucopia and the new, and we have the commodification of human emotion, nature itself, all of space, and all of time (Chapter 3). The space of revolution and of the maelstrom of the early twentieth century (Chapters 4 and 5) would replace the worlds of the commodity and of power, but instead we get modernity as fragmentation—or are we to call it postmodernity? The first half of this century carries another dream however: Emancipation will come in the universal fellowship of humankind and in the internationalizing of all institutions, and architecture and urban design are to represent the new unity—an "international style," and space replacing place (Chapter 6). That dream also crumbles, so it seems, and to confront the fragmentary can no longer be postponed (Chapters 7, 8, and 9). None of this account is ultimately about the past, but rather about the present— How is space, the (con)text of our lives, to be read? This is the theme of the first conclusion to the work (in Chapter 10): It will draw heavily on Walter Benjamin and on Susan Buck-Morss's (1989) excellent speculation on Benjamin's unwritten *Passagen-Werk*, to seek new ways of seeing that can lead to "new social theory" and "new geography."

The account is resumed in two final chapters (11 and 12), which ask where emancipation in the present age is to be found and how the purposive production of spatial meaning, in architectural and urban design, is to be seen in that enterprise. Accordingly, in those chapters, I address the second guiding question of the work: Wherein lies the most likely path to human enrichment and fulfillment, and what do the present endeavors of the designers, their dreams and disasters, tell us of that path? Here the conclusion leans in part on Nancy Fraser's reconstruction of Habermas's argument and on the more general feminist reconstruction of the field of art criticism: The emancipatory endeavor will always have to negotiate a diversity of paths, of voices that are different to the point of discord, and of different ways of seeing, and the pursuit of that goal is going to involve "new architecture" and "new urban design."

CHAPTER 2 # Space and Power: The Enlightenment

*To articulate the past historically does not mean
to recognize it "the way it really was." . . . It
means to seize hold of a memory as it flashes
up in a moment of danger.*

—WALTER BENJAMIN, "Theses
on the Philosophy of
History" (1969, p. 255)

*One consequence of recent critical theory is the
realization that literary texts have no self-sufficient
or autonomous meaning, no existence apart from
their after-life of changing interpretations and values.*

—CHRISTOPHER NORRIS, Editor's Foreword
to Holub, *Jürgen Habermas: Critic in
the Public Sphere* (1991, pp. viii–ix)

The Enlightenment, claimed Foucault, made Man, that autonomous subject of modernity, who seems to define himself by new
modes of separation—from nature, from others, most fundamentally from his own unreason (though these three are but different
aspects of each other). This, of course, is a modern observation, not an
Enlightenment one—the "seizing hold of a memory" in the dangerous
moment of new self-definition. This chapter will tell three short stories—texts—on (modern) texts about other texts from the Enlightenment. The stories are about the present more than the past. The first
turns to that first aspect of seeming Enlightenment separation.

|POWER OVER NATURE

In 1745, William Shenstone, a poet of some inflated repute, created the Leasowes in Shropshire. "A master of the artificial–natural style in poetry" (Barbara Solomon is quoting Saintsburg), he was allegedly inspired by "a type of rural gardening that was classical"; Solomon quotes a French critic: "It is designed for the shepherds of Guarini and of Fontanelle. There are no pastures here, no closures, no animals, nor any of the farm buildings which are included in the *genre pastorale*." There were however "Virgil's Grove, a Temple of Pan, a new ruin of a Gothic priory, a root house, a lead statue of a peeping Faunnus, a Latin inscription to the goddess of health, and innumerable philosophical inscriptions" (Solomon, 1988, p. 76). Shenstone left nothing to chance—every corner and glimpse contrived, every view framed and surprise designed, no opportunity for a classical allusion missed; and everywhere there appeared fashioned "nature" complemented by in-scriptions, exhortatory doggerel, and instructions on how to view and what to contemplate.

> And tread with awe these favour'd bowers,
> Nor wound the shrubs, nor bruise the flowers; . . .
> But harm betide the wayward swain,
> Who dares our hallow'ed haunt profane!
> (William Shenstone, Root House inscription
> at the Leasowes, quoted in Pugh, 1990, p. 151)

"No pastures . . . no closures, no animals," and certainly no labor-ers—"harm betide the wayward swain" (that spoils the view!). For this is the countryside at the end of its centrality to the mode of production, residual feudalism in the age of industrial and commercial expansion; and Shenstone typifies a new class: a newly idle gentry uncomprehend-ingly watching the world slip away, "the pastoralist." Pugh (1990) speaks of "Shenstone the idler": "Idleness is a parody of self-generating nature that seemingly requires no labour, for the more dependent the rulers are on the work of others the more work is despised and idleness becomes a virtue" (pp. 148–149). Pugh cites Graves's 1772 satirical novel on Shenstone: Make-believe workers can be employed to lend rural authenticity to the perfect landscape, and a hermit can sit with "book and crucifix" outside the hermitage, for "keeping a hermit may be cheaper than keeping a wh-re, or . . . a pack of dogs" (quoting Graves, 1779, Vol. 2, pp. 121–124). Adds Pugh (1990), "rhetorically linked, worker, whore and dogs are adornment and amusement" (p.

149). And they, and the vision of nature that all three occupy, are masculine constructions. Certainly there were idle women, and they too saw nature outside, but differently. If the pictures they painted and the gardens they purportedly endlessly tended and pruned are indicators, then *their* nature was more one of intimate objects and places, and a wider range of sensory experience than the intellectualized gaze toward set pieces and allegorical "landscapes" of the male, would-be pastoralist.

In exploring what he calls the "semantic recoil" from the voyages of discovery (those of Cook in the 1770s ending the age of limitless space and the great unknown), Stephen Bann has observed the different responses ("recoils") of the French and the English landscapists to shifting experiences of space, nature, and the countryside. The distinguishing characteristic of English practice was "to establish limits through a pictorial, mythic or cultural framing"—pictorial vistas, a cultural otherness through displacements to "the utopia of the Roman idylls" or the imaginary world of a Claude or Giorgione. What lies at the root of this equivocalness is, "as the Pre-Raphaelites and William Morris recognised [in the next century], a mythic representation of the Earthly Paradise, which is always on the point of reversing itself into the Garden of Eden from which, in so far as we are knowledgeable, we have always already been expelled" (Bann, 1990, p. 219).

The French garden, by contrast, is "a minutely graded series of transitions, rather than a system of mythic rupture." It begins at the house itself (the English houses are quite dislocated from their gardens), with phased *broderie*, then topiary, then trained trees, then avenues, until untrained nature can be deferred no longer and the forest can finally signify "unlimited wildness" (p. 220). Continuities rather than ruptures; yet both are attempting the same thing: to mediate, through representation as landscape, the profound disruption of an urban world and mentality invading a rural world.

The Enlightenment was also the age of writing and the explosion of literacy. What Simon Pugh's text reveals, most saliently, is an early instance of spatial representation in the language of spatial forms themselves (graded transition, mythic rupture) *and* in the language of writing—poetic evocation. The inscriptions are as necessary as the views and the closures, for *meaning* is dependent on language standing against language—space, in an age of literacy, is to be read intertextually. Missing are the texts, in either language, that can represent other experiences of space—of women, of rural labor, of the embryonic urban proletariat whose prior expulsion made possible the transition from productive countryside to bucolic landscape.

|POWER OVER THE SELF

We recede to a century before Shenstone and to another (modern) text that attempts to seize the memory of that great disruption in the experience of space and nature. In *The Reenchantment of the World* (1984), Morris Berman sees the Enlightenment as "the disenchantment," the gathering triumph of a new science that separated observer from observed, that was concerned with how things work rather than why, and that experienced nature as something controllable, to be measured and put to human use. And the state of nature from which we were to be enlightened . . . ?

> The view of nature which predominated in the West down to the eve of the Scientific Revolution was that of an enchanted world. Rocks, trees, rivers, and clouds were all seen as wondrous, alive, and human beings felt at home in this environment. The cosmos, in short, was a place of *belonging*. A member of this cosmos was not an alienated observer of it but a direct participant in its drama. His personal destiny was bound up with its destiny, and this relationship gave meaning to his life. This type of consciousness— . . . "participating consciousness"—involves merger, or identification, with one's surroundings, and bespeaks a psychic wholeness that has long since passed from the scene. (Berman, 1984, p. 2)

The new "nonparticipating" consciousness of nature and self, and with it of space and time, had been a long time emerging however— traces of it are found, we are told, in the antianimist tendencies of the old Greek and Jewish traditions in particular; and elements of that earlier, participating consciousness have persisted throughout the progress of modernity. The great divide is indeed located for us in *scientific* revolution—ideas about explanation; and the exultant clarity of ideas finally rings out in the mechanistic philosophy of René Descartes (1596–1650). The universe is to be seen as "a vast machine, wound up by God to tick forever" (p. 21). To know nature was to stand outside it, detached, denying any ultimate "purposes":

> The identification of human existence with pure ratiocination, the idea that man can know all there is to know by way of his reason, included for Descartes the assumption that mind and body, subject and object, were radically disparate entities. Thinking, it would seem, separates me from the world I confront. (Berman, 1984, p. 21)

But this perception had to be learned, and that involved the purposive suppression of affective knowledge of the natural world; the ecstatic union with nature, akin to what the seventeenth century termed "enthusiasm" and encompassing sublime anxiety as much as sublime harmony, had to be repressed as "irrational." The repression however—like its opposite, celebration—is forever ideological; that is to say, it has to do with those structures of beliefs that sustain a prevailing worldview that provides *meaning* to life and *cohesion* to society. As Berman is forced to conclude, it is not just "that men conceived of matter as possessing mind in those days, but rather that in those days, matter *did* possess mind, 'actually' did so" (p. 83).

There are two long stories told to represent this "learning as suppression." The first is of the end of alchemy. The alchemist of the late Renaissance would proceed through "purification, solution, distillation, sublimation, calcination, and coagulation" (Berman, 1984, p. 78); there is however no agreement in the alchemical literature on how "actually" to perform these steps; but there are reputable reports of their effectiveness to the alchemists and their observers, and manifestations of gold were indeed recorded. So the real question is, What was the alchemist "actually *doing*"? But the question is a red herring, as "the worlds constructed by participating and nonparticipating consciousness are not mutually translatable"—there are different languages, borne on different voices. "What we really mean," argues Berman, "is what *we* would be doing, or what a modern chemist would be doing, if we or he could be transported back in time and space to an alchemist's laboratory. But what was 'actually' going on was what the *alchemist* was doing" (p. 81). The difference—and thereby the Enlightenment itself—is relocated in the realm of language, which Berman elsewhere attempts to identify in the different forms of reasoning for which different social languages and their carrying voices are the medium[1]:

> The language of alchemy, as well as of dreams, follows a type of reasoning which I have termed "dialectical," as opposed to the critical reason characteristic of rational, or scientific thought. . . . Descartes regarded dreams as perverse because they violated the principle of noncontradiction. But this violation is not arbitrary; rather, it emerges from a paradigm of its own, one that could well be called alchemical. This paradigm has as a central tenet the notion that reality is paradoxical, that things and their opposites are closely related, that attachment and resistance have the same root. (Berman, 1984, pp. 68, 71)

So what was alchemy (Berman's "paradigm science of participation")? It was "poetic clothing for unconscious psychic processes" (Dobbs, 1975, p. 32); thereby perhaps "a map of the human unconscious" (Berman, 1984, p. 67). It was a "real" science, "the last major synthetic iconography of the human unconscious in the West" (p. 73), the geography of dreams and the psychic. The gold of the alchemist was not the means for obtaining other things, but the end: to surpass the bounds of space and time, to liberate the space of the unconscious. The iconography of the alchemists is linked in Berman's text to Jung's representations of dreams, and to the melted time of Dali and the space of dreams of the Surrealists Magritte and Dali, though Berman could equally have referred to de Chirico or Tanguy, and even to the antidreamers of the dadaist movement, including Walter Benjamin. The difference (the Enlightenment) is seen as one of different world views and different voices; and the conclusion is that our inability to embrace a participating consciousness of nature reduces our humanity. Foucault is quoted: Divination "is not a rival form of knowledge; it is part of the main body of knowledge itself" (Berman, 1984, p. 64).[2]

The narrative of the fall of alchemy is followed by a second: the rise of Newton (1642–1727). Berman quotes John Maynard Keynes, writing in 1934: "Newton was not the first of the age of reason. He was the last of the magicians"—the universe is a riddle that might be read from clues that God has set in the heavens and in the elements, or a riddle that might be read in texts handed down by the esoteric brotherhood in an unbroken chain that stretches back to the original revelation to the ancients. The universe is "a cryptogram set by the almighty" (Keynes, quoted in Berman, 1984, p. 108). Newton, we are told by Berman, believed that his own birth was propitious, that he was "endowed with extraordinary powers" (p. 110), that he was even a prophet, in a long line of great thinkers, part of that " 'golden chain' of magi or unique figures designated by God in each age to receive the ancient Hermetic wisdom" (pp. 109–110). He was also an alchemist, "connected to alchemy by something that was integrally related to his megalomania about inheriting the sacred tradition: his conviction that matter was not inert but required an active, or hylarchic, principle for its motion" (p. 112).

Through alchemy Newton sought the system of the world, the "secret of the universe." His interest in the Hermetic tradition was suppressed in later years as the result of "politically motivated" self-repression: "What Newton did . . . was to delve deeply into the Hermetic wisdom for his answers, while clothing them in the idiom of the mechanical philosophy" (p. 115). But additionally, Berman notes, it became "imperative for Newton to dissociate himself from these ideas . . . in what amounted to a rigorous self-censorship" (p. 116). The suppression of "one half of the human" saw Newton gradually transformed into a mechanical philosopher: "In the end, however, we see the rigidity of the mechanical world view, the Newton who denied his own internal principles . . . for the sake of social approval and outward conformity. We see, in effect, the tragedy of modern man" (Berman, 1984, pp. 120–121).

The shift from alchemy to modern science may have been far more complex than mere suppression, however. Kenneth Knoespel (1989) points to the nature of alchemy as narrative; each step is local narrative ("conclusions are not end points alone but points of departure"), plotted in the larger chain of a metanarrative that is, in its simplest form, a story of perfection (p. 100). But the method of the new chemistry was physical allegory—with the spiritual or anagogical allegory of the baroque poets as its necessary obverse, one could add. Newton's dilemma was to be caught between modes of representation (Castillejo, 1981); his achievement, in his alchemical work, was to realize alchemy's dependence on intertextuality—a realization seemingly missing from Berman (Dobbs, 1975; Westfall, 1984, cited in Knoespel, 1989, p. 105). The end of self-conscious intertextuality in the realm of "objective" science is matched by its rise in the realm of art—the nonsense of Shenstone is one with the symbolism of the late baroque and of romanticism.

Renaissance geography, akin to the medieval romance, was similarly narrative and intertextual—stories of journeys and adventures (every conclusion a point of departure), episodes of learning and self-perfection. In geography we come to the supreme physical allegory: Mystical geometries of space, to represent the linked narratives of the pilgrimages (the quest for perfection as the metanarrative) or to represent Michell and Rhone's (1991) "twelve-tribe nations" and sacred geographies, give way to that ultimate metaphor (metanarrative) of the Cartesian grid. We advance from the space of collective spiritual self-discovery (for which the alchemist's laboratory was the microcosmic complement, as the space of individual psychic discovery) to space emptied of all meaning, bar its physical universality and differentiability.

| POWER OVER THE OTHER

And in that differentiable space, there were new institutions of differentiation: The Age of Reason can only be represented if its opposite is glaringly visible. Here the modern text is the vast *oeuvre* of Michel Foucault (1926–1984), the archaeology of modernity, to trace the insidious links between language, space, and repression.[3] The rational city of the Enlightenment only comes into existence when language can be mobilized to define rationality's "other"—madness, illness,

criminality, sexual deviance—and when institutions can be invented
for the "other's" confinement or else repression (in asylums, clinics,
prisons, confessional boxes) and when both institutions and inhabitants are banished from that rational space to the melancholy state of
wild nature, itself the "other" of Shenstone's bucolic world.

Foucault's first major text was *Histoire de la folie*, (1961; or *Madness
and Civilization: A History of Insanity in the Age of Reason*, 1967): The
earlier world can be conceived as a chaotic space where madness had
many points of contact with wider society, but the advance of the
Enlightenment saw a progressive stigmatization (largely through language) and spatial exclusion from the sites of "normal" social interaction to those new, exurban, horrific, rational institutions—a "geometry
of negativities," of "inside" and "outside"; the "geography of haunted
places." In Foucault's *Surveiller et punir* (1975; or *Discipline and Punish:
The Birth of the Prison*, 1977), discipline arises through "the distribution
of individuals in space": Bentham's *panopticon* (see Figure 2.1) becomes
all of space as we sink into self-surveillance and self-repression. Denis
Hollier's reading of Foucault would push the argument to a simpler
assertion: The text of *Histoire de la folie* is a critique of architecture,
which must bear the responsibility first for the invention of madness
and then for its production; and *Surveiller et punir* similarly describes

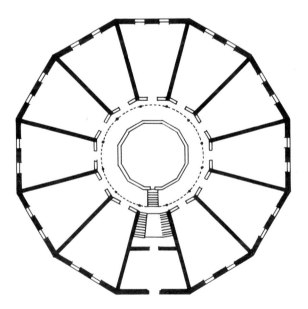

FIGURE 2.1. The ideal prison ("surveiller et punir"): Jeremy Bentham,
Panopticon Prison, 1797. Author's drawing, based on Vidler (1987).

architecture's "invention of criminality through techniques of spatial planning" (1989, p. x).

Another reading and extension of Foucault is that of Anthony Vidler: In the late Enlightenment, for the first time, the dreams of a rationalized, self-controlled social life spilt over into architectural discourse, with two interlocking effects. The first, a response to social and political necessity in a collapsing world, had to do with institutional reform and ideal programs for factories and industrial competition, hospitals, poorhouses, health care and poverty, judicial and penal reform, markets, cemeteries, and the whole gamut of public activity. The second was historiographic: Whereas the Newtonian mechanistic model of causes and rational consequences had been extended by Etienne Bonnot de Condillac into language and by Jean-Jacques Rousseau into society, with the abbé Laugier it was architecture that was similarly traced back to "natural origins." With the widening of geographical horizons, architecture was also increasingly seen to be culturally bound and to stand as a kind of language or system of symbols (Vidler, 1987, pp. 2–3), the active, purposive production of spatial meaning.

The shock of the urban forms, for the most part, matched the radicalism of the advocated programs. Etienne-Louis Boullée (1728–1799) must claim some historical priority, with his preoccupations with the Burkean notion of "the sublime," translated into reformist (even "enlightened") designs for prisons, museums, and other projects. By the 1770s his schemes were so vast in scale, and so concerned with "meaning" rather than "function," as to be quite unrealizable. His cenotaph for Isaac Newton (of 1784) would have consisted of a sphere seemingly hundreds of meters in diameter, pierced to admit sunlight to resemble the night sky and the stars by day, and with a flame to represent the sun and the daytime sky by night—time inverted, space reversed. Boullée asserted that architecture's effects are caused by light, and its first principles are to be found in geometric solids—pyramids, cubes, and, preeminently, spheres. Claude-Nicholas Ledoux (1736–1806), disciple of Boullée and arguably the most inventive of the French architects of his time, extended this architectural confrontation of the institutions of society into the very mode of production itself: "I wanted to dwell on the needs and conveniences of a productive factory where the utilization of time offers the first economy" (Ledoux, 1804, p. 122; quoted in Vidler, 1987, p. 37).

Ledoux's most notable early achievement was for the saltworks and model town of Chaux (see Figure 2.2), designed in the early 1770s and built between 1775 and 1778. The "first economy" presented the dilemma of the integration of processes and functions for optimum

FIGURE 2.2. C.-N. Ledoux: The ideal town of Chaux, 1775–1778. From Ledoux (1804). Copyright 1804 by Princeton Architectural Press. Reprinted by permission.

efficiency versus their articulation and separation for health and safety. The resolution was sought in the ideal geometry of a circular urban form. More fundamental was that ultimate dilemma of capitalism (*state* capitalism in this instance), of community versus control. The director's house stood at the very center of the town, a symbol of both centralized power and a hierarchy of surveillance; but the surveillance was implied rather than real, and the workers in fact were separated from the director's sight by rows of trees and were more oriented to their own communal spaces and "the smaller community of hearth and home" (Vidler, 1987, p. 39). It was an attempt at architectural reconciliation of centralized versus dispersed production. Finally, in its architectural detail it had an elaboration and magnificence (to mark the "sublime" vision of work and community) that had, by Ledoux's account, markedly vexed an aging Louis XV (Ledoux, 1804, p. 40) (see Figure 2.3).

Between 1775 and 1800, Vidler's text recounts (on the authority of Ledoux's own), Ledoux prepared schemes for all sorts of factories, housing, and institutions that would together represent a new dispersed, almost Rousseauian reconstruction of industrial production— humankind would exist in a refound innocence, in a harmony of forest, river, and factory (see Figure 2.4).[4] Collected together in his publication of 1804, these utopian projects constituted something of an architectural extension of the *Encyclopédie*. His was certainly not the only such attempted extension, but it was the one that came nearest to confronting constructively the ascendant production relations of the time. It also provides a link to yet further and more radical attempts at a new society through new urban form.

Conflating of disparate discourses, leveling of distinctions, totalizing, reductionist, are among the charges brought against Foucault's accounts of the Enlightenment: Everything comes down to a naked play of power through knowledge—we read space as the medium through which the struggle is endlessly refracted and fragmented, and we look for chinks and cracks in the edifice of the rational world, to break it apart.[5] Christopher Norris (1992) summarizes the objections (of mutually dismissive Habermas and Derrida):

> What is the status of a discourse that reduces all truths to the level of an undifferentiated power-knowledge; that denounces reason as merely an agency of ever-increasing surveillance and control; and that claims not only to speak on behalf of that madness which reason has constructed as its outcast other, but moreover to speak the very language of madness from a standpoint beyond any rational accountability? (p. 135)

FIGURE 2.3. The cemetery of the town of Chaux. From Ledoux (1804). Copyright 1804 by Princeton Architectural Press. Reprinted by permission.

24

FIGURE 2.4. C.-N. Ledoux: House of the directors of the River Loe. From Ledoux (1804). Copyright 1804 by Princeton Architectural Press. Reprinted by permission.

25

Though Foucault would escape from the Enlightenment's privileging of the rational, he must ultimately speak for the irrational in the language of the rational. Derrida objects that discourse must escape madness—"By its essence, the sentence is normal." Where Habermas sees only the dangerous leveling of the distinction between reason and unreason—the anti-Enlightenment—Derrida however suggests a critical force in Foucault's antireason, demystifying despite its own avowed purpose and suggesting to us that "there are crises of reason in strange complicity with what the world calls crises of madness" (quoted in Norris, 1992, p. 186). There seem to have been attempts throughout the Enlightenment to represent, if not the space of unreason, then certainly prereason—Newton's other, suppressed voice. Thus, among Vidler's chapter headings are "Spaces of Production," "The Theatre of Industry," "Confinement and Cure," "The Design of Punishment"; but also "The Architecture of the Lodges" (rituals and the symbols of Freemasonry, as well as the search for a spatial representation of the realm of the occult) and "Asylums of Libertinage" (the space of the erotic and, indeed, the antirational, of de Sade, Lequeu, and Fourier). And from chapter to chapter, both voice and language are constant; the sentences are normal.

But the ambivalence in Foucault goes well beyond this rationality-bound critique of the rational. For against the reductionist intent (all social life seen as the play of power in knowledge) stands a profound antireductionism. Chris Philo picks up on the notion of "spaces of dispersion" in Foucault: At one level of understanding, space "disperses" these processes, makes them heterogeneous; space fractures the unities, so that the one process is manifested differently in one place simply because it is a place different from other places (the Hôtel-Dieu at Paris will be different from the Hôtel-Dieu at Lyons because there are different people, events, régimes of control—thus, dispersion!). At another level, any phenomenon—say, the exercise of power through knowledge in the madness industry—will unfold in a vast multiplicity of places, in debates and interplays of texts and lives, over a chaotic, heterogeneous, muddled-up space without conceptual pattern.

The point that Foucault's critics seem to have missed is that the ambivalences in the text mirror the contradictions of the Enlightenment and the ambivalences that must necessarily arise in any sensitive reading of Enlightenment events: Newton's single vision against the intertextuality of his own inclination—the mechanical philosophy, the autonomy of intellectual spheres, and the seeming triumph of instrumental rationality, against the unstilled yearning for some higher meaning and purpose—the search for a right representation of the universe (nature, the self, others) so as to control the very path of human progress, achievable however only by the suppression of all other visions and representations (of women, the poor, the poetic, but also the mad, the bad, and the otherwise excluded). These polarities would seem to define the very dimensions along which the paradigm shift of the Enlightenment—a thoroughly modernist concept—can be observed.

CHAPTER 3

Space and the Commodity: The Nineteenth Century and the Rise of Modernity

Constant revolutionizing of production,
uninterrupted disturbance of all social relations,
everlasting uncertainty and agitation, distinguish
the bourgeois epoch from all earlier times. All fixed,
fast-frozen relationships, with their train of
venerable ideas and opinions, are swept away, all
new-formed ones become obsolete before they can
ossify. All that is solid melts into air, all that is holy
is profaned, and men at last are forced to face with
sober sense the real conditions of their lives and their
relations with their fellow men.

> —Karl Marx and Friedrich Engels, *The*
> *Communist Manifesto* (1952, p. 25)

The fundamental event of the modern age is the
conquest of the world as picture.

> —Martin Heidegger, "The Age of the
> World Picture" (1977, p. 149)

There is no moment when modernity begins. The storming of the Bastille was one signal ("against the monuments that are its real masters," in George Bataille's [1971] unmasking of architecture [pp. 171–172]); another was the marvelous profusion of the novel that could, by the 1820s, suggest the coming cornucopia of a new (industrial, modern) age. And the succeeding economic collapse of 1846–1848—the first to engulf the whole capitalist world and the first clearly *not* to be attributed to wars or natural disasters but to bourgeois virtues of overproduction and speculation—demonstrated conclusively the impossibility of any universal agreement on bourgeois–democratic hegemony and likewise signaled the coming of the modern.

In *The Condition of Postmodernity* (1989), David Harvey begins a perceptive essay on "modernity and modernism" with a comment from Baudelaire: "Modernity is the transient, the fleeting, the contingent; it is the one half of art, the other being the eternal and the immutable" (p. 10). Both elements of this dialectic of modernism were present in the Age of the Enlightenment. The century dominated by the French Revolution was scarcely untroubled; but the chaotic, transient, and fleeting were themselves seen as the necessary conditions in which the triumph of reason would be won. By the middle of the nineteenth century, that then-old vision was more difficult to sustain. For one thing, with the compression of space and time—the seeming speeding up of history—the fleeting and contingent could no longer be seen as a mere step to a new age. Transience was not at all transient, but permanent. Second, if one did on occasion believe that there was a path out of the turmoil, how was one to choose that path from the chaotic range of options variously presented?

In this new uncertainty, then, how were we to understand the world—to represent it to ourselves? What was the representational task? At the more superficial level of aesthetic disputation, the alienated artist saw his mission as one of never-ending struggle and resistance to "the eternal and the immutable"—every path might be tried, and we entered the age of the avant-garde. A second level is that of the tension in cultural production itself. While resisting bourgeois art, what is in fact being fought for? Within that transience and contingency of struggle, what values are to be represented? An unalienated nature, the aspirations of the human soul, the dignity of labor . . . ? At this level, the dialectic of modernity became the dialectic of the avant-garde.

Again, as in the previous chapter, it is through more recent texts and voices—Walter Benjamin, Louis Althusser, Friedrich Nietzsche, Luce Irigaray, "seizing a memory" in a moment of more recent danger— that we read something of this birth of modernity. And again the reading will be as a series of short stories—Benjamin, Nietzsche, Irigaray—but in the context of reactions to the shattering, fragmenting space of the nineteenth century.

| THE COMMODITY WORLD

Walter Benjamin (1892–1940), from 1926 until his death, worked on
assembling a vast collection of verbal and graphical images to represent
that maelstrom of modernity—ostensibly of Paris in the nineteenth
century. This was the *Passagen-Werk*, or Arcades Project. The material
was organized as thirty-six massive files (*Konvoluts*); but the file on
Charles Baudelaire was over twenty percent of the total collection.
Benjamin also wrote a separate treatise on Baudelaire as the archetypal
poet of the nineteenth century. Baudelaire was concerned with the
decadence of modern life—material progress is chimerical, innovation
becomes mere fetish ("change-as-progress" is but progress as "Hell"),
and the splendor of the newly constructed city is an "urban phantasmagoria." The world is "but a shop of images and signs"; Paris in that age
was a world where all things were in the process of losing their reality,
to become mere commodities. The prostitute was the final symbol of all
commodification, whereby even human emotions and happiness were
eroded to the status of commodity; worse, things finally became just
signs.

Like the painted smile of the *Folies* dancer or the street-woman,
hollowed out and empty, the "nature" of the city is also hollowed out.
The space of the city becomes an allegorical space—baroque and
melancholy, the symbol of fallen nature.

> Paris changes, but nothing of my melancholy
> Gives way. New palaces, scaffolding, blocks,
> Old suburbs, everything for me becomes allegory,
> While my dear memories are heavier than rocks.
> (Baudelaire, "Le cynge," *Les Fleurs du mal*,
> quoted in Buck-Morss, 1989, p.179)

The arcades of Benjamin's title were the iron-and-glass-roofed
alleys of shops that proliferated through Paris in that great speculative
boom that started in the 1820s, the first new building type of modernity, with the first artificial materials (iron and glass), glowing and
magical (the first gaslight), brimming with wave after wave of new
commodities—the first flood of industrial mass production and colonial exploit: "The great poem of display chants its stanzas of color from
the Madeleine to the gate of Saint-Denis" (Balzac). But by Baudelaire's
time the arcades were already in decay, eclipsed by the new department
stores, as commodified space was itself swept into the endless, hypnotic
cycles of innovation, supersession, and decay that is the fate of every
commodity—by then abandoned to the marginal and the demimonde,
part of that world of women-as-commodity.

Baudelaire was not the only one to see modernity as decadence and to see the real value of things eroded by the commodity. Friedrich Engels (1820–1895) read Baron Haussmann's Paris of the Boulevards ("new palaces, scaffolding, blocks") as the city's becoming pure spectacle in order to mask the commodity's grip on urban space as capital swept away the slums that would immediately reappear in a thousand new locations as the corrupting cause persisted; and Karl Marx (1818–1883) saw the economic relations that yielded the commodity as the central fact of history itself. The distinguishing characteristic of the human (vis-à-vis the lower animals) is the *production* of one's means of subsistence, and human history is most fruitfully approached through the perspective of change in the modes of such production (Marx and Engels, 1965). Thus, too, do we privilege "the characteristically masculine activity of production as the *definitively human* activity" (Owens, 1985, p. 63)! Women are situated outside this glorious distinction, "in a state of nature" (p. 63). Lyotard (1978) asserts, "the frontier passing between the sexes does not separate two parts of the same social activity" (p. 15).

Always immanent in human behavior, in this Marxian construction, is a mighty contradiction whereby actions in our individual self-interest can be antithetical to the collective interest of the broader group or society. This translates, in a mode of production, into a potential contradiction between the forces and relations of production: The *forces* are typically dependent on collective action, but the *relations* of production—the egotistical appropriation of socially created wealth or, alternatively, the avoidance of one's "fair share" of the labor of production—undermine the cooperative basis of that socialized action.[1]

The total social formation is of course far more than the forces and relations of production. But the Marxian argument is that these forces and relations constitute the societal *base*, on which all the institutions of the political and cultural spheres (including sustaining worldviews and beliefs—forms of consciousness) stand merely as a *superstructure*:

In the social production of their existence, men inevitably enter into definite relations of production appropriate to a given stage in the development of their material forces of production. The totality of these relations of production constitutes the economic structure of society, the real foundation, on which arises a legal and political superstructure and to which correspond definite forms of social consciousness. The mode of production of material life conditions the general process of social, political and intellectual life. It is not the consciousness of men that determines their existence, but their social existence that determines their consciousness. (Marx, 1970, pp. 20–21)

The narrow interpretation of this argument is that the economic sphere *determines* the political and cultural spheres and that social evolution derives from contradictions and instabilities arising simply between the forces and the relations of production (again, the economic sphere). It is a view that is reductionist—all explanation brought down to a single, assumed cause—and scarcely illuminating. The contrary interpretation comes most coherently and compellingly through the later, twentieth-century voice of Louis Althusser (1969): The contradiction that seems always to develop between the forces and relations of production is a necessary but not sufficient condition for the historical transformation from one mode of production to another. For what is also necessary is the rise of further, secondary contradictions in the superstructure of *political* and *ideological* relations, whose reverberations compound the basic contradiction. Althusser insists that a mode of production comprises a complex structure operating at all three levels—the economic, the political, and the ideological—that contradictions arise both within and between each level, and that the basic economic contradiction can become "overdetermined" as other contradictions develop at other points in the system. The result can be a "ruptural fusion" of these various contradictions, and the mode of production itself is transformed.

Relations at the economic level (i.e., the relations of production) determine the relations between the three levels; they also determine which level is to be dominant in that mode of production. For different levels perform the dominant function depending on the economic relations of that mode: In ancient empires the political was dominant because of the crucial role of the state in maintaining the unity of the system; in the feudal mode of production it was the ideological, because of the central role of religion in maintaining unity; in the capitalist mode of production, it is the economic level itself that is dominant. Although the economic is determinant to this extent ("in the last instance" is Althusser's term), it never determines how each level is to develop; each has its own degree of autonomy, although each also has effects on the others—it is, after all, the one system. Thus, crucially important contradictions can arise in any level or at any point in the complex relations between levels.

Finally, in this Althusserian model of modes of production and forms of contradiction, there can develop contradictions between different, coexisting modes of production. For the system described above is a mode of production *in its pure form*. However, any given society will exhibit elements of a variety of modes of production—residual from previous epochs or from contact between different societies (colonialism, neocolonialism, etc.), new experimentations, or forms of resistance. Each is likely to stand in some contradiction to a dominant mode of production.

The real value in Althusser's argument is that it focuses attention on the idea of contradiction and instability in human society: Social evolution is somehow to be linked to the continual working out of a fundamental contradiction in all human nature, wherein our individual and our collective interests are logically opposed and mutually undermining. Althusser's argument additionally forces us to look at the shifting connections between economic relations, political relations, and motivating ideas or worldviews, as that working out of contradiction reverberates through all aspects of social life. The edifice however is cracked, and Foucault-like we must find the substratum. "Every thought of society and of history," observes Cornelius Castoriadis (1987), "itself belongs to society and history" (p. 3). Therefore, to continue Castoriadis's (1987) argument, if in antiquity "the dominant categories under which social and historical relations are grasped are essentially *political* categories"—such as the relations between city-states and between power, force, and right—while the economic gets only marginal attention, this was not because understanding or reflection was less advanced or because there was some absence or neglect of economic material. Rather, the reason is that "in the reality of the ancient world, the economy was not yet constituted as a separate 'autonomous' moment (as Marx would say), 'for itself,' of human activity." No real analysis of the economic was possible until after the seventeenth century, and more particularly after the eighteenth, "that is with the birth of capitalism, which in fact set up the economy as the dominant moment of social life" (Castoriadis, 1987, p. 13). It is a moment that will pass.

Certainly there is an objective, material reality; but we know it through the ways in which we represent it to ourselves. Marxism is one brilliantly illuminative representation that could only have been painted (like any representation) at a specific time in history. At other moments, reality will be more tellingly represented to us in other ways. As the commodity is suppressed by the image, new representations are already, necessarily, emerging.

| SPACES OF RESISTANCE

The first of the six "provisional chapter divisions" of Benjamin's never written *Passagen-Werk* was to have been titled "Fourier or the Arcades." It shifts the attention back to that tumult of the 1820s as late-Enlightenment certainty seemed to overlap with modernist rejec-

tion and doubt; for it is in both worlds that we might locate Charles
Fourier (1772–1837). "Conceived and realized on the level of text, . . . "
argues Vidler (1987), "the apparent content of the critical utopianism
[of Fourier] . . . was less determining than its linguistic form, which . . .
took the methods of reason and enlightenment to their logical and
ultimately 'mad' conclusions" (p. 103). The content of Fourier's
utopianism derived in part from the models of Ledoux (for a new,
postcivilized society and new, more harmonious relations of production
through architecture and urban design) and of Rousseau (for a remerging of humanity with broader nature); and his starting point was
the new, lower-density, bourgeois, residential quarters of Paris of the
late 1790s, with their freestanding houses in "English" gardens. Fourier
proposed the idea of a garden city (as early as 1796), not as an end in
itself, however, but as a necessary stage in the progress from the urban
shambles of the present to the ultimate, unified architecture of the
final state of social evolution. The garden city would be followed by a
further stage, the *tribustère*, or home of the associated tribe, to house
about a hundred people of differing social status and fortune: The city
would be reorganized block by block on this model, blocks linked by
covered galleries (the arcades, appropriated and subverted at the moment of their first emergence), all to engender a new form of "association" as prelude to universal association. Then, in that final, universal
state, the city would be replaced: It would be the "new industrial
world," a nonrepressive society of ideal communities, or "phalanxes,"
each of some eighteen hundred persons, again of different levels of skill
and fortune, and housed in a *phalanstère*, to be located in the open
countryside and predominantly agricultural in its economy. In its
physical form the phalanstère seemed to be modeled on the layout of
Versailles—somewhat incongruously for an altogether new, nondomi-
native world, as Frampton has observed (1985a, p. 22). In its detailed
program, however, the phalanstère was indeed revolutionary. Two
components were central to its role in social transformation: the gallery
and the exchange. The former would run above the ground-floor
service arcades, connecting each wing and enclosing each courtyard,
unifying the phalanstère physically and symbolically, extending over
all three stories with all apartments overlooking it, glass-roofed, as a
great winter garden. The 1800s, when Fourier formulated his ideas, to
the 1820s, when he published them, was the high moment of the Paris
arcades—the birth of the bourgeois world of "the commodity as fetish."
The gallery was to take the physical form of the Aladdin's cave of the
arcades, but then to create its dialectical opposite, in a world freed from
the commodity. Where the gallery "deconstructed" and then "reconstructed" the arcade and the urban street, the exchange did the same to

the new, capitalist Bourse. Here not money but pleasure, entertain-
ments, and information were to be exchanged. There would be new
languages of signaling and new modes of social interaction. As Roland
Barthes (1976) has observed, it is an architecture and urban design that
is almost totally *preoccupied with communication*. Anthony Vidler's
(1987) judgment on Fourier is worth quoting:

> [His] method is clear: he transforms the evil practices of civilization
> into their opposites, solely by means of language. He uses the tricks
> of neologism and dialectics to redefine the old codes. The magic
> wand of linguistic play, disguised by an apparently exhaustive sys-
> tematization, turns every bad into a good. As in writing, so in
> architecture: the gallery and the Exchange are only two of the
> well-known spatial elements to which he gives beneficent connota-
> tions . . . all [are] turned inside out and upside down. (p. 113)

The interplay of the language of writing and speech with that of
space itself (iron, glass, arcade, exchange) will enable reconstruction of
the very mode of production—will transform modernity itself. This is
the lesson of Walter Benjamin's reading of Fourier (in the Baudelaire
Konvolut): The myth of inevitability in modernity's subjection of both
human beings and the natural world is deconstructed. In Buck-Morss's
(1989) transcription of the *Konvolut* material (where she quotes Benjamin, 1982, pp. 455–456), to be confronted is "the illusion that raw
material receives 'value' only through an order of production which
rests on the exploitation of human labor"; for if this exploitation
ceases, then "human labor for its part will cast aside its characteristic
exploitation of nature" (p. 276). Rather, labor will be after the model
of children's play, the basis of the *travail passionné* of the phalanstère.
Fourier's achievement is "to have situated play as the canon of a form
of labor that is no longer exploitative"—to have offered the image of a
world where, at last, "activity would be sister of the dream [Baudelaire]"
(p. 276). The gallery (arcade) and the exchange belong to that present
(though they will resonate into the future, to our own time); the
intertextuality (of space and speech) are of both past and future; but
the instrumentalist faith in the power of design seems only of an earlier,
Enlightenment past: "I am going to prove that a man of taste could, on
his own, perfect a general architecture to metamorphose civilization"
(Fourier, notebook in Archives Nationales; quoted in Vidler, 1987, p.
110).

Fourier published his ideas as *Traité de l'Association Domestique
Agricole* of 1822, and *Le nouveau monde industriel* of 1829. Although
generally rejected in their own time as the ramblings of a madman,

they have persisted through the utopian socialism of late-nineteenth-century urban ideals, the urban programs of the Russian avant-garde in the 1920s, the arguments and projects of Le Corbusier in "high modernity," and the postmodernists after 1970. These are stories for later chapters. The appropriation of ideas is always transformative—both present and past are unstable.

| SPACES OF TRIUMPH

If the arcades were a step in the commodity's insinuating colonization of everyday life, then the World Expositions, from the Crystal Palace Exhibition of 1851 onward, were the triumphant march. Another of Benjamin's "provisional chapter divisions" would have been "Grand-ville or the World Expositions": Grandville, a graphic artist contemporary with Marx, satirized humanity finally remerged with nature in . . . the commodity! There are "fish fishing for people, using various desirable items [commodities] as bait"; a dog takes his man for a walk (the commodity roles reversed); nature already cooked and ready to eat falls from the sky or else sprouts marvelously in the Fourierist utopia; people vanish and their possessions take over. The halls of the World Expositions took the iron and glass of the arcades, but also their derivative, backward-looking classicism, and their function of the display of every new commodity at the moment of its invention. If capitalists were to reproduce themselves as a class, Marx had observed, they had continually to expand the basis for profit; but this endeavor always came up against the barrier of fixed consumption; so the task was to push that barrier ever outward—to find new markets (to breach national boundaries) and within every market to find and promulgate new commodities ("desirable items as bait"). Thus, the World Expositions became the ultimate halls of fantasy—a dreamworld between past and present—that also rendered the commodity geopolitical. And as the nation-states thereby increasingly tried to establish national identity through their commodities, the two became indistinguishable. The nation itself became the commodity paraded. For the first time architecture was also swept up in the enterprise of geopolitics; colonial expansion was its apotheosis.[2]

Barbara Rubin (1979) translates this story from glasshouse Paris to the open, also-new world of North America. The Chicago World's Fair of 1893—to mark the fourth centenary of Columbus's discovery of the New World—provided "the opportunity for the [old] culture elite, in alliance with professional taste-makers, to create the first world's fair explicitly intended to set a standard for architectural and urban design," against the garish city of brand names of the new entrepreneurs (Rubin, 1979, p. 343). The function of this grand exemplar was, however, different from that of the European beaux arts models from which it derived, for this "had not to reconcile new urban construction with sanctified architectural relics; American cities were too new to be so demanding of architects' sensitivity and erudition" (p. 344). Rather, it was "to codify, by virtue of its 'high culture' associations with Europe and Antiquity, the hierarchical framework by means of which 'good taste' in America could be distinguished from 'bad taste' " (p. 344).

The taste setter was architect and urban designer Daniel Burnham, and Haussmann's Paris was the dreamworld. Though celebrating capitalist progress (and promulgating it), the Chicago Fair's "White City," as it came to be known, was supposed to be above the crude economics of the market. But by that time, the international expositions had generated a class of petty entrepreneurs who exploited the commercial opportunities presented; so at the 1876 Philadelphia Exposition, these outsiders had developed an amusement zone beyond the city-owned exposition grounds, in what became known as "Shantyville." For Chicago in 1893, however, the amusement zone and its honky-tonk were acknowledged in a separate quarter *within* the grounds—"Midway Plaisance." "Good taste" could only survive provided that "bad taste" was also successfully accommodated. The "ideal" and the "real," observes Rubin.

White City was also an exemplar in another sense. Burnham's collaborator in this vast scheme was Frederick Law Olmsted (1822–1903), by far the most important landscape architect of the nineteenth century and advocate of "scientific" urban planning. Olmsted was also principal progenitor of the American parks movement that accounted for the systems of major and often interconnected urban parks characterizing so many North American cities and democratizing the aristocratic English garden and the objectification of nature—landscape as commodity—though without the intertextuality and literary allusions of the original. Olmsted's contribution to the fair was its overall plan of axes, basins and ponds, and interlaced formality and informality in park and landscape design. The plan, a blending of clear strength and fine subtlety, stood in purposeful contradistinction to the crude grid of the city it adjoined, just as the more or less unified style of its architecture stood against the cacophony of competing entrepreneurs that lined the streets of that grid. Paraphrasing Tafuri and Dal Co (1986), the exemplar was methodological as much as stylistic, to assert through difference or otherness (p. 39).

The Chicago fair was largely credited with triggering the "City

Beautiful" movement in the United States. Civic beautification programs translated the fair's architectural vocabulary to new banks, city halls, urban squares, and the like throughout the country—the example that Rubin gives is Dewey Arch in New York City, which however was immediately confronted by an equally grand advertising sign (among others) for "Heinz Pickles" and "57 Varieties"—the *new* intertextuality, though vastly more fragmented in its momentary grabs for meaning than anything in the contrived sequences of Shenstone's allusions. The paradox of White City versus Midway Plaisance—the ideal versus the real (" 'The Real,' unlike the 'The Ideal,' had to pay its own way" [Rubin, 1979, p. 347])—was thereby reproduced in dual, contradictory aesthetics of the North American (and capitalist) city.

⌐THE PUBLIC, THE PRIVATE, THE FLÂNEUR

Another reading of the fragmenting space of the late-nineteenth-century city returns the focus to Paris. It was quintessentially the city of the avant-garde; to Walter Benjamin it was the "capital of the nineteenth century." The novelists, painters, and poets from Baudelaire to the 1920s depicted the world of the boulevards, cafés, bars, brothels, the *Folies*, and above all the comfort of the crowd, and the *flâneur*—the stroller, the dandy, the urban idler, detached, with distanced gaze, watching the world go by. That this new urban world was the object of avant-gardist representation was not merely incidental; as Doreen Massey (1991) observes, "the spatial and social reorganisation, and flourishing, of urban life was an essential condition for the birth of the new era." However, she adds, this reorganization led to a city that was increasingly *gendered*, first in the sense of "the distinction between the public and the private": The mid-nineteenth century was crucial to the ideological "separation of spheres" and its spatialization, with women increasingly relegated ("ideologically if not for all women in practice") from the public to the private sphere of home and suburb. According to Massey, "The public city which is celebrated in the enthusiastic descriptions of the dawn of modernism was a city for men. The boulevards and cafés, and still more the bars and brothels, were for men—the women who did go there were for male consumption" (p. 47).

The celebration of the world of the flâneur in avant-garde art effectively elevated the commodification of women to conscious bourgeois acceptance, and the public space of the city to "men's world" (every man the voyeur), much as the pastoralist William Shenstone and his ilk had marked the commodification of nature.

> For the flâneur, the city is a "show-place": in the streets, "the
> product surrounded by a flow of customers" (Benjamin) gives the
> illusion of reconciliation with the wilderness of the big city, just as
> the privatised spaces of the garden tramped by a succession of
> visitors make nature into a side-show. Both are landscapes, the
> unknowable made domestic, controllable, "reconciled" (Benjamin).
> (Pugh, 1990, p. 155)

Simon Pugh goes on to observe how the flâneur, in a sense, grew
out of the pastoralist; both privatized the public realm by objectifying
it, as the distanced voyeuristic gaze replaced participation as the path
to the production of knowledge. A bourgeois idle class complemented
an aristocratic one ("like the pastoralist who does not work, the flâneur
does not trade" [Pugh, 1990, p. 155]), and the worlds represented—in
landscape gardening as in the nineteenth-century avant-garde—were
equally false and ultimately repressive (of broader nature, of women,
and, accordingly, of the real potential of human experience). Above
all, their reigns marked "progressive" steps in the commodification that
came to distinguish modernity.

The erotic gaze of the flâneur and the lecher compelled the commodification of women in a second sense. For it is from that gaze that
good women are to be kept, and the private realm becomes ever more
private as the century advances. The house, enveloping and protecting,
is the preeminent locus of the confinement; it and its street—the
milieu of quiet, discrete, respectful surveillance—and its comforting
neighborhood become the new panopticon: Women become their own
keepers, and the new, bourgeois suburbia produces and reproduces an
ideology of self-surveillance of those most precious of all possessions.
The institution of suburbia has always been linked to the gender
division of labor; more hidden have been the links within the space of
suburbia at all levels (the house, the privacy-reinforcing street, the
broader neighborhood and its anonymity), the power relations thus
reproduced (a space for the little woman, a good place to bring up kids),
the environmental, spatial masking of the consequent repression and
self-repression (getting greener, getting better), and the different experiences of women and men (the idyllic world of the suburbs—or is it
the world of isolation and the mortgage trap?—against the "real world"
of capitalist production and bureaucratic guidance).

As suburbia becomes preeminently the realm of consumption—of
the ever-changing, ever-new commodities essential to the keeping of
women—the gendered, fragmenting, isolating space of the city becomes increasingly linked to capitalism's great nightmare: how to push
out that barrier of fixed consumption.

| SPACE AS THE VOID: NIETZSCHE

The most explicitly spatial of all readings of the coming of modernity is that of Friedrich Nietzsche (1844–1900). His hero Zarathustra asks: "And where does man not stand at an abyss? Is seeing itself not—seeing abysses?" (Nietzsche, 1961, p. 177).[3] To which a far more recent text replies: "On the edge of this precipice, you seek the secret of your birth and of your death" (Irigaray, 1991, p. 55).[4]

Once modernity is viewed through the lens of its spatial fracturing, fragmentation, and ambiguity—the cacophonous spaces alluded to in this chapter represent only a surface trace—all faith in modernity-as-progress cracks; the triumph of rationality is revealed as delusion (the gas chambers are foreseen); the commodity world is empty, all meaning has been lost, and we are before the void—the abyss. The most troubling philosophical text of the nineteenth century has to be *Thus Spoke Zarathustra*, written between 1883 and 1885. It is "a spiritual odyssey through the modern world," a savage unmasking of its hollowness, a vast parable of the space of modernity; and, like all parables, it is ambivalent, paradoxical, unstable in its meanings, but thereby insinuating into all sensibilities and deconstructive of all illusions—the certainties come tumbling down.

"Where has God gone?" cries the madman in *The Gay Science*. "I shall tell you. *We have killed him—you and I*" (Nietzsche, 1974). The collapse of faith in the Christian God is an event of such magnitude that its consequences will take us centuries to grasp (one of those centuries has now passed); all we know "must collapse now that this faith has been undermined because it was built on this faith, propped up by it, grown into it" (p. 279). All of Western morality comes down. So with what are we to replace this death (of God, of morality)? The "Superman" (*Ubermensch*), answers Nietzsche—the man who has "overcome" man, that is, himself.[5] The only path is self-overcoming: The Superman is he in whom the "will to power" is sublimated into *creativity*—he who rises above the overcoming of others, to the overcoming of self (Hollingdale, 1961, p. 23). "And life itself told me this secret: 'Behold,' it said, 'I am that which must overcome itself again and again'" (Nietzsche, 1961, p. 138). But now we are standing before the sea, not the abyss. "Behold, what abundance is around us! And it is fine to gaze out upon distant seas from the midst of superfluity. Once you said 'God' when you gazed upon distant seas; but now I have taught you to say 'Superman'" (p. 109). Self-creation—becoming—involves both the sublimely calm and the sublimely tempestuous, and the sea is metaphor for both.

This is the first doctrine of *Thus Spoke Zarathustra*; the second is that of the eternal return. The voice of Courage, the destroyer even of death: " 'Was *that* life? Well then! Once more!' " (p. 178). The idea of the eternal return is not some cosmological thesis that everything has been before and will recur again (though there is something of that in it); nor is it a call to us to will that our actions may live forever (though something of that resides there too) (Caygill, 1993, p. 201). Far more it is the call to take responsibility for the positing of time. The philosopher affirms life in the totality of its details: Every moment is repeated infinitely, so every moment is infinitely important—"history" is repudiated. Nietzsche would deny the significance of *ends* or *purposes*; the notion of *progress* is absurd. We do not try to escape the past (linear time) nor to repeat it (cyclical time), but to accept, creatively, the responsibility for the giving of time: We seize immortality in a new form. Now the space of modernity is a path: Zarathustra struggles upward toward the future, but weighted down (back toward the abyss) by the grievous burden on his back—a dwarf, "the Spirit of Gravity, my devil and arch-enemy" (p. 177). They come to a gateway, from which run two paths, eternally long, one into the future, the other to the past: "They are in opposition to one another, these paths; they abut one another: and it is here at this gateway that they come together. The name of the gateway is written above it: 'Moment' " (p. 178). This new immortality invests life with a great quality—a new morality to replace that which is dead: "So live that you may wish to live again" (Hollingdale, 1961, p. 24).

Distinctively different readings of Nietzsche run through the major texts of both Martin Heidegger and Jacques Derrida in the twentieth century, and both mediately and immediately his voice resonates through most of the philosophy of the present era. That voice itself, however, was always ambivalent; intonations changed. For Nietzsche is described as a "double thinker," celebrating life as a wonderful flux of energy and affirmation (Dionysian), but also preoccupied with images, beautiful illusions, calm restraint, order, and even authority (Apollonian) (Schutte, 1984; Vasseleu, 1993). It is this very instability that distinguishes Nietzsche as *the* philosopher of late modernity. Three themes in particular are taken up (seized in that present "moment of danger"). The first is the seeming rejection of Enlightenment rationality: Attention focuses on the texts not only as a "philosophy of the body" and of human experience and emotion but also as a deconstruction of the logocentric basis of Western thought—the privileging of logic over the poetic, as a mode of representation and, thereby, revelation. Nietzsche alone, of the philosophers of modernity, is spared Derrida's dismissal as still stuck in metaphysics. Nietzsche takes us to "the play of the world" (it is the play of the child, but also of the artist—Fourier's travail passionné again—mixing "being and semblance," and it is the source of new worlds). But Nietzsche also takes us to the loss of play, passion, and affirmation that comes with all language. For language is but a pale reflection of two originary truths: One is of metaphor (only "the forgetting of that primitive world of metaphor" allows us to postulate logical and conceptual "truth" [quoted in Haar, 1992, p. 55]); the other is of music (the affective world, the "originary melody of pleasure and displeasure" [pp. 55–56] crossing, pulsating, and mixing). Writing, in turn, is yet a further diminution:

> What is most comprehensible in language is not the word itself, but the tone, the intensity, the modulation, the tempo with which a series of words is pronounced—in short, the music behind the words, the passion behind this music, the person behind this passion, thus everything that cannot be *written*. This is why it has nothing to do with literature. (*Nachlass*, 1881–1884; quoted in Haar, 1992, p. 58)

Yet, up to a point, writing for Nietzsche *can* restore something of language's double source—the metaphorical and the passional. The "double thinking" has purpose, and philosophy must begin afresh: "Are not all words made for the heavy? Do not all words lie to the light? Sing! speak no more!" sings Zarathustra (Nietzsche, 1961, p. 247).

Habermas's reading of Nietzsche reverses Derrida's enthusiasm. The achievement of the Enlightenment, the reign of human reason, has been denied, and Nietzsche is the enemy of the philosophical project; instead of emancipation—the very focus of that project—we are offered a purely aesthetic, ecstatic abandonment (Habermas, 1987). Habermas's censure extends to Derrida, Lyotard, and all the philosophical heirs to Nietzsche. (One cannot critique rationality except rationally—as Hegel did!) But the lesson that most immediately leaps from the discord of these voices relates, not to the question of which path is to be followed in the quest for human emancipation, but rather to the realization that the question has been there for a century: It is itself part of modernity.

The second theme that the present seizes from Nietzsche is the spatial metaphor for the representation of the modern condition—the void, but preeminently *distance*, "that longing for an ever increasing widening of distance within the soul itself" (Nietzsche, 1972, p. 173). Rosalyn Diprose (1993) paraphrases the argument of distancing's inevitability: "A distance or difference within the self, between the present self and an image of self towards which I aspire, is necessary for change to be incorporated in the constitution and enhancement of the bodily self" (p. 6). The human endeavor is the creation of oneself ("the will to power to be sublimated into creativity"); but the self as work of art is not the same as the self as artist. Rather, "the image which the artistic self creates is a moment beyond the present self which creates it" (Diprose, 1993, p. 6)—the "pathos of distance." Elsewhere it is called "difference," the image of "the other." Gilles Deleuze (1983) observes that Nietzsche is *the* philosopher of difference. Space, not time, is the medium of modernity, and Nietzsche hurls us back into space—the void, the sea (the "oceanic feeling"), the path on which we would will ourselves to travel eternally (even time can only be represented spatially), distance.

Woman may be distance itself, suggests Jacques Derrida, and that equation brings us to the third theme from Nietzsche appropriated into the present age. All too easily does Nietzsche present as the misogynist ("Are you visiting women? Do not forget your whip!"); but, as ever, the voice is ambivalent. Woman is the distanced, complementary image that man posits in constituting himself; so woman can never be possessed by man, for the distance must forever be maintained. "Everything about woman is a riddle," says Zarathustra, "and everything about woman has one solution: it is called pregnancy." Thus, that ultimate image of man as self created is forever unattainable. "For the woman, the man is a means: the end is always the child. But what is the woman for the man?"—danger and play (1961, p. 91)! For Luce Irigaray (1991), the strength of Nietzsche is in his insistence on unbridgeable difference and in his refusal to sustain the fantasy supporting rational discourse—that there is only one sex. Derrida also sees the difference as Nietzschean distance between ways of being/becoming in the world:

> That which will not be pinned down by truth is, in truth—*feminine*. This should not however, be mistaken for a woman's femininity, for female sexuality, or for any other essentializing fetishes which might tantalize the dogmatic philosopher, the impotent artist or the inexperienced seducer who has not yet escaped his foolish hopes for capture. (Derrida 1979, p. 55)

But suddenly *truth* is the ultimate male fetish—the Enlightenment heritage. A feminist response: That which constitutes women may be the distance/difference between female sexuality (the surface wherein, at any particular moment, the woman is represented) and the feminine (the undecidable concept that truth will not pin down) (Diprose, 1993, p. 23).

AFTERWORD AND FOREWORD

Modernity presents as fragmentation itself, and the nineteenth century was the age when its opposite, in the unitary dreams of the Enlightenment, finally disintegrated. Just as Marx could only have seen explanation for human history in contradiction—in the economic—at a precise moment in that history, so too was Nietzsche's reflection on the distance between the male and the female—the constitution of the human—only possible at a precise instant. Despite the shattering of the glass, the century had its triumph, and it was the triumph of the bourgeoisie. Paris of the boulevards, the arcades and the expositions, like Chicago or Philadelphia or any other aspiring metropolis of the trans-Atlantic—but not yet Los Angeles—could all reveal the glories of the commodity world, its perpetual breaking into a million parts, and the million entrepreneurial opportunities thus made. The gathering stories of the triumph and of its fragmenting space—the reassessments—are a preface to a reading of the twentieth century.

CHAPTER 4

The Space of Revolution: 1900 and the Maelstrom

This confusion was only a facade. Our provocations, demonstrations and defiances were only a means of arousing the bourgeoisie to rage, and through rage to a shamefaced self-awareness. Our real motive force was not rowdiness for its own sake, or contradiction and revolt in themselves, but the question (basic then, as it is now), "where next?"

—HANS RICHTER, *Dada: Art and Anti-Art* (1965, p. 9)

We bring new cities. We bring the world new things. We will give them other names.

—KASIMIR MALEVICH, "UNOVIS—The Champions of the New Art," reprinted in L. A. Zhadova, *Malevich: Suprematism and Revolution in Russian Art, 1910–1930* (1920/1982, p. 297)

The epoch of the bourgeoisie was also the epoch of the avant-garde and brought a new question into focus: Can architectural and urban design—the production of spatial meaning—adopt an effective revolutionary stance? The thought of painting, sculpture, poetry, or literature to unmask repression, to offer a vision of a better world, even of a new mode of production and form of social integra-

45

tion, or to inspire to some revolutionary violence—to cast off the chains—is not especially problematic. At first, abstracted glance, a similarly intentioned, purposively produced urban meaning might also seem conceivable. At second glance, however, the doubts must gather.

For one thing, while the meanings (signifieds) might with difficulty be nominated—aspects of a world without palaces, a world of equality, of difference without hierarchy, the nobility of human labor, or whatever—designers must ultimately design signifiers, physical objects to convey those meanings. So what are *they* to be? How do we get from abstracted ideas to buildable images? Second, it would seem far easier to get one's revolutionary-intentioned painting exhibited or poem published than to have a similarly intended building or part of the city built—neither capital nor the state is likely to knowingly self-destruct, and who else is there to pay for it? Designers have of course periodically found the signifiers appropriate to their intended meanings; and even though their outrages have not been built, they too have been exhibited and published like the paintings and poems. Fourier's *phalanstère*, Le Corbusier's *Ville contemporaine*, and the architectural and urban designs of the Russian constructivists leap to mind. So, third, has there been any revolutionary *effect*? One could certainly derive but little encouragement from the cases of Fourier, the utopian socialists (the new social worlds of Robert Owen, the Proudhonists and their ilk subverted to company towns), and the arts and crafts movement (the attempted rejection of the capitalist mode of production descending, with William Morris, into marvelously lucrative *capitalist* production).[1] However, before any conclusion can be suggested, it is necessary to consider the most extraordinary collision of revolutionary ideas in the production of the built environment and of its meanings in the modern age. The time is around and immediately following World War I.

THE REVOLT AGAINST
THE BOURGEOIS WORLD

In the individual's experience of space, time, and the self, World War I brought a profound disorientation—a rupturing of the old continuities and certainties—that rendered bourgeois representations of that old experience painfully nostalgic to some and grotesquely anachronistic to the avant-garde. Symptomatic of the reaction, Hugo Ball founded the Cabaret Voltaire in Zurich, on February 1, 1916, thereby launching the dadaist "provocations, demonstrations and defiances." The virulence of the rejection really preceded the war: Picasso's *Les Demoiselles d'Avignon* dated from 1907; Stravinsky interposed the musical chaos of

The Rite of Spring in 1913; even more significant was Schönberg's discarding tonality (most notably in *Pierrot Lunaire* of 1912) as prelude to the complete break of the twelve-tone system (in 1923); and 1913–1914 also saw breaks in literature from Proust, Lawrence, and Joyce (see, e.g., Bradbury and McFarlane, 1976). The extraordinary flowering of avant-garde activity is not however to be seen merely as iconoclasm or despair; it was, rather, an attempt to represent a profoundly new experience of space and time and of the self—a tension between the protean hero and the working class (and neither was bourgeois).[2] Electronic communications had brought the phenomenon of *simultaneity*—there was both distance (in travel, in the movement of commodities and labor power) and no distance (in communication and the movement of information). The compression of space and time was now increasingly *differentiated*. So *Les Demoiselles d'Avignon* and the cubist *oeuvre* generally are not to be viewed simply as distortion or rejection of the bourgeois representations of nineteenth-century space (though they were also that), but as an attempt to represent that simultaneity and differentiation. The new ambiguities could scarcely be represented through perspectivist conceptions of space and sequential accounts of time. (We must, in our creativity, accept the responsibility for the giving of time and the picturing of space—Nietzsche.)

I would agree with Gregory Ulmer (1985) that "by most accounts, collage is the single most revolutionary formal innovation in artistic representation to occur in our century" (p. 84; Ulmer especially cites Kostelanetz, 1978). Though ancient, collage's elevation to "high art" is attributed to Picasso and Braque, as a solution to problems raised by cubism, thereby providing "an alternative to the 'illusionism' of perspective which had dominated Western painting since the early Renaissance." Ulmer (1985, p. 84) quotes an account by Edward Fry:

> In a still-life scene at a café, with lemon, oyster, glass, pipe, and newspaper [*Still-life with chair caning* (1912), the first cubist collage], Picasso glued a piece of oilcloth on which is printed the pattern of woven caning, thus indicating the presence of a chair. . . . For just as the painted letters JOU signify JOURNAL, a section of facsimile caning signifies the whole chair. Later Picasso would go one step further and incorporate into his collages actual objects or fragments of objects, signifying literally themselves. (Fry, 1966, p. 27)

A similar shift in signification characterized dada (Richter, 1965). The preoccupation with simultaneity, and with the emergent ambiguities in the experience of space and time, also permeated the new high modernism in literature (Proust, Joyce, Pound, among others); even more so it permeated architecture. A new aesthetic based on inter-penetrating planes, spaces, and volumes, and on a designed ambiguity between spatial containment and disintegration and between enclosed and open space, characterized the architectural ideas emanating from the Bauhaus, proclaimed at Weimar in 1919. It emerged even more strongly in the early designs of Le Corbusier (Charles Edouard Jean-neret, 1887–1965). From 1925, the date of his *Pavillon de l'esprit nou-veau* for the Paris Exposition des arts décoratifs, there began a long series of published designs and completed projects that represented a far more radical break with all previous (bourgeois) design than any-thing in the Bauhaus output.[3] Preceding these extraordinary designs, and, I would argue, establishing their essentially *revolutionary* program, were the first of Le Corbusier's visions for a new space of urban life.

URBAN DESIGN AS TRANSFORMATION, 1: LE CORBUSIER

Le Corbusier was not the first to conceive of an architecture and urban design that could represent this new experience of space and time in those first decades of the twentieth century. Two visions especially stand out: Antonio Sant'Elia's *La Città nouva* of 1914 and Tony Garnier's *La Cité industrielle* of 1904–1918. The latter was significant mainly for its program: a "socialist city" (no church, police, barracks, law court, or private property), based on industry (but separating and even counterposing the industrial zone with that of civil society), civilizing, low density, with all unoccupied land as green parkland and with not only its urban morphology resolved in detail but even its construction methods specified (principally reinforced concrete and steel) (Garnier, 1917/1932; Wiebenson, 1969). Garnier's beaux arts credentials were impeccable—student of Gaudet, winner of the 1899 Prix de Rome—yet it was during his tenure of that prize, and in apparent reaction to the vacuity of his beaux arts background, that *La Cité industrielle* was conceived. And significantly, the formality of the beaux arts tradition persisted in *La Cité industrielle*, despite the reaction. By contrast, the significance of *La Città nuova* was in its imagery. Some time around 1912, Sant'Elia had teamed up with the Italian futurists, whose rejection of bourgeois design and embracing of new technology, the speed of modern communication, and the destruction of the mu-seum and of all tradition were more protofascist than socialist. It was also, incidentally, an explicit rejection of Ruskin, William Morris, and

the arts-and-crafts movement, though an adoption of their moral preoccupations. Whether Sant'Elia is to be labeled a futurist is debated;[4]
scarcely contestable however are the futurist ideas behind his numerous drawings for a "new city": electricity-generating stations, airports
atop central railway stations (and suicidally flanked with skyscrapers),
airship hangars, illuminated skyline advertising, "bringing together
skyscraper towers and multi-level circulation in an image that has
dominated modern ideas of town-planning right down to the present
time" (Banham, 1960, p. 119) (see Figure 4.1).

In 1907, Le Corbusier met Garnier in Lyons; he also visited the
functioning commune at the Charterhouse of Ema, in Tuscany. Both
events had a profound effect on the development of his own socialist
ideas and program. Also influential was his experience, in the work of
Auguste Perret, of the Hennebique system of reinforced concrete columns and floor slabs, where walls would merely be non-load-bearing
screens. These various elements came together in a project of 1910 for
a school of applied art: three-stepped tiers of studios, each with an
enclosed garden, around a communal, glass-roofed space (*Le Corbusier,
1910–1960*, 1960, p. 23). Kenneth Frampton's (1985a) more recent
voice represents the project as an exercise in multivalence and interpretation.

> This free adaptation of the Carthusian cell form, with its connota-
> tions of communality, was the first instance on which Le Corbusier
> reinterpreted a received type in order to accommodate the pro-
> gramme of an entirely new type. Such typological transformations,
> with their spatial and ideological references, were to become an
> intrinsic part of his working method. Since this synthetic procedure
> was impure by definition, it was inevitable that his works should
> become charged with references to a number of different antece-
> dents at once. (p. 150)

(It is worth emphasizing that these were "typological *transformations*," and not explicit references. Le Corbusier was already some
distance from cubism and collage, and was by 1918 to reject them
outright, in favor of "purism."[5])

Frampton (1985a) comments on another aspect of Le Corbusier's
"method": a dialectical "habit of mind"—"that ever-present play with
opposites . . . that permeates his architecture and is evident as a habit
of mind in most of his theoretical texts" (p. 149). The method anticipates a postmodernist aesthetic of "in-betweenness." Frampton suggests its derivation from an Albigensian background and its Manichean
worldview. Certainly the opposites loom in the first major demonstra-

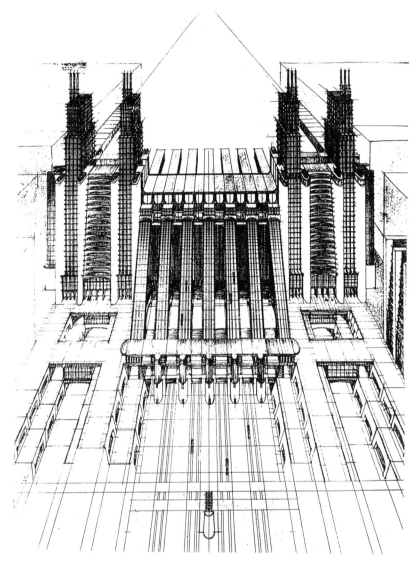

FIGURE 4.1. Antonio Sant'Elia: Airplane and railroad station, with cable cars and elevators on three street levels, 1914. From Caramel and Longatti (1987).

tion of his urban design ideas: the Ville contemporaine for three million people, of 1922 (*Le Corbusier et Pierre Jeanneret: Oeuvre complète 1910–1929*, 1935) (see Figure 4.2). There is first the dialectic of a beaux arts formal plan (major axes, diagonals, ronds points, all far more formalist than anything in Garnier) versus an unashamedly futurist commitment to technology, communications, and a totally new urban imagery (at the city center there are no fewer than seven superimposed levels of circulation, with the Sant'Elian element of an airport on the top level, again suicidally surrounded by skyscrapers, and a central railway station underneath). There is also a dialectic—even paradox or contradiction—between a commitment to communal housing forms and a clear acknowledgment of the hierarchical, information-dominated nature of the modern, capitalist–bureaucratic state:

> These skyscrapers [of the city center] will contain the city's brains, the brains of the whole nation. They stand for all the careful working-out and organisation on which the general activity is based. Everything is concentrated in them: *apparatus for abolishing time and space*, telephones, cable and wireless; the banks, business affairs and the control of industry; finance, commerce, specialisation. (Le Corbusier, quoted in Banham, 1960, p. 254; emphasis added)

The elitism of this acknowledgment (thereby, reproduction) of capitalist centralized control, and its contrast with Le Corbusier's avowedly socialist ideals, did not pass unnoticed at the time; the communists, in particular, were highly skeptical of Le Corbusier's intentions (Frampton, 1985a, p. 155).

A third dialectic characterizes the approach to landscape: The relentless formalism of axes and diagonals was opposed to a picturesque, "English garden" treatment of the natural landscape. Indeed, claimed Le Corbusier, "the English garden is destined to be the logical extension of the heart of the city," linking it in turn to the surrounding countryside (*Le Corbusier, 1910–1960*, 1960, p. 288) (see Figure 4.3). We are back to that French preoccupation with "transitions" from the built world (spaces of manly control) to the space of untrained nature, in contrast to the "mythic rupture" of the English garden (Bann, 1990, again). But the languages of representation are now mixed, and the imagery is English, not French.

By any standards, the Ville contemporaine is an extraordinary achievement of both synthesis and innovation and is the most complete of all visions of an alternative urban space. And note that Le Corbusier termed it "contemporary," not a "future," city—he insisted on its imme-

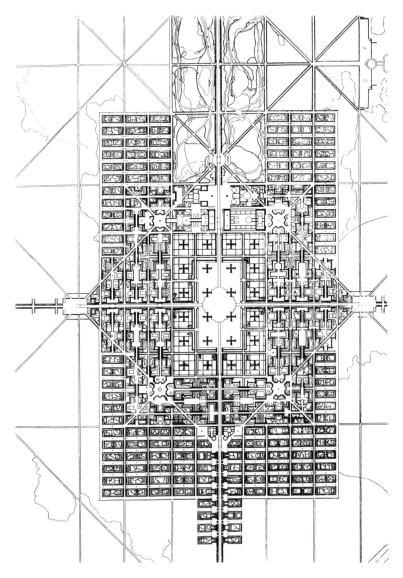

FIGURE 4.2. Le Corbusier: La Ville contemporaine for three million people, 1922. Beaux arts formality, an antibourgeois aesthetic, a futurist dedication to new technology, a socialist program, and an English garden landscape. From *Le Corbusier et Pierre Jeanneret: Oeuvre complète 1910–1929* (1935).

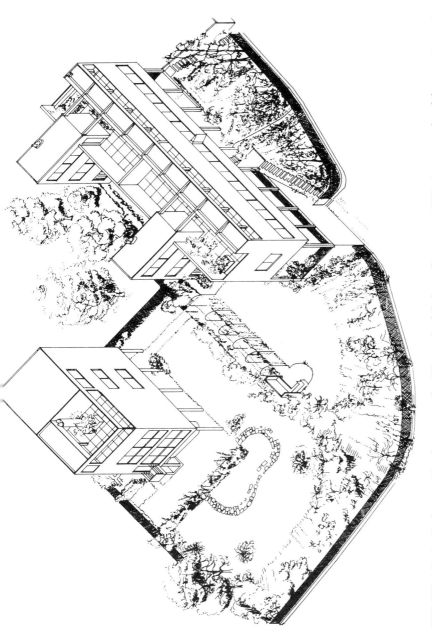

FIGURE 4.3. Le Corbusier: Two houses in the Weissenhof Colony, Stuttgart, 1927. An example of the superimposition of a purist, antibourgeois aesthetic on an English garden landscape. Author's drawing, based on *Le Corbusier et Pierre Jeanneret: Oeuvre complète 1910–1920* (1935).

diate relevance and feasibility. It was exhibited at the 1922 Salon
d'automne in Paris and then again in 1925 in the Pavillon de l'esprit
nouveau alongside an even more provocative demonstration of his
intentions. The Plan Voisin for Paris, acknowledging that the automo-
bile had destroyed Paris, proposed that it now become a central element
in its (futurist?) resurrection: Most of the historic city north of the Seine
would be demolished and a development of the Ville contemporaine
would be constructed in its place. Two great motor roads extend endlessly beyond the city—both symbolically and functionally "urbanizing
all space"—with the office towers mainly on the north–south axis and
the immeubles villas mostly on the east–west, with only a few monuments of the past preserved. Both the boulevard of the flâneur and the
bourgeois park are rejected. Certainly Le Corbusier anticipated the
outrage, even from "progressive" circles, and countered it in the accompanying polemic. He also subsequently acknowledged that the plan
"seemed as much an amusing utopia as an extended study in bad taste"
(Le Corbusier, 1910–1960, 1960, p. 292). But from its serious intent and
immediate feasibility, he never resiled. The new, "high modern" experience of space and time was to be functionally accommodated and
symbolically represented in a new form of urban space. The bourgeois
city had run its course, its overthrow was imminent.

Though the intent was emancipatory, the contradictions were over-
whelming. The greatest was revealed when, also in 1925, Le Corbusier
published his ideas on the city, as Urbanisme; its last illustration was an
engraving of Louis XIV commanding construction of the Invalides. Its
caption read: "Homage to a great town-planner—This despot conceived
great projects and realised them. Over all the country his noble works
still fill us with admiration. He was capable of saying, 'We wish it,' or
'Such is our pleasure' " (quoted in Banham, 1960, p. 256). "We love the
solution," he declared (Banham, 1960, p. 250); and elsewhere, "The
situation called for a man of resolute will charged with the authority of
going about and getting a solution to the question of the city. A Colbert
was needed!" (Le Corbusier, 1910–1960, 1960, p. 292).

Instrumental rationality and action triumph. Many schemes of
extraordinary vision for new cities followed: Rio de Janeiro (1929),
Algiers (1930–1934 and again in 1942), Antwerp and Nemours (both
1933), Hellocourt (1935), the University City of Brazil (1936), Paris
again (1937), Buenos Aires (1938), La Rochelle-Pallice (1945–1946),
Saint-Dié (1946), Bogota (1950), Chandigarh (1951–1954). More
generalized, and without reference to any specific site, was La Ville
radieuse of 1935—effectively an update of the Ville contemporaine,
intended to be linear, extendable, and classless (attempting to avoid
both the spatial and social hierarchy of the earlier project), and far

more resolved in its architectural and detailed urban design. There was also a design for "the agrarian Reorganization, the cooperative Village" ("the key to the economic solution"), of 1934–1938 (*Le Corbusier, 1910–1960*, 1960, p. 315), and for a linear industrial city of 1942–1943. All of these schemes would represent the universality of the new civilization, and the radical break; and all would address "the solution" rather than any process. However, as the most persistent images and exemplars of "the city" of high modernism, they shaped the very idea of urban planning and design in this era, and thereby became part of "the process." At least in the 1920s it was far from a universally accepted process however.

URBAN DESIGN AS TRANSFORMATION, 2: THE SOVIET UNION

Architecture and urban design in the Soviet Union are of special interest in the 1920s, for here occurred the twentieth century's most sustained reaction to capitalist society. And in the aesthetic sphere, the central dilemma was this dialectic between solution and process.

By the time of the 1917 Revolution, Frampton observes, two avant-garde movements had arisen in Russia.[6] The first was "apocalyptic," promising to "transform everyday life into [a] millenial future," akin to futurism, adopting a highly abstract, nonobjective, nonutilitarian expression, and best represented in the poetry of Kruchonykh and the graphic arts of Malevich, Kandinsky, and Lissitzky. It is especially well documented in Lissitzky-Küppers (1967). Kasimir Malevich was the movement's clear leader; his struggle between 1910 and 1915 to find an "escape route from the impasse of Russian Cubo-Futurism" (Zygas, 1981, p. 65) somewhat predated Le Corbusier's similar shift from cubism to purism, and the resulting aesthetic was similarly austere. Malevich's (1928) own claim was that

> Suprematism arose in 1913 (a planar phenomenon) in its static and dynamic phases and was painted predominantly in black, red and subsequently, white; white Suprematism appeared at an exhibition in 1918 (the works were done in 1917). Volumetric Suprematism began to develop in 1918, although the elements of it had emerged as early as 1915. (quoted in Zygas, 1981, p. 66)

It is "volumetric suprematism" and the related scaleless, ambiguous architectural models of intersecting and overlain planes and rectangles that were subsequently taken up in the architectural and urban design ideas of Mies Van Der Rohe and the International Style of the 1950s.

The second avant-garde was "synthetic," aiming to "forge a new cultural unity from the material and cultural exigencies of communal life and production" (Frampton, 1985a, p. 168). This latter had derived from the Slavophile arts-and-crafts movement that blossomed following the liberation of the serfs in 1861 but was transformed toward a grassroots cultural force through the "scientific" cultural theories of the visionary doctor, philosopher, and politician A. A. Malinovsky (who styled himself "Bogdanov"). Gorky, Bogdanov, and Lunacharsky believed in *bogostroitel'stvo* ("God Building")—that the anticipated revolution and socialism would effect a mystical, religious unity of the proletariat, bringing individuals to their true, godlike potential. Together they were responsible for organizing the party schools on Capri and in Bologna in the decade preceding the 1917 Revolution (with Lenin establishing a rival school at Longjumeau to counter the heresy). Bogdanov argued that the advance to socialism would be along three autonomous paths: the economic, the political, and the cultural. The proletariat had made some progress in the economic and the political but none at all in the cultural. The role of that cultural path was crucial: to effect "the organisation of social experience, in cognition as well as emotions and aspirations" (Lodder, 1983a, p. 75)—in other words, to unmask present experience, partly through the critical study of past culture, and to represent a motivating vision of a socialist world. As artistic production is just another instance of human labor, needing to be emancipated from present production relations, this new proletarian art will necessarily involve everyday, accessible, theoretical and technical knowledge, but it will also need to be catalyzed by an ideologically pure, proletarian elite. To this end, Bogdanov and his colleagues founded Proletkult (Organization for Proletarian Culture), which aimed to regenerate society by unifying traditional culture with the material product of a new proletarian collectivity, thereby yielding a new (essentially Saint-Simonist) principle of social integration. Utilitarianism replaced the nonutilitarianism of the Malevich persuasion.

The 1917 Revolution focused the antibourgeois thrust of these two movements, but it also exacerbated the conflict between them. Kasimir Malevich in 1919 established a "suprematist" school of fine art in Vitebsk (based on the former Institute of Art and Practical Work, from which he had ousted symbolist Marc Chagall) and founded the UNOVIS group—the Affirmers of the New Art. Opposed were the "productivists," furthering the Bogdanov line, and including Tatlin and Rodchenko; there was also a strongly rationalist tradition, represented especially in the increasingly significant constructivist movement that included Ladovsky, the brothers Vesnin, and the brothers Stenberg. At an institutional level, Inkhuk (the Institute for Artistic Culture) and Vkhutemas (the Higher State Art and Technical Studios) were founded in Moscow in 1920 to advance education in art, architecture, and design; and both served as fora for debate between these various artistic paths. At the same time, graphic art was actively mobilized to fulfill the communication needs of the Revolution among a mainly illiterate population: The art was essentially proletarian and relatively spontaneous, taking the form of street theater, film, exhortatory graphics to cover every available urban surface, street art displayed in "Agit-Prop" trains and boats—all most simply produced and easily transportable (see, e.g., Kopp, 1970, pp. 43–51; Zygas, 1981; see Figure 4.4). This production especially became the task of the Proletkult artists of Bog-

FIGURE 4.4. An urban design of pure messages: A. Rodchenko, Agit-Prop kiosks, 1919–1920. Author's drawing, based on Khan-Magomedov (1986).

danov's group. The new "urban design"—the purposive production of urban meaning—was productivist (and activist), mobile and demountable, and diffuse in its forms and media.

As Tafuri has observed, these attempts to transform the whole city, and in turn to urbanize the countryside by transporting the new messages of the city beyond its limits, seemed to be realizing one of the central myths of the avant-garde: "a total work of art which . . . would exorcise the separateness of all artistic products, the partiality and alienated individuality of the objects floating on the waves of the metropolitan universe" (Tafuri and Dal Co, 1986, p. 175). It was Marx's "productivist aesthetic"—the search for knowledge (about a new mode of production and of social integration) as "potential within the object, the material," and "the return of artistic experience to the life of the masses."[7]

In view of this central role of street theater, it is worth observing V. Meyerhold's "Octobrist" proclamation of 1920 setting out three principles of the "agitatory" theater: (1) the unification of audience and actors, (2) antinaturalistic, mechanized production (with the circus as something of a model); and (3) the exclusion of illusion and the symbolist ideas still characterizing the bourgeois theater (Frampton, 1985a, p. 170; also Lodder, 1983a, pp. 170–180; see Figure 4.5).

By 1920, however, Proletkult and its advocacy of the central role for agitational cultural production in the revolutionary enterprise were

FIGURE 4.5. The machine invades the theater, and both invade the city: Lyubov Popova, stage design for Meyerhold. Author's drawing, based on Khan-Magomedov (1983) and Lodder (1983b).

running into trouble. Bogdanov's somewhat Weberian notion of the threefold path to socialism sat ill with Lenin's more Marxist ideas; and the insistence on the autonomy of the cultural sphere—its "necessary" separation from an always-compromised politics and its critical function relative to evolving political and economic relations of society— meant that Proletkult was emerging as virtually an alternative workers' party. Bogdanov was accordingly repudiated, and Proletkult was subjected to Narkompros (the People's Commissariat of Enlightenment, directed by Bogdanov's still enlightened ex-colleague Lunacharsky). Much of the Agit-Prop program persisted however in Meyerhold's theater, and in the continuing Proletkult output of kiosks, tribunes, and other information structures, in what Frampton (1985a) calls "the first attempts to formulate a nonprofessional socialist style of architecture" (p. 170).[8]

Something of the brilliant turmoil of the time can emerge from two stories. The first is that of Gustav Klucis. He is reputed to have been a revolutionary from the age of ten (in the 1905 uprisings), a soldier in 1917 (with a notoriously ruthless, revolutionary regiment), studied art with various schools, but most notably with Malevich in 1919, producing strongly architectural paintings (e.g., *The Dynamic City* of 1919) that were markedly akin to Malevich's and Lissitzky's architectural compositions from that time. He exhibited with the UNOVIS group in both Vitebsk (1920) and Moscow (1921) and opened a UNOVIS studio in the Vkhutemas school prior to his graduation there in 1921. But at the same time, he moved from suprematism to a more constructivist approach and from abstraction to agitational and analytical art. The most notable output from the shift was a series of agitational stands and "radio-orators" of 1922, to overlay a city of revolutionary meaning (both analytical and exhortatory) on the city of preexisting meanings (see Figure 4.6). The second story is of Aleksei Gan, whose progress was from futurism, to association with the ubiquitous Malevich by 1918, experimentation with photomontage, then responsibility for revolutionary festivals and mass urban spectacles with Narkompros from 1918 to 1920. In 1922 he published his seminal aesthetic treatise *Constructivism*, "the first theoretical text of the Soviet era to link the problems of artistic creation with the problems posed by the building of a socialist society" (Kopp, 1985, p. 8). By 1924 he had split with most of the constructivist groups, turning instead to agitational kiosks and stands, furniture, photography and cinema. Constructivism, to Gan, was to provide, through the informational city and countryside, a complete vision for life and the world; the path to that city and countryside, however, was going to compel an almost dadaist fury—

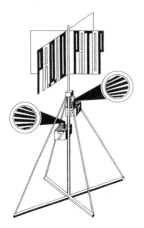 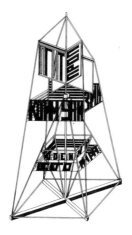 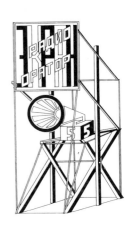

FIGURE 4.6. An urban design of revolutionary agitation: Gustav Klucis, agitational stands, 1922. Author's drawing, based on Khan-Magomedov (1983) and Lodder (1983b).

"We declare uncompromising war on art," was his slogan (Lodder, 1983a, p. 244). Both Klucis and Gan died in a Stalin labor camp.

More at the level of solution than of artistic production as process, and tending to link both productivists and suprematists, was a series of technologically visionary, "constructivist" designs to actively represent new conceptions of collective life and production, the new unity of social life, and the internationalist goal of socialism. There was also something of a turning back to *meaning*—to what James Wertsch (1991) has called the Russian "priority of semantics," the ways that "language and other semiotic systems could be used to produce meaning, especially meaning as it shapes human action" (p. 67) (see Figures 4.7 and 4.8). The most notable essay was Tatlin's symbolically charged tower as a monument to the Third International (1919–1920)—two intertwining logarithmic spirals, enclosing (and counterpointing) four suspended, transparent volumes rotating at progressively faster speeds (and representing the new time frames of legislation, administration, information, and cinematic projection), all constructed of glass and iron (see Figure 4.9). To be expressed was the new, dynamic (socialist!) experience of space and time that must challenge the static (bourgeois) experience represented in the static Eiffel Tower. It was to stand at 400 meters, 100 meters higher than its bourgeois precursor. Also outstanding were the brothers Vesnin's Pravda Building for Moscow (1923) (see Figure 4.10), Melnikov's USSR Pavilion for the 1925 Exposition des arts decoratifs in Paris, and Lissitzky's "cloud-hanger" (1924), intended

FIGURE 4.7. New languages: All previous worlds must be rejected. Project for the top elevation of the city, A. Rodchenko, 1920. From Khan-Magomedov (1986). Adapted by permission, Idea Books Edizioni, Milano.

as a dialectical response to both the capitalist skyscraper and the classical gate. There was also a preoccupation with simpler building forms to facilitate the new mode of social integration—workers' clubs, recreation facilities, and the like. El Lissitzky, who brought almost a Choisyesque rationalism to architectural and urban theory of the 1920s and apparently first coined the term "constructivist" to symbolize his argument (Banham, 1960, p. 194), could describe the Pravda Building thus (Lissitzky, 1930, p. 13):

> The building is characteristic of an age that thirsts after glass, iron and concrete. All the accessories that a metropolitan street imposes on a building—illustrations, publicity, clock, loudspeaker, even the

lifts inside—are all drawn into the design as equally important parts
and brought to unity. This is the aesthetic of constructivism.
(quoted in Banham, 1960, p. 195)

Kestutis Zygas (1981) refers to these "accessories" as the "compo-
nent fixation" of the Russian avant-garde (p. 72). Elsewhere it is
described as elementarism–constructivism: The components or elements are to be separately expressed and assembled, the building (and
the whole city for that matter) effectively analyzed for its program
before the observer's very eyes. As well as expressing the structural cage
in all its elements, there were almost invariably radio antennae, sound
horns, illuminated screens, billboards, projectors—all there for the
explicit purpose of political agitation. Clocks were also indispensable:
A new society had to live in a new sense of time—of modernist (and

FIGURE 4.8. Again, the top elevation of a new city in a new world: A.
Rodchenko, 1920. From Khan-Magomedov (1986). Copyright 1986 by Idea
Books. Adapted by permission, Idea Books Edizioni, Milano.

socialist) progress replacing both the cyclical time of peasant life and the linear but regressive time of capitalist repression. Both in their projected buildings and in the ubiquitous Agit-Prop kiosks, tribunes, and theater sets, the design "method" was one of architectural collage. And the concern was almost entirely with urban space as theater: The structural cage, components, and agitatory messages were everything, internal spatial arrangements were neglected. As Zygas (1981) concludes, "The interest in architectural space had yielded to a fixation on the external, space-enclosing elements" (p. 74); and on their meanings, one should add. In other words, on urban design.

With Lenin's death in 1924, the Revolution effectively ended. The problem of housing and of forms of settlement dominated architectural discourse and was especially pursued in the investigations of OSA (the Association of Contemporary Architects), founded in 1924

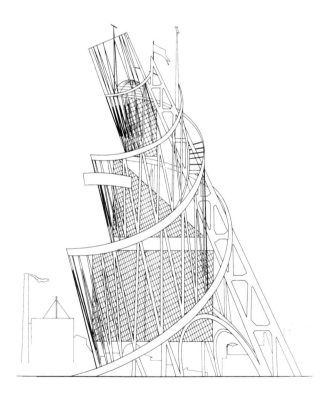

FIGURE 4.9. Vladimir Tatlin: Tower to celebrate the Third International, 1919–1920. Drawing by Matt Spinaze, based on Kopp (1970) and Khan-Magomedov (1983).

under the leadership of Moisei Ginzburg. The essential task for constructivist architecture, argued Ginzburg, was the creation of "social condensers": buildings, complexes, or even whole cities that could not only perform their immediate functions but also motivate users (or, if necessary, constrain them) to new actions, new habits—and, thereby, new ways of living. Collectivity was invariably implied, with workers' clubs, communal child care, laundries and sewing rooms, communal dining facilities, and the like. Although the short-term goal was the improvement of immediate, everyday life, especially for women, the ultimate intention was a transformation of all aspects of human existence—the end of an ego-centered human experience. The political revolution had been won; now it was time for the cultural revolution—

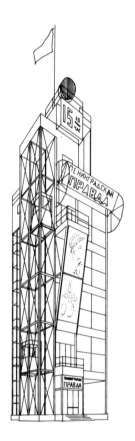

FIGURE 4.10. The Brothers Vesnin: Pravda Building, Moscow, 1923. Author's drawing, based on Frampton (1985) and *Architectural Drawings of the Russian Avant-Garde* (1990).

the profoundest of all forms of revolution, through which the shift to a socialized form of production could be achieved, everyday life replacing the ego-focused worlds of capitalism and the family and supplanting that "quality of ego-strength" that Morris Berman (in turn, echoing Freud) sees as distinguishing the modern. The architecture to achieve this cultural revolution was something of an "elementarist" version of Fourier's phalanstère (the "elements" separately expressed, then recombined, like the Vesnins' Pravda building), overlain with Leninist ideas and rhetoric. Certainly Ginzburg and his colleagues remained acutely aware that collectivization could not be achieved overnight, nor by architectural means alone: The design of buildings and the relations between urban elements could "stimulate but not dictate" the transition to a "socially superior mode of life." The communal houses were therefore transitional (still only halfway to the final, collectivized world) but inspirational (showing that way); they were also, by most accounts, sad failures. Though Anatole Kopp (1985, p. 80) tends to excuse the architects for the disasters, putting blame instead on the officials who ordered the study and building of communal houses, nevertheless the designers were preeminent in the early debates on an architectural program for social revolution and took to the directives with enthusiasm. There was some mild advance, most notably in the shift (albeit tentative) away from a gender-based division of labor in the domestic sphere, though here the earlier Agit-Prop programs may have been as determinative as the motivational social condensers of the OSA group.

The constructivists were also caught up in another debate of the late 1920s involving *forms of settlement*. The context was set with the political–economic battle between the ideas of N. I. Bukharin (for a continuous, balanced development between industrial and agricultural sectors) and those of E. Preobrazhensky (for an uneven development favoring the industrial over the agricultural, with open conflict between the two). The outcome was that the 1928 Five Year Plan went for rapid development of basic industry, but without the political sophistication of Preobrazhensky's thesis; the result was the profound dislocation of both city and countryside of the 1930s. Some 354 new cities were to be built around the new production nodes; numerous European architects were brought in to assist the design task, and avant-garde ideas survived for a time; but the resource problem and the backwardness of the building industry were ultimately defeating. A frustrated avant-garde increasingly turned to more utopian ideals, as Tafuri has observed (Tafuri and Dal Co, 1986, p. 186): The "urbanists" for example, allied with Ginzburg's OSA group, proposed new settlements that were based on communal houses, socialized life replacing the family, and centralized activities that would in turn transform peasant life. Opposed were the "disurbanists," calling for industrial and residential dispersion and a fusion of city and countryside: A model was the linear city theory of Soria y Mata, with ideas of anarchist origin.[9] Ultimately, the urban program failed to cope with the resource problem; and the very diversity of Soviet architectural urban design and planning thinking was anathema to the paranoia of the Stalinist era.

Though finally suppressed in the Soviet Union, the Russian avant-garde was not without lasting influence, in architecture and urban design as in other fields. Wassily Kandinsky and Naum Gabo (Pevsner) moved to the West following Lenin's 1920 curbing of the avant-garde, the former joining the Bauhaus in 1922; after 1923, the Bauhaus and Vkhutemas apparently influenced each other substantially. In 1922 as well, El Lissitzky, one of the most significant theoreticians of the modern movement, moved to Berlin and introduced suprematist ideas into the aesthetic discourses of Western Europe. Productivist ideas were also introduced, for example in lightweight, demountable "constructivist" furniture; but the participatory, "communist" design practice advocated by Bogdanov and the Proletkult movement seems to have left little trace—except in those tired graphics of socialist–realist urban art that persisted in Eastern Europe until the political collapses of 1989–1990 and in the Soviet Union to 1991.

Three forms of legacy from that extraordinary era remain. First is the vast reservoir of constructivist images from the formalist experiments of Inkhuk and Vkhutemas, most notably from what was referred to as "laboratory work"—models and drawings, exhibited and published (but never built), structurally adventurous and geometrically dynamic, and intended as a language of forms appropriate to a new society oriented to social action. There is a poignancy in the eventual adoption of those forms, sixty years later, for a different society and program, as the society they were intended to serve collapsed.

The second legacy is in the geometric purity of suprematist painting and sculpture, most strongly represented in Malevich's "Volumetric Suprematism"—intersecting and layered blocks and beams known as *Tektonics*—and in El Lissitzky's *Prouns* (Project for the Affirmation of the New), "a half-way station between architecture and painting" (Lodder, 1983a, p. 249), and taking the form of superimposed and compacted circles, squares, surfaces, and lines.[10] Both the images and the method have also surfaced in the layered and compacted designs of self-avowed postmodernists in the 1980s (Jencks, 1988a).

The most potent images proved to be those of "late constructivists," who brought the formal disciplines of suprematism to bear on the previous wild geometries of constructivism, most specifically the urban design projects of Leonidov and Chernikhov (see Figure 4.11). There was, as Catherine Cooke has observed, a shift from the real, three-dimensional space of constructivism to the exploded, dematerialized space of "new communication technologies, whereby 'distance would now be measured by time' and 'proximity' or 'connectivity' between individuals was no longer a correlate of their spatial contiguity" (Cooke, 1988a, pp. 14–15; also 1988b). It was a shift linked to the "disurbanist" tendency of the late avant-garde, referred to earlier, much as the OSA group was linked to the "urbanists"; its appeal to the 1980s we will return to. The final form of legacy is the *memory* of a *productivist* aesthetic practice: the city as theater-workshop, for the discovery of new forms of social life and reempowerment.

A postscript: Le Corbusier made three trips to Russia between 1928 and 1930, principally to design his problem-plagued Centrosoyus office complex. By then the ferment of the 1920s had virtually run its course, but there were at least three significant effects on his ideas: His socialist predilections were recharged, he was exposed to OSA housing prototypes (specifically the cross-over duplex apartments above and below a communal corridor, or "internal street," which subsequently emerged in his Unités d'habitation), and he observed the 1930 industrial, zoned, linear city models of N. A. Milyutin (which in turn emerged in the 1935 Ville radieuse—also linear, zoned, and more "socialist" than the Ville contemporaine).

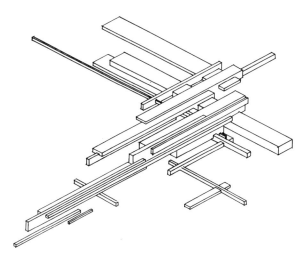

FIGURE 4.11. Iakov Chernikhov: A complex factory building of functional character, 1931. Author's drawing, based on Chernikov (1931).

THE SOVIET TRANSFORMATION: OTHER VOICES

*It is a fact that great revolutions are born of the
contradictions between that which is old, that which is
directed at the destruction of what is old and a striving of
the most abstract kind for that which is new, which must
be so new as not to contain even a grain of the old, and the
more abrupt such a revolution, the longer will be the time
during which such contradictions will persist.*

—V. I. LENIN, "Better Less, But Better," quoted in
L. A. Zhadova, Malevich: Suprematism and
Revolution in Russian Art, 1910–1930
(1982, p. 89)

Before turning to that other quest for a revolutionary urban program in
the 1920s—of the German avant-garde and the Bauhaus—it is useful
to listen, briefly, to other responses to the great cataclysm of Russia.
Lenin's observation, made at the very end of his life, provides an
extraordinary twist (forty years ahead!) to Althusser's argument on the
accumulation and "ruptual fusion" of contradiction as cause of that
fundamental social collapse that precedes transformation to a new form
of social cohesion and integration. *Revolutionary* transformation, we are
told, flows from a tripartite contradiction between *three* mutually opposed yet mutually constituting principles: the old order of things and
its defense (only "old" because an alternative is presented to it), the
anger and violence thrown against it (where agitational art, street
theater, and urban design find their place, in the new "city of meanings" to be superimposed upon the old), and the visions of the new
(suprematist and constructivist representation, productivist reinvestment in proletarian cultural action, as much as the dream of a collec-
tivist utopia, giving meaning both to the old—as its dialectical opposite!—and to the struggle for its destruction). The observation has
plausibility. It tends especially to focus attention on the role of the
motivating vision—"the most abstract kind for that which is new"—
and to support Cornelius Castoriadis's (1987) insistence on the primacy of the "imaginary" in the production of society.

Lenin was not alone in trying to make sense of those events. We
owe James Wertsch (1991) a debt for drawing attention to the advances being made in Russia, at the time of the Revolution, in the field
of psychology and semiotics. The task, he observes, was "to help construct what they saw as the first grand experiment in socialism" (p. 5).
Especially significant in this enterprise were L. S. Vygotsky (1896–
1934) and M. M. Bakhtin (1895–1975); the ideas of the former, argues
Wertsch, were characterized by three themes.

The first was a focus, following Darwin and Engels, on genetic or developmental analysis, where the transition from elementary to higher mental functioning (hence, the definition of the human) is reflected in the shift to *representational tools* such as language and other sign systems, whereby humans have the representational means to overcome the contextual factors that would enslave them. Development does not stop there however, for there is a further transition from "rudimentary" to "advanced" higher mental functioning (the objective of the revolutionary enterprise?), played out in terms of the abstraction and "decontextualization" of the semiotic means mediating communication and thinking (Wertsch, 1985).

The second theme of Vygotsky's thought is the claim, this time following Marx, that higher mental functioning in the individual derives from social life. More problematic is Vygotsky's extension of this claim: that the idea of mental function ("think," "remember") can be applied to social as well as individual activity. It is an extension of some increasing present respectability, however (Wertsch, 1991, p. 27).

The third is the claim that all action, whether on the individual or the social plane, is mediated (made possible, but also given its form) by tools and signs—the influence is from Marx and Engels. The approach to language and other sign systems is to be in terms of how they are a part of and *mediate* human action (p. 29); and the inclusion of new signs in action fundamentally transforms the action (p. 32).

Vygotsky, as far as I know, did not address the realm of those mediating signs that constitute the city and architecture. Yet at one level his concerns are at one with the constructivists: To change fundamentally the actions of individuals and social groups—to transform "the mind of the age"—it will be necessary to transform the mediating signs, to add new signification to that already existing (his "dual stimulation method"), whether in child development (Vygotsky's area of work); in Proletkult graphics, street theater, and kiosks; in elementarist–constructivist skylines; or in OSA social condensers. Signs are central to revolution.[11]

Bakhtin shared Vygotsky's main preoccupations, but his essential focus was on another idea that would seem to address yet a further aspect of the Revolution and its times. *Dialogicality*, he asserts, informs every utterance, every text (as it must inform the text of the city, one could add):

> To understand another person's utterance means to orient oneself with respect to it, to find the proper place for it in the corresponding context. For each word of the utterance that we are in process of understanding, we, as it were, lay down a set of our own answering

words. . . . *Any true understanding is dialogic in nature.* (Voloshinov, 1973, p. 102; quoted in Wertsch, 1991, p. 54)

There are two important corollaries to this. The first is "that multiple authorship is a necessary fact about all texts, written or spoken" (Wertsch, 1991, p. 49), or the significations of urban meaning, for that matter. Second, no single voice can be privileged over any other; rather, what must be privileged is "multivoicedness," and "heterogeneity in thinking." By 1929 such ideas were out of official favor, and so was Bakhtin. He was consigned to internal exile and his work suppressed.

AFTERWORD

From the perspective of 1990, Hal Foster's voice resonates with new agendas:

If Russian Constructivism is notoriously difficult to define [a modernist project, surely!], then its relationship to Western art after 1932, the year of its official suppression in the Soviet Union, is almost impossible to delimit. This relationship cannot be described in terms of style or medium alone, not only because of the extraordinary multiplicity of Constructivism, which sought to exceed or even to void these categories, but also because of its complex reception in the West, where its many practices were variously condensed and displaced, repressed and recoded. Indeed, the posthistory of Constructivism is a field of effects in which its significance is never fixed. To see its genealogy in this way is also true to its spirit, for if there is one thing that unifies Constructivism it is the demand always to transform cultural practice in relation to productive mode and social formation. (Foster, 1990, p. 241)

Yet in the 1960s, midway between these poles, the answering words were few and scarcely heard, and the constructed space that presented the most potent images of an emancipated life seemed Corbusian rather than constructivist. But Foster is correct as much as incorrect: The Russians were present and not present—in words (cited, torn from context) rather than sentences (narratives, meanings, contexts); in fleeting images, distorted, rather than grand remembered landscapes. It is a consequence of the ambivalence of translation.

CHAPTER 5

The 1920s as Crucible: Translation, Vkhutemas, and the Bauhaus

Every sign, linguistic or non-linguistic, spoken or written (in the current sense of this opposition), in a small or large unit, can be cited, put between quotation marks; in so doing it can break with every given context, engendering an infinity of new contexts in a manner which is absolutely illimitable.

　　　—JACQUES DERRIDA, "Signature Event
　　　Context" (1977, p. 185)

For just as the tenor and the significance of the great works of literature undergo a complete transformation over the centuries, the mother tongue of the translator is transformed as well. . . . Translation is so far removed from being the sterile equation of two dead languages that of all literary forms it is the one charged with the special mission of watching over the maturing process of the original language and the birth pangs of its own.

　　　—WALTER BENJAMIN, "The Task of the
　　　Translator" (1992, p. 74)

Space here enters the exploration in a new way. Ideas and images have always been translated translinguistically *and* across space—from one place or city or hemisphere to another. But in these decades from 1900 to around 1930 they are also translated across political economies—different worldviews and fundamentally different social constructions of space (and time) itself. All translation confronts a dilemma: Where is it that ideas and images are to be found? . . . in the utterance, or in the voice on which it rides? So what, ultimately, *can* be translated?

For Bakhtin, context and contingency are inescapable; so "the most important thing for making sense of meaning is not the sign [e.g., the word and its sound], but the whole utterance into whose composition the sign enters" (Ivanov, 1974, p. 237, summarizing Bakhtin). In turn, the utterance can only be understood in the context of the text, the text in yet a wider framework, and so on. The utterance is "the *real unit* of speech communication," and it is always "situated"—it has a context, away from which it cannot be understood. But the utterance is inexorably linked with the idea of "voice," "the speaking personality, the speaking consciousness" (Holquist and Emerson, 1981, p. 434; quoted in Wertsch, 1991, p. 51). Clark and Holquist's (1984) account can be quoted:

> An utterance, spoken or written, is always expressed from a point of view [a voice], which for Bakhtin is a process rather than a location. Utterance is an activity that enacts differences in values. On an elementary level, for instance, the same words can mean different things depending on the particular intonation with which they are uttered in a specific context: intonation is the sound that value makes. (p. 10)

The voice modulates all communication, both written and spoken, it reflects the person's "perspective, conceptual horizon, intention, and world view"—their "agenda." The voice is always socially contingent; as Wertsch (1991) observes, no voice exists "in total isolation from other voices" (p. 52). The utterance reflects both the voice producing it and the voice to which it is addressed (Bakhtin, 1986, p. 99). Thus arises "dialogue," involving the "double logics" of speaker and listener. Wertsch adds, "in the formulation of an utterance a voice responds in some way to previous utterances and anticipates the responses of other, succeeding ones; when it is understood, an utterance comes into contact with the counter word of those who hear it" (p. 53).

Both subjects, Bataille would later insist, are transformed in the process: Communication is never the transmission of some message "existing independently, as a signified, between two subjects whose identity remains intact and untouched in the process" (Hollier, 1989, p. 67). Communication, rather, "is loss of self in the absence of message on both sides, in the nonsense that is the absence of a transcendental signified" (p. 67). One person's utterances "interanimate" those of another. As the landscape, spatial meaning, that "way of seeing the world," is spawned in conversation, it becomes "not only 'graphically visible' in space but also 'narratively visible' in time, in a field of discourses all attempting to account for human experience" (Folch-Serra, 1990, p. 258). All readings of space and landscape become intertextual, as well as dialogical.[1]

Sharing its era with Bakhtin, though certainly not its context, is Walter Benjamin's 1923 essay, "The Task of the Translator" (Benjamin, 1992). That task, we are told, is decidedly *not* to transmit (information, meaning):

> Art . . . posits man's physical and spiritual existence, but in none of its works is it concerned with his response. No poem is intended for the reader, no picture for the beholder, no symphony for the listener . . . [thus] any translation which intends to perform a transmitting function cannot transmit anything but information—hence, something inessential. This is the hallmark of bad translations. (p. 70)

For Benjamin, rather, a translation is to strike that effect upon the new language "which produces in it the echo of the original," enriching the new (p. 77). In contrast to a literary work, a translation "does not find itself in the center of the language forest but on the outside facing the wooded ridge; it calls into it without entering, aiming at that single spot where the echo is able to give, in its own language, the reverberation of the work in the alien one" (p. 77).

But *what* is to reverberate? The original *mode of representation* is the answer—stated otherwise, the mode of intention rather than some intended object (the voice on which the motivating agenda is still detectable): "A translation, instead of resembling the meaning of the original, must lovingly and in detail incorporate the original's mode of signification, thus making both the original and the translation recognizable as fragments of a greater language, just as fragments are part of a vessel" (Benjamin, 1992, p. 79).

This will be achieved through "a literal rendering of the syntax," focusing on "words rather than sentences . . . [as] the primary element of the translator" (p. 79). To privilege the word over the sentence shatters the coherence and linearity of the latter, rendering it "transparent" to that search for the intonation of voice and value: "For if the sentence is the wall before the language of the original, literalness is the arcade" (p. 79).

The archetypal case of all translation—of words and images, across languages, spaces, and worldviews—arises in the first decades of the twentieth century, as highly localized avant-gardes collide. Ideas are

torn from context, engendering Derrida's (1977) "infinity of new contexts in a manner which is absolutely illimitable" (p. 185)—the emancipation of words and images themselves from the reifying effect of a
specific place and time;[2] both old and new contexts are thereby transformed. Text (modes of representation) survives over context.

ARCHITECTURE AND URBAN DESIGN
AS TRANSFORMATION,
3: THE BAUHAUS

The Bauhaus can rather superficially be viewed as successor to the
German arts-and-crafts movement, as Vkhutemas and the constructivists were, equally superficially, to the Russian.[3] The Deutsche Werkbund was founded in 1907 by Prussian civil servant Herman Muthesius,
as a cooperative association that brought together creative designers and
productive industry; its objective was the radical transformation of German design, production, and marketing, thereby breaking through the
anti-German barriers to trade and achieving economic expansion
through *quality*—new design, new economy! The model, to be translated
across languages and worldviews, was the English arts and crafts: Muthesius had served as an attaché at the German Embassy in London from
1896 to 1903, with the brief to draw lessons from the reputed excellence
of English art and architecture (the monumental outcome was Muthesius's three-volume *Das Englische Haus* of 1904–1905). At the Werkbund's Congress of 1911, Muthesius clarified the congress's aesthetic
direction, extolling *standardization* and *"form."* This latter implied rationalism—in architecture, the geometric clarity of the Doric order, Gothic
structure, the internal volumes of Roman thermae, the aesthetic unity of
the Enlightenment—and would be universal in its application (though
Germany would unquestionably play the leading role in its development
and promulgation in the modern age!). To be rejected were impressionism, postimpressionism, and art nouveau. His audience on that occasion
apparently included Mies van der Rohe, Walter Gropius, Bruno Taut,
and Le Corbusier (still calling himself Charles Edouard Jeanneret); if one
had to accord an emblematic starting point to the quest for the modern
movement in architecture, then that might be it.

In that year also, Gropius and Adolf Meyer began the design for
the Faguswerke at Alfeld; two years later, in 1913, they designed their
pavilion for the 1914 Werkbund Exhibition in Cologne. Both complexes displayed walls of industrial glazing and other "machine aesthetic" detailing, but were strongly classicist in their planning. Together they represented precisely the sort of corporate world that the

Werkbund advocated and still remain potent images of the modernist project.

The Bauhaus came about with the 1919 amalgamation of two institutions in Weimar: a long-established, traditional Academy of Fine Arts and a Grand-Ducal Applied Arts School founded in 1903 in that flush of enthusiasm for improved design that also triggered the Werkbund. Walter Gropius (1883–1969) was appointed director, largely on the recommendation of Belgian painter-designer-architect Henry Van de Velde, previous head of the Applied Arts School: During a celebrated brawl at the Werkbund's 1914 conference, Gropius had apparently displayed a combination of functionalist pragmatism and, simultaneously, belief in the power of artistic genius, which had attracted Van de Velde's attention (Willett, 1978, p. 20). The idea that education spanned all branches of craft and design, culminating in architecture, was far from original and fully consistent with Deutsche Werkbund principles (Banham, 1960, p. 276); what was original was the zeal of the pursuit of this idea at the Bauhaus, as well as the extraordinary ebbs and flows in its theories and programs.

For there were three other traditions running through the Bauhaus debates. The first was that of German expressionism. In the age of the bourgeoisie and the avant-garde, a dominating debate in aesthetics had been that of objective realism, anti-idealist, the representation of nature and life freed from our emotions toward it, the evocation of beauty itself (classicism, but quintessentially impressionism), versus the expression of the artist's inner emotions (fauvism, expressionism, ultimately the exploration of the subconscious itself in surrealism). The debate was paralleled in architecture by that of functionalism and the craft tradition (looking for value in the work—for which one could read meaning—in its materials and process of production) versus expressionism (the conscious representation of ideas and feelings about space, place, and institutions). The German trend toward expressionism in art had received its sanction with Immanuel Kant and the idea that neither reason nor material reality has absolute value, only appearances are accessible to us, and the judgment of taste "is not a cognitive judgement; hence it is not logical but aesthetic, that is, the principle that determines it is purely subjective" (quoted in Huyghe, 1962, p. 212): Art will express the personal vision. The philosophical tradition that dominated German thought from that time continually reinforced the sanction. The tragedy and trauma of 1914–1918 in Germany, and the need to explore and represent the anguish and protest, brought an especially poignant focus to this Kantian worldview and to the visions and output of the expressionists.

In its architectural translation, expressionism notably embraced the ideas of light and glass—more vicariously, progress, the new, the fire of creativity. Paul Scheerbart published his somewhat fantastical *Glasarchitektur* in 1914—a futurist vision of a world of glass, flashing lights, and things that whiz around; Bruno Taut published *Die Stadtkrone* in 1919 to advance an altogether new form of town planning. Garden cities, zoned cities, and all the other types advocated in that age lacked the one thing that ultimately makes a city—a symbolic heart, a *Stadtkrone*. Taut's drawings for this new type of city show something not dissimilar to Le Corbusier's Ville contemporaine of three years later—axial and gridded, though lower density. The difference was in the generating conception: The crown, the heart of the city, would not be Le Corbusier's functionalist tower blocks for business and administration but would be public buildings that accumulated toward a great symbolic glass tower—modernity's equivalent of the Gothic spire or Assyrian ziggurat. The clearest demonstration of this architecture of glass and light had been Taut's Glass Pavilion at the 1914 Cologne Exhibition—standing in some dialectical, "expressionist" opposition to Gropius and Meyer's "functionalist" Werkbund pavilion for the same occasion.

Now the genesis of the Bauhaus may well have been in the Werkbund and the arts-and-crafts tradition, but the staff that Gropius recruited was largely expressionist; certainly expressionist ideas and sentiments dominated the debates and programs. The Proclamation of the Weimar Bauhaus had on its cover a woodcut by Lyonel Feininger of the purely Scheerbartian image of a Gothic cathedral topped by high-tech beacons and lights. Gropius writes of a building like a "crystal symbol" and echoes both Scheerbart and Taut in calling for the transformation of all work by the elimination of the distinction between hand work and brain work. The ideology quickly plunged even further toward the messianic: The head of the *Vorkurs*, or preliminary course, was Johannes Itten who brought a wild mixture of oriental mysticism, peripatetic gurus, vegetarianism in the school's kitchens, communes, Tolstoyism, utopias, and pseudoreligions.[4] By 1921 the cracks were showing; by 1922 Gropius was forced to abandon neutrality in the storm of ideas and movements and to counter the expressionist putsch.

As painting instructor Oskar Schlemmer could observe, "Retreat from Utopia. . . . In lieu of cathedrals the machine for living in. In short, retreat from medievalism" (quoted in Willett, 1978, p. 81). The writings of Le Corbusier and the influence of the constructivists seem to have had much to do with the swing back.

Indeed, the second "other" tradition running through the Bauhaus debates and programs—counterposing, together with expressionism, the Werkbund functionalist thrust—was constructivism. There was an active German–Hungarian constructivist group focused on Berlin, of which the most significant member was László Moholy-Nagy; and it was Moholy-Nagy whom Gropius brought in, early in 1923, to replace Itten as head of the Bauhaus preliminary course. During 1922 there were meetings and congresses of "creative persons of revolutionary outlook" (Willett, 1978, p. 77), notably in Düsseldorf and Weimar (partly to give the narcissistic Bauhaus expressionists a fright), and with some vague idea of forming a "Constructivist International." In that year there was also a major exhibition of the new Russian art in Berlin, again with great impact. Finally, for this part of the story, there was the progressive flight of figures from the Russian avant-garde, both constructivist and elementarist, to join the Bauhaus staff and effectively end the expressionist domination.

The third "other" factor was more ephemeral in its effect. The dadaist movement had been founded in Zurich (in 1916), but there were almost immediately groups in a variety of other centers, each quite distinctive in personnel and character. As examples, Paris dadaism was decidedly literary (or perhaps *antiliterary*, deconstructing and then reconstructing language, sound, words, and associations in ways taken up by Scheerbart, Ball, Apollinaire, and Joyce and prefiguring Derrida half a century later); New York dadaism was dominated by Marcel Duchamp and the "ready-mades" (found objects—a bicycle wheel, a urinal—exhibited for the delectation of the art lover) but also by Francis Picabia (who seems to have been in most places most of the time) and pioneer photographers Alfred Stieglitz and Edward Steichen; and Berlin dadaism was especially characterized by photomontage (deconstructing and reconstructing images as well as language and words). And everywhere it was intent on creating outrage, being rowdy, insulting its audience, giving offense, creatively discovering new obscenities, making noise, and absurdity. The dadaist media were painting, sculpture, and the ready-mades; cabaret and street theater; poetry—more aptly, strings of words and letters freed of context—and anything else coming to mind. Indeed, everything was to be freed from context and meaning (paint, said Duchamp, comes from a tube, so a painting is merely a *ready-made aided*); and the dadaists accordingly proclaimed anti-art in place of art, as aesthetic pleasure is eschewed, "not works of art but of non-art, the results of discursive rather than sensory insights" (Richter, 1965, p. 92). But it is not discursive in the usual sense, since they also proclaimed *chance* over *reason*: Theirs is an environment of *found objects*, where the Mona Lisa (with a moustache drawn on it) is not privileged over a urinal.

Certainly there was an antibourgeois intent in all of this activity (even actively revolutionary on occasion—Berlin dadaism joined in the 1918 revolution in Berlin), but there was more. So Hans Richter (1965), a member of the Berlin dadaist group, quotes with approval Karsten Harries on nihilism: "Freedom is identified with the spontaneity of life," which is to be preferred to "the spirit which is seen as stifling" (p. 92). Life is described (by Heidegger, Nietzsche, James) "as an infinite stream; any attempts to exhaust this richness must be inadequate. Life and concepts are incommensurable . . . to seek them is to hack the fundamental unity of life into pieces" (p. 92). We are to seek emancipation from the myth of the wilful, autonomous subject, the myth of "the great artist."

Dadaism is therefore the opposite of expressionism. But we need to see what this means. The concern of expressionism is meaning: The signified is everything, and the signifier seemingly forever inadequate. With the drift of expressionism towards surrealism, and the aim to represent not just emotions but the subconscious itself, the symbolism always immanent in expressionism became far more purposive. Here the play is with *surpluses of meaning*: The signified becomes unstable, there are no boundaries; the effect, says Ricoeur (1974), is to link "the multiplicity of meaning to the equivocalness of being" (p. 13).[5] Dadaism, on the other hand, would deny the signified altogether—at the least to stress the material of the signifier over the meaning of the signified, at the most to hold out a new level of emancipation where the poignant discovery of the meaninglessness of a world at war with itself (in 1914–1918) is revealed to flow from the supreme delusion that there was some meaning in the first place. (There was no meaning, no loss; our dashed expectations of higher meaning must be unmasked, and we must get on with life. So, it seems, say the dadaists.)

At a figurative level (of "modes of representation") there was quite some affinity between dadaism and constructivism. The constructivist penchant for seemingly unstable structures and mechanical devices is paralleled, for example, in the more composed works of Marcel Duchamp (and even in the assemblage of many of the ready-mades)— in the *Great Glass* of circa 1918, most notably—and in much of the work of Francis Picabia, Hans Arp, Kurt Schwitters, and others. Similarly, the dadaist preoccupation with typography flowed into constructivist graphics. There was also affinity in their social programs. Both aimed to confront and destroy avant-gardist "establishments"— dadaism to unmask the expressionist preoccupation with the profounder emotions and, thereby, to break down all (essentially bourgeois) reliance on "meaning" as the cement of society; the constructivists to expose the vacuity of the fashionable (again bourgeois) cubo-symbolist Russian theater, painting, poetry, sculpture, and architecture prevailing at the beginning of the century. There was,

however, an important difference semiotically. Whereas the constructivists may have aimed for images without meaning (Zygas's [1981]
"form follows form")—structures refer only to themselves, and the
signified loses significance in those abstract urban forms of Leonidov
and Chernikhov—nevertheless, it was always imagined that a world of
new, motivating, *proletarian* meaning would ultimately arise and that
these forms would carry the signification of that world.

There was certainly something of a Werkbund image of a better
city in a better world, with Gropius and Meyer's Faguswerke and
Werkbund pavilion arguably such a world's clearest manifestations.
Similarly, an expressionist vision emerges in the writings of Scheerbart and Taut: The representation of material progress and emancipation through new design and technology and the elimination of
divisions in human labor, characteristic of the Werkbund idea, is
replaced by a picture of emancipation through new artistic action.
The constructivist city is more complete in its representation: The
city is to be instructional theater, to present a new image of a workers'
paradise—antibourgeois, international in its potential—and to show
a world of new technology and new communication. There was
however no dadaist urban vision, though the characteristics of one
might well be imagined. It might be an urban space of "found objects": What is already there is accepted and there is no "grand
vision" but a thousand mutually tolerated private worlds. Such tolerance might not be extended to "the absurdity of bourgeois life and
values," of course; but even that rejection has only to last until the
privileging of the bourgeois vision is effectively unmasked. It is interesting that, some fifty years on, such an urban design does emerge,
explicitly and self-consciously pursued.

The account of the Bauhaus needs to be concluded. The shift from
expressionism to elementarism—the free composition of ensembles
using clearly separable elements (Banham, 1960, p. 21)—finally occurred in 1923. In high rancorous disputation, Itten was removed from
the *Vorkurs* (preliminary program), to be replaced for brief periods by
Paul Klee and Wassili Kandinsky, then finally by Moholy-Nagy. Klee's
contribution was to take that era's preoccupation with Newtonian
versus Einsteinian conceptions of space and to present it as a representational task for the graphic arts, architecture, and urban space.[6] In
his drawings he also represented space often as transparent geometric
solids in a way that was both Sheerbartian and elementarist: Moholy's
(and Gropius's) final push to the elementarist–constructivist aesthetic
of clear composition with lines, planes and geometric solids was effectively prefigured. Moreover, with Moholy's constructivist predilections
came the final acceptance of the machine aesthetic, the end of mysti-

cism and funny dress-ups, and the Bauhaus's second age. Despite the changes in program, style, and public image, the Bauhaus met with mounting opposition from a Weimar public and political establishment that saw it as a threat to the middle class and the stability of society. By Easter 1925, it was on the brink of closure; salvation, however, came with an offer of relocation from a progressive city administration of Dessau, and the school moved en masse. At the end of 1926, it occupied its new home, designed by Gropius and Meyer, and arguably the first *realized*, large-scale masterpiece of the modern movement (see Figure 5.1).[7] By 1933 the Bauhaus was closed and its participants dispersed.

REVOLUTIONARY INTENT, REVOLUTIONARY EFFECT?

The confrontations of this and the previous chapter—avant-garde attempts to represent and, thereby, to effect a new urban world—lasted little more than a decade. Was the revolutionary intent of the artists and designers anywhere matched by real transformation in the patterns of social life—emancipated, remotivated; and could any such effect plausibly be attributed, even in part, to the visions, ideas, and battles at this level of aesthetic discourse and cultural production? Or is the "last instance" always economic, and are both the individual vision of the

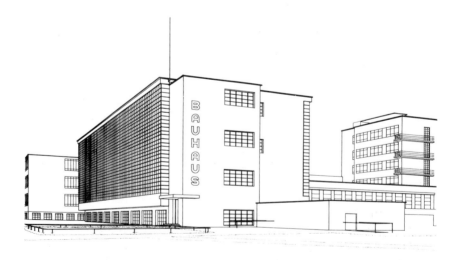

FIGURE 5.1. Walter Gropius and Adolf Meyer: Bauhaus, Dessau, 1926. Drawing by Matt Spinaze, based on Foster (1990).

rebel and some Vygotskian "collective vision" of an avant-garde "class" (if such a notion has any meaning) ultimately to be dismissed as mere surface manifestations of the real changes in society? We turn again to these three interlinked stories—of Le Corbusier, the Russians, and the Bauhaus—but reversing the order from that preceding.

That the teetering instability of Germany at the beginning of the century was economically determined (in some last instance!) seems unexceptionable. Contradiction and conflict seemed most clearly manifested in economic crisis (with German economic expansion increasingly blocked by the denial of foreign markets), national identity versus colonial frustration (the late unification of Germany meant that it had missed out on the great age of European colonization), increasing militarism (to try to break the chains of both continental and colonial containment), and domestic political tensions (Prussia vs. the appropriated states, the rural gentry vs. the urban bourgeoisie and the intellectuals, capital vs. labor). Each aspect of the accumulating crisis, however, became a target for avant-garde outrage and posing of alternatives. So bourgeois banality and the posturing of the aristocracy were confronted by the dadaist revolt; more profoundly, dadaism denied the signification on which all political legitimacy and commodity fetishism stands. Constructivism at one level reinforced the denial of the signified and the assertion of the signifier; at another level it insisted on an altogether new meaning that pointed to new institutions and social organization in a new world. Both the constructivists and the dadaists, incidentally, saw urban space as didactic theater—the former to lead us forth to new relations of communication and production, the latter more to shocked self-recognition and unmasking of present self-delusion. The expressionists attacked the seeming materialism of the new Germany, posed new spiritual values, and after 1914 especially focused revulsion toward Prussian militarism, war, and carnage. The arts-and-crafts movement and its partial culmination in the Deutsche Werkbund differed from these other forms of response in being reformist in intent rather than revolutionary (though to tired, conservative capital it presented itself as threatening and revolutionary enough). Economic crisis and political containment were to be confronted not militarily but through new design, new products, demolition of the division between handwork and headwork—all to be represented to the world in new architecture and urban meaning.

In *The Imaginary Institution of Society* (1987), Cornelius Castoriadis observes that we can never have complete understanding of the society we wish to change or of the state of society that we wish to change it to (so the informed revolution of a politically enlightened class, foreseen by Marx, is forever impossible). All we have, rather, is our individual experiences of the conflicts and contradictions in which we are enmeshed and some vague idea of a better alternative. The effect of the cultural realm—in this instance, the German avant-garde (and, at least potentially, in every other instance in modernity)—was to bring into focus two forms of experience that effectively reinforce each other: the nature of the myriad conflicts that beset each individual, and the possibility of alternatives. Those two forms function dialectically: I can only see the absurdity, repression, and self-repression of my condition if I can see that there is a real alternative; and an alternative only takes on reality by reference to my present condition. It is close to Walter Benjamin's distinction between consciousness raising and redemptive criticism (Habermas, 1979b). The cultural realm—of representations of reality (consciousness raising) and of possibilities (redemption)—rather than the chaos of (economic) disintegration, is what enables direction in change.

The two effects also yield the basis for the rejection of the old and for the motivating vision of the new and constitute the second and the third terms—with the old and its defense as the first term—in Lenin's tripartite contradiction underlying "great revolutions." Now the Bauhaus, in all this, was the crucible (perhaps, more appropriately, *one* crucible—the streets of Berlin in 1918 and again in 1919 were another, though at an altogether different level). Dadaism, expressionism, constructivism, elementarism, and their variants were all *translated*: fragmented, torn from other contexts and places—hence, freed and *appropriable*. Benjamin's metaphor of the transparency of arcades (words shattering the coherence and linearity of the sentence) rather than the barrier of the wall (the sentence) is apposite. Yet what is translated is both text (the pamphlets, poems, plays), recalled or imagined utterances (what Lenin, or Malevich, might have said or wanted to say),[8] and visual images (shattering, here, the coherence of place and space); and the fragments, inevitably, become context for each other, suggesting connections—this image with that idea!—alien to any intentions of the original authors. The point is that Benjamin's insistence that only the original's mode of representation, rather than its meaning, can reverberate through the translation, must be taken with caution. Meanings do reverberate. But they are not those of the original, and they are in new contexts.

This storm of images, words, and fragments of meaning, seized as they flashed up in that new "moment of danger," massively transformed the perceptions and understandings of the new disintegrations and, more positively, the possibilities facing the disparate, cosmopolitan coteries of expatriates that constituted the Bauhaus. Its internal conflicts and crowding threats would seem to have been the necessary fire in which to forge an image of an alternative, possible world from these fragments. That alternative was of new relations of production, hand and mind fused in new design and high technology, the magic of a machine age, the nobility and excitement of the factory, universalism in place of the old, paranoid German insularity, a global civilization in place of local culture (but with a new Germany in the vanguard of that new, universal, industrial, technological order). To many on the left, the vision was a sellout, and the communists in particular railed against it. To others, however, it was indeed revolutionary—a new world being purchased at altogether too high a price, the loss of local richness and diversity and of local culture as source of all innovation. And it was profound unease at this invasive uniformity and universalism of high modernity—all the world to be the same, the vast diversity of human experience to be expunged, and everywhere "the same technological frenzy"—that lay at the heart of Heidegger's rejection of this path and opting for the appalling right-wing alternative.

The Russian Revolution differed fundamentally from the German. Certainly, the realm of cultural production and aesthetic discourse were significant (as both "consciousness raising and redemptive criticism") in the sharpening of political disputation preceding the February uprising of 1917 that saw the fall of the monarchist regime and again preceding that of the following November that brought the Bolsheviks to power. The ideological worlds and supporting tastes of gentry, urban bourgeoisie, military, and church were attacked in suprematist poetry, theater, and graphic arts and in productivist linkings of design and production. But the proselytizing was to a very small, urban, intellectual class in a vast, dispersed, unhearing, illiterate mass, and the uprisings were similarly elitist. November 1917 had the effect of sweeping aside many of the political constraints on building the new workers' paradise, though the contours of that world had still to be worked out; and in the working out, the avant-garde found itself in the near-novel position of being hand in hand with the new instrumentalities of the state. In the immediate task of consciousness raising, the streets had the significant role as didactic medium (not as battleground as in Germany), with street theater, banners, kiosks, exemplary structures, Agit-Prop boats and trains, monumental pageants, and the rest—an entirely new form of production of urban meaning, to be overlain on the text of the still-existing czarist city. The next step was to extend the propaganda to the countryside. With the elementarist–constructivist turn, the concern shifted to an architectural and urban design language with which to represent the new world that was sought—unless it can be represented, it cannot be achieved! Later still, the turn was to more immediate concerns of the crises threatening the Revolution itself:

forms of housing, the "social condensers" and ways of living, affordable building methods, urbanization or disurbanization—and, thus, the form of the city itself.

With the Germans, so with the Russians: The avant-garde and the production of new urban visions were central to the finding and transmitting of *direction* to the revolution. Accumulating contradiction and instability can well account for the disintegrations of the old—with the far more spectacular collapse in Russia easily attributable to its greater economic ("last instance"?) instability as rapid modernization of the means of production faced the logical inconsistency of virtually feudal relations of production. But the new order to replace the old must be sought in the realm of ideas, and here cultural production and aesthetic discourse are central to both the critique of the present and that motivating vision of something better. It must appear surprising that the space of disintegration presents itself as order, while that of the new is chaotic, and as diffuse as the serendipitous flashes of ideas themselves. The purposive, consciousness-raising critique of the present text of the city—the meanings transmitted in its architecture and urban design—would seem to occur early in the revolutionary project; the search for alternative visions and their appropriate representation may also come early, but it seems to be followed by a time of attempted synthesis—to many, the sellout. (Lenin's tripartite contradiction needs to be anchored in time and space.) One cannot fail to be moved by the extraordinary efflorescence of ideas, the assurance, and the brilliant originality of so many in the Russian avant-garde. For a fleeting moment in history, it almost seems that we are indeed witnessing Marx's "revolutionary class"—but it is the intellectuals and visionaries rather than the proletariat.

Another reading, another translation:

> Another theory, coming from afar, of a super Cartesian rigour, "Russian Constructivism" . . . seemed to demand the supremacy of a pitiless design—steel, glass, mathematics. . . . They are poets in steel and glass. Form takes precedence of function, and the plan and construction is still rudimentary. What emerges from Moscow is an enthusiastic declaration of faith in the architectural poem of the modern age. (Le Corbusier, quoted in Zygas, 1981, p. xvii)

The fascination with Le Corbusier is that he stands far more alone than these "classes" of the Russians or Germans. Although his method was synthetic, even eclectic, bringing together diverse spatial and ideological references, translated, dialectically opposed and even contradiction ridden, the results of that method always stood unique at the time of their production and entered sometimes immediately and sometimes after long delays into the discourse and practice of other designers. The isolation is, however, an illusion. The significance of Le Corbusier's "method" is that it is so explicitly an instance of the "multiple authorship of all texts" that Bakhtin insisted upon (and Bakhtin, it must be remembered, was writing at precisely the time of this effusion of the avant-garde and was having to come to terms with the seemingly limitless novelty of its texts); and the uniqueness of the product—of the "utterance," in Bakhtin's terms—similarly points to the dialogic nature of every utterance, every text. Le Corbusier's ideas are *read*—nobody's, surely, more so than his, unless they be Marx's— and no one reading can ever be privileged over any other (though, of course, some readings have indeed been privileged, as the next chapter recounts).

Multivoicedness characterizes the producer as much as the receivers. "Architecture or Revolution" was one of Le Corbusier's catch cries. But was it a call for revolution in the cultural sphere as an alternative to political revolution? Or was it a considerably less radical exhortation to reform—repair the slums or risk the time bomb, in Anatole Kopp's (1985) interpretation? Or was it a proffered hope to the bourgeoisie and its bureaucratic state that, by a new, internationalist, machine-age environment, a new society could be built and revolution permanently avoided? Was it for revolution or stability? Possibly both, as Le Corbusier's own life and practice (like Lenin's) oscillated between vision and pragmatic compromise. The point is that the text—the idea, the vision—is probably always ambivalently produced, certainly variously read. Something of the process is suggested in Bakhtin's account of a *social language*, the discourse peculiar to a specific social stratum (profession, age group, etc.) in a specific social system and time: Every unique utterance is of one voice speaking ("ventriloquating") *through* another voice or voice type in a social language (Wertsch, 1991, pp. 57–59).[9]

In all translation—whether of words or of images, translinguistically or across space, time, or political economy—something of that animating voice as well as the interweaving of meanings arising in the old context, is always lost. We can elaborate Walter Benjamin's (1992) aphorism that opened this chapter: "Translation . . . of all literary forms . . . is the one charged with the special mission of watching over the maturing process of the original language [Vkhutemas and constructivism, dadaism, expressionism] and the birth pangs of its own [the Bauhaus, cosmopolitanism, the internationalist project, universal space supplanting local place]" (p. 74).

CHAPTER 6 | # The Universal Space of the Twentieth Century: Voyages against the Ebb

What threatens man in his very nature is . . . that man, by the peaceful release, transformation, storage and channeling of the energies of physical nature, could so render the human condition . . . tolerable for everybody and happy in all respects.

> —MARTIN HEIDEGGER, *Poetry, Language, Thought* (1971a, p. 116)

There is the paradox: how to become modern and return to sources; how to revive an old, dormant civilization and take part in universal civilization.

> —PAUL RICOEUR, *History and Truth* (1965, p. 277)

Greater than any threat to external nature is that of "technological thinking" to internal, spiritual nature "should technology solve all our problems": The concern is "the human *distress* caused by the technological understanding of being."[1]

The 1920s were unique for the proliferation of original ideas in the sphere of art and for the attempts—especially in architecture and urban design—to argue the links between art, technology, and politics or morality. The great debates of this heroic age of high modernity may well have centered on the Bauhaus, Le Corbusier and his group in

Paris, and the Russians—each part of the broader avant-garde of Germany, Paris, and Moscow in that era. However, these groups were not alone. Though the expressionists and their ideas were in part appropriated into the Bauhaus and there, by 1923, effectively supplanted, the vision nevertheless persisted for a glass paradise as emancipation from the older experience of finite, limited space. The *Neue Sachlichkeit* (New Objectivity), more geographically diffused, opposed the Berlin-centered expressionists with a technical rationality akin to that of elementarist–constructivism (indeed El Lissitzky and the dadaist Hans Richter were especially involved in it). The Dutch De Stijl movement promised "a new plastic unity" of art with everyday life, though stylistically it was ultimately superseded by Russian constructivism. Mies van der Rohe was designing increasingly minimalist (elementarist) houses and pavilions and, in 1921, his first glass skyscraper, strongly expressionist in inspiration (see Figures 6.1 and 6.2). And all the time there was the enormous influence of Frank Lloyd Wright (1869–1959), dating mainly from the publication of his works in the German Wasmuth volumes of 1910 and 1911 (Wright, 1910, 1911).

By the mid-1920s, the tumult of the radicals was well broadcast in both specialist and popular media; but there was also a gathering view that if governments were to be persuaded to embark on the hoped-for transformations of social life, then a unified voice (and unified vision?) was needed. The near-thirty-year debate to define such a voice began with an initiative from the Swiss section of the Werkbund to call a

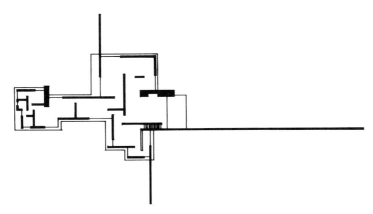

FIGURE 6.1. Ludwig Mies van der Rohe: Project for a brick house, 1923. A new representation of space, the indoor–outdoor dichotomy deconstructed, and the influence of Frank Lloyd Wright. Author's drawing, based on Frampton (1985) and Zukowsky (1986).

symposium of the leading European architects at La Sarraz, Switzer-
land, in 1928. From this resulted the Congrès internationaux d'architecture moderne (CIAM) and its first Declaration. Though CIAM I
was little more than an exchange of opinions, the La Sarraz declaration
clearly revealed the dominance of Le Corbusier and the Neue
Sachlichkeit architects. The past and the Academies are to be rejected,
for the problem of architecture is the problem of *building*. In consequence, economic efficiency is demanded as are "rationalization and
standardization" and the universal adoption of industrialized production methods, especially in the sphere of housing; the consumer must
readjust to the new conditions of social life flowing from this rationalization; and the urban problem is likewise one of rational, functional
order, and a socialized land policy.[2]

CIAM II (Frankfurt, 1929) was initiated by Frankfurt city architect and low-cost-housing expert Ernst May, to address the *Existenzminimum*—the low-cost-dwelling unit as a function of industrial rationalization (freed at last from the sentimentality of broader culture
and meaning!). CIAM III (Brussells, 1930) moved on to *Rationelle
Bebauungsweisen*—the most efficient height and spacing of the building blocks to contain those functional dwelling units and, in consequence, the organization of land itself. This was the era of Sachlichkeit
preeminence, where the utopia to be represented was that of technological rationalization and universal civilization. The professed socialism was, however, poorly informed: Means of production were seen as
technology narrowly conceived; relations of production—as well as the
household and gender divisions of labor on which the *Existenzminimum*
must ultimately be contingent—were scarcely seen at all. And despite

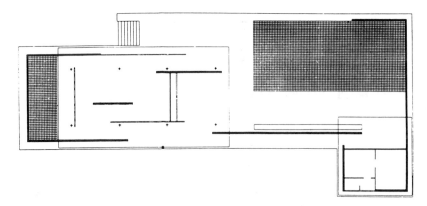

FIGURE 6.2. Ludwig Mies van der Rohe: German Pavilion, World Exhibition, Barcelona, 1929. Suprematist references replace Wright. Author's drawing, based on Frampton (1985) and Zukowsky (1986).

the goal of a socialized control of land, the paths to such an end were also not understood.

CIAM IV was to have been in Moscow, but ended up instead and more agreeably on a yacht between Marseilles and Athens, in 1933. With it, dominance shifted from the "objective" Germans to the more critical, complex, questioning Le Corbusier, and the focus shifted more to "the city." The architects had ample time to compare their ideas, to analyze the conditions of some thirty-three European cities, to be filmed by Moholy-Nagy, and ultimately to produce the Athens Charter, the most significant document to emerge from the CIAM. The charter held forth on the conditions of contemporary towns and then on proposals for dealing with them, under five main categories: "Dwellings," "Recreation," "Work," "Transportation," and "Historic Buildings." Those proposals boiled down, in the main, to two devices: land-use zoning, with greenbelts separating different functions; and high-rise, widely spaced apartment blocks wherever densities must be high. It is hard to avoid Reyner Banham's 1963 judgment: "At a distance of thirty years we recognise this as merely the expression of an aesthetic preference, but at the time it had the power of a Mosaic commandment and effectively paralyzed research into other forms of housing" (in Lampugnani, 1986, p. 69). One could go further: The "motivating vision" represented in that expression only ever succeeded in motivating the architects themselves and, after 1945, the public housing officials that gave some of them rein; but by then, CIAM had itself largely moved on from that vision of the world.

The real significance of CIAM only becomes clear with the realization that, by 1933, the focus of debate was overwhelmingly *the city* and urban life: Building form and "style" were no longer problematic *except in their contingency on the form of the city and of urban life*. The "voice" with which to represent this new world was already, by that time, *in part* defined: It would comprise agreed ways of portraying an elementarist approach to spaces, components, and institutions; a purist geometry; a Sachlichkeit commitment to standardization and technological rationalization; the machine aesthetic—all akin to what Bakhtin would term a new "social language" in which every architect, universally, could henceforth ventriloquate. And it would comprise agreed ideas—however uncritically accepted—of what a house, an apartment block, an office building, a factory will be. Above all, both the "social language" of the new architecture and the building types or "genres" in which it could be employed—the *modern movement*, in short—were to be universally applicable.[3] It was the architecture of a new, universal civilization. The disaster was that the text in which social language and genres were to be employed—the forms of social

life that the modern movement was to represent and thereby facilitate—remained largely empty.

|OTHER VOICES, OTHER VISIONS

Walter Benjamin could observe that, in the nineteenth century, flowers, gardens, and landscapes could be "transposed" indoors, under the
glass roofs of the arcades and exhibitions. But now, "Today the slogan is
not transposing, but transparency (Corbusier!)" (Benjamin, 1982, p.
528; Buck-Morss, 1989, p. 303). There is a new vision of space; and
new technology is a facet of "new nature"—a now-possible world—
"the waking world toward which the past was dreaming" (Benjamin,
1982, p. 1058).[4]

To Martin Heidegger (1889–1976) in the 1930s, by contrast, new
technology (and *Neue Sachlichkeit* as one mode of its representation)
would reduce all entities, including humans, to mere resources to be
put to efficient use: It is "the priority of machination, of discipline, and
of method over what it is that goes into them and is affected by
them"—"the priority of ordering over what it is supposed to accom-
plish" (Heidegger, 1989, pp. 336, 397; in Guignon, 1993, p. 20).[5] But
we need first to take a step back. In *Sein und Zeit (Being and Time)* of
1927, Heidegger had confronted the very basis of Western metaphysics
in its Platonist distinction between enduring substance and ephemeral
properties—the either/ors, the detritus from abstract theorizing far
removed from real lived experience but ultimately structuring both
language and our understanding of existence. Instead, he attempted to
recover some original, prereflective sense of being (*contra* Nietzsche:
Becoming is all the being there is): How things show up, are disclosed
to us, in human existence itself—*Dasein* (being there)—What are the
conditions for the intelligibility of things, for disclosedness? The answer lies in our embeddedness in a practical, concrete, local, meaning-
ful world of the everyday—the "life-world." We *start* with context and
meaning. (Only local place can have meaning, and universal space
must be a delusion.) To recover "originary" experience and thinking,
we must "do violence" to commonplace assumptions and their underpinning "Cartesian ontology of modernity" (Guignon, 1993, p. 7); and
in this enterprise of emerging "from the grip of modern rationalism,"
Heidegger must be accorded priority (Taylor, 1993, p. 317).[6]

Through the 1930s, the voice changed: The historicity of being—
existence as a journey from birth unto death—had always permeated
Heiddegger's writing and lectures, but now it came increasingly into
focus. He would deconstruct the "history of ontology": There was a
"first beginning" when the pre-Socratic Greeks first brought to con-

scious reflection the "ontological difference" between being and things (then aware, albeit dimly, of how language and human practices will structure what is significant in making a world). But the history of metaphysics has been "a progressive masking or concealing of what was revealed in that primordial experience"—what it is that makes presence possible (Guignon, 1993, p. 17). So the task is to break through to a new beginning, to retrieve the "wellsprings": "The beginning, conceived in an originary way, is being itself," and the new beginning is "realizable only in a dialogue with the first" (Heidegger, 1962, p. 58).

As modernity advances upon us, then, we get "a totalising, homogenised understanding of things," a world of objects drained of all significance ("origin")—"use values" only: *the commodity.* Universalizing space and reductionist technology mark the destruction—"the priority of machination," "the priority of ordering" (Heidegger, 1959, pp. 336, 397).

"Every thought of society and of history itself belongs to society and history," to repeat Castoriadis's dictum. If Benjamin is of the avant-garde, linked to the dadaist preoccupation with collage and the disrupting juxtaposition and to a Jewish messianic trace, then Heidegger is likewise context bound in the profound, gathering conservativism, between 1870 and 1933, of a Germany reeling from the seeming cataclysms of unification, rapid industrialization and urbanization, and erosion of tradition. The horrors of 1914–1918, the ignominy of defeat, the injustice of Versailles and war reparations, the economic collapse, hyperinflation, the ineffectiveness of the Weimar republic and the bourgeois cupidity of its politicians composed the context for both the reactions of the avant-garde and those of the conservatives—which, in turn, were reactions against each other. National renewal, proclaimed Heidegger in 1919 in his first Freiburg University lecture, demands "return to the authentic origins of the spirit"—"Man, become essential!" The rest of his life would be the search for those "authentic origins." Where Walter Benjamin in March 1933 left Germany permanently, for Paris and the *Passagen-Werk,* eventually to die in 1940 at his own hand while fleeing the Nazis, Heidegger on May 1, 1933 joined the Nazi Party: Perhaps in the turn to the "blood and soil" of the German soul, a *volk* retrieved and renewed, one could find the "new beginning" in the escape from universal space and technological understanding.[7]

THE MODERN MOVEMENT
AND THE MODERNE

The abstracting tendency of the modern movement presented a problem. How was the power of the state (capitalist–bureaucratic, National

Socialist, Soviet, etc.) to be represented and its legitimacy reinforced, and how were underlying structures of domination (capitalist, surveillant, self-surveillant, etc.) to be reified? The case of the Third Reich is instructive, caught in a Puginesque tension between the representation of a heroic destiny and the return to old values—uprooted by the economic and political upheaval of 1870–1933, but also, after 1933, by the industrialization of the military and of violence: How does one represent the promised domination of a "modern," industrialized world—and simultaneously the escape from its values—by the means of that world. The former was invoked in an arid, stripped-down neoclassicism, with Albert Speer as its master, and as its models the Prussian classicism of C. F. Schinkel (1781–1841) and Haussmann's brutalizing reconstruction of Paris. Berlin must exceed such glories: "Wasn't Paris beautiful?" Speer reports Hitler as saying, but then to add, "when we are finished in Berlin, Paris will only be a shadow. So why should we destroy it?" (Speer, 1970, p. 172).[8] Walter Benjamin (1982) states: "Empire style is the style of revolutionary terrorism, for which the state is an end in itself" (p. 1212). The other term in the contradiction—the return to old values, the new beginning "in a dialogue with the first," "blood and soil"—found expression in quaint, folksy, Hansel-and-Gretel-revival housing estates under party auspices (pitched roofs against the "bourgeois–internationalist" flat roofs of Weimar housing estates), the party political schools in mock medieval guise, but also the more serious rhetoric of Paul Schultze-Naumburg (almost Heideggerian) and the Teutonic–expressionist tendency of such architects as Tessenow, Häring, and Scharoun (Taylor, 1974). Though the ideological cacophony was mobilized to suppress the Neue Sachlichkeit architects and lead to their dispersal, where true mechanized efficiency had to be represented, the officially banned styles would be readily appropriated.

In 1937 yet another of the great Expositions was held (they were endemic in the 1920s), in Paris, with the almost Fordist theme of peace through unity and of national solidarity *with* labor, against the internationalist slogans of the solidarity *of* labor. It presented one supremely bizarre image: the German pavilion, in high-Teutonic, neoclassicist, soul-reawakening monumentality confronted, across the "Avenue de la Paix," the Soviet pavilion in its own solidarity-of-the-proletariat, Stalinist monumentality. And they complement each other marvelously. They could be interchangeable. The Soviet state was never troubled with the ideological intricacies and subtleties that contorted the Nazis; and by the late 1920s, there could be a simple, brutal "battle of styles" over how to represent the workers' paradise. The seminal event was the 1931 competition for the Palace of the Soviets. Le Corbusier's entry was the most constructivist essay of his whole output and was a preeminent example of spatial arrangement for didactic social purpose. There were other international and domestic entries covering the whole gamut of the debates. In the event, the winning entry (by B. M. Iofan, who would later design the 1937 pavilion in Paris) was a classicist throwback to prerevolutionary national romanticism. In April 1932, the social–realist line was adopted by the Central Committee, the constructivist and elementarist tendencies were suppressed, and Anatole Lunacharsky finally abandoned his enlightened protection of diversity and threw in his lot with the winning side.[9] Architectural and urban design went the overblown, neoclassicist way of Speer and Iofan, though extraordinarily bastardized with thrusting vertical elements, statues of proletarian virtues, and bits of nationalistic confectionary.[10]

The universalist project of the modern movement also withered on the other side of the Atlantic. There the turn was to the "moderne" the art deco style of the North American skyscrapers of the 1930s. It was stripped-down Gothic rather than stripped-down neoclassicism (its lineage being from the neo-Gothic Woolworth Building of 1913, to Hood and Howell's winning design for the Chicago Tribune tower of 1922, to Van Alen's art deco Chrysler Building of 1928–1930, to the almost cubist art deco of Rockefeller Center of 1932–1939); but there was also a strong German expressionist streak running through it (the Flash Gordon imagery of the Chrysler Building, for instance, and the preoccupation with glass and lighting). The new style seems to have been "necessary," not for the legitimation of the state, but to celebrate the new, North American capitalist hegemony: a new beginning in a New World after the discredit and destruction of the old in 1914–1918 and a new belief in *the inherent goodness of capitalist progress.*

THE INTERNATIONAL STYLE AS SYNTHESIS

The economic collapse of the early 1930s—what Harvey (1978) has termed "the first global crisis of capitalism" (though the events of 1846–1848 might challenge for that title)—and its aftermath in the 1939–1945 period, left governments globally with a legitimation crisis and, in the broader cultural sphere, with what Habermas (1976) terms a *motivation crisis*—a crucial deficit of action-motivating meaning. For what sort of world was the war being fought? In many societies—Britain, the United States, Canada, Australia, as examples—discourses increasingly addressed societal goals (that "action-motivating meaning") and the redemption of validity claims underlying prevailing

relations of production. The capitalist mode of production was certainly to be questioned—and, in some views, to be replaced.

The bourgeois responses to this crisis were varied, but increasingly
from the late 1940s they involved signifying a break with the past and
a new faith in material progress. This would call on both architectural
style (as sign) and broader aspects of an aesthetic program—what
would be built, how it would be built, and how it would be used. The
moderne was discredited, associated with a discredited era and vanquished regimes (in Germany, India, etc.); the new actors, however,
were already veterans in the wings.

Four themes seem to have woven their paths through the aesthetic
practices and theoretical disputations of high modernism: (1) the
search for agrarian origins, the "first beginning," the vernacular (the
arts-and-crafts movement, to some extent both Vkhutemas and the
Bauhaus, and reflected by Heidegger); (2) the celebration of technology (the Deutsche Werkbund, again the Bauhaus, CIAM in its Neue
Sachlichkeit era, and of course Le Corbusier); (3) the search for "pure
form" and the escape from signification (the pioneers were Adolf Loos
in Vienna and later Paris, Malevich and the suprematists, yet again the
Bauhaus, Mies van der Rohe, but preeminently Le Corbusier); and
finally (4) the idea of popular empowerment (a new mode of spatial
production was always implicit in the work of William Morris and
writings of Marx, but its classic expression was with the Russian productivists). The aesthetic program and stylistic language eventually
appropriated in the later 1940s drew upon the second and third of these
traditions of high modernism—the machine aesthetic, and the pur-
ist/suprematist escape from signification—to yield, in the International
Style, the putative representation of universal space.[11]

GLOBAL BOOM
AND THE INTERNATIONAL STYLE

The International Style was implicated in the extraordinary growth in
the Western capitalist economies of the 1950s and 1960s, just as the
beaux arts tradition—whether called Victorian, Second Empire, or
Italianate—was associated with the expansions of the second half of
the nineteenth century and just as the moderne or art deco was linked
with the good times of the 1920s. By implying progress, functionalism,
and technical efficiency, the International Style gave expression to
that material growth; and in turn the association led to its increasing
signification of the "economic miracle" and all that it stood for: Western democracy, the American way of life, the New Germany, La Gloire.

The guaranteed signification (build this way and you too will be identified with Western progress!), together with the international penetration of Western economic influence and the growth of the transnational corporation, ensured that the International Style would indeed be the world's first truly *international* style.

It was, however, far more than just "style." Meanings were also universal: An office building was recognizable as an office building wherever it was built—likewise for a railway station, an airport terminal, a factory. The social relationships signified were likewise universal. To continue the Bakhtinian analogy, both the social language and the genres were universally accessible, and their appropriation and use in the production of new urban meaning seemed everywhere to ensure the vision of the final apotheosis of modernity.[12] The world was *nearly* a single space.

At first, superficial glance, there is little difference between the "International Style" of the 1950s and 1960s and the "modern movement" architecture of the 1930s, and the sudden success of the former scarcely warrants a change of label.[13] There is, however, the profoundest of differences, for the signified has changed. The intent behind the radicals of the avant-garde and CIAM was a new world and form of social life ("new architecture, new society"), whether or not they knew how to achieve it: Socialist in the main, antibourgeois, technologically *modern* (*rational*, in Le Corbusier's parlance), it was a world *yet to be achieved*. Those architectural firms of the 1950s and 1960s were one with the new corporate world (and often continuous with anti-modern movement firms of the 1930s), building that new, agreed-upon world whose achievement seemed imminent and turning their often considerable talents to ways of representing it. The signified had slipped from the third of Lenin's mutually contradictory terms (the vision of the new, radically opposed to the world of the old) to the first (the old, the established—albeit a new, modern "old"). If the represented world changes, one would expect the signifiers to change also—and they did: There *is* a difference, even at the level of surface appearance. By the 1950s, the glass walls are smoother, the packaging more urbane, the buildings and their plazas more geared to the advertising function (see Figure 6.3).

The revolutionary, emancipatory intent reemerges, however, in the way one might expect: through an attempt to represent a new experience of space and time contingent on a redefinition of the self that can oppose individual experience—a principle of difference—to that dream of universal order represented in the International Style. Again, the central figure was Le Corbusier; but we need first to take a step back.

HEIDEGGER, SPACE, AND THE WORK OF ART

By 1936, Heidegger's National Socialist zeal was waning. The Nazis had somehow failed their high calling: Being and entities were yet again being reduced to the level of the commodity, as the preoccupation with the *volk* marked merely an extension of subjectivism and humanism, the dead end of Western metaphysics. It could amount to nothing more than "a *'völkische'* expansion of 'liberal,' 'me-centered' thinking and of the economic representation of the maintenance of 'life'" (Heidegger, 1971a, p. 319). A Nazi slogan, "Everything must be at the service of the people," would commodify all entities.

Instead, Heidegger (1993) comes to argue that, in order for enti-

FIGURE 6.3. The street broken apart, context denied, buildings as objects: Mies van der Rohe and Philip Johnson, Seagram Building and Plaza, New York, 1958. Author's drawing, based on Zukowsky (1986).

ties to manifest the full, billowing richness of their being, we must cease to see things as merely bits of the "world picture" of our representations: To repeat, "The fundamental event of the modern age is the conquest of the world as picture" (Heidegger, 1977, p. 149). Rather we must seize that experience of our being "thrown" into a setting where, as Guignon (1993) paraphrases it, we are "called" to the task of letting things show up in their full significance and belongingness together (p. 33). Heidegger will call that experience "insistent [standing-in-a-site] caring"—"dwelling"; again and again he speaks of a "clearing" where things can gather the surrounding environment into a coherent whole, a "play of time-space." This clearing for dwelling—a fundamental mode of abiding upon the earth—is to bring together a "fourfold" oneness of mortals, gods, earth and heaven. How might this be? Heidegger's (1971a) essay "The Origin of the Work of Art" gives the example of the Greek temple:

> Standing there, the building holds its ground against the storm raging about it and so makes the storm itself manifest in its violence. The luster and gleam of the stone . . . first brings to light the light of the day. . . Tree and grass, eagle and bull, snake and cricket first enter into their distinctive shapes and thus come to appear as what they are. (p. 42)[14]

The great work of art (here, of architecture) is a world-disclosing and world-transforming event "that crystallizes an understanding of being for a people, giving them a coherent focus and direction for their lives," again in Guignon's (1993) paraphrase (p. 22). Somewhere here, then, is the "new beginning," and Heidegger's space is the space of transformation, where mortals, gods, earth, and sky are gathered together "into a kind of cosmic dance which frees up the inherent luminosity of things" (Zimmerman, 1993, p. 250).[15] "Beyond what is," writes Heidegger (1971a), "not away from it but before it, there is still something else that happens. In the midst of beings as a whole an open space occurs. . . . Only this clearing grants and guarantees to human beings a passage to those entities that we ourselves are not, and access to the being that we ourselves are" (p. 53). The space of the clearing is however *constituted by a thing* (natural, or artefactual): "There must always be some being in [the clearing], something that is, in which the openness takes its stand and attains its constancy" (Heidegger, 1971a, p. 61)—the temple, or the cathedral, or the peasant dwelling in the Black Forest?

Da-sein now refers, in the later Heidegger (1971a), not to humans but to "the self-opening medium of the interplay of calling-forth and belongingness; . . . the *between* between humans . . . and gods" (p. 311). *Things* are increasingly central in letting a world happen—constituting the clearing. So we come to the "ecological turn" in Heidegger (1971a): The task is "to be simply *'for the sake of being,'* not for the sake of man [modernity, the Nazis] but for the sake of the being of entities in totality" (p. 16). But suddenly human existence itself is the clearing, the openness, in which things can manifest themselves (though the dimensions of this space are always temporal—past, present, future). We are as one with the "Divine Nothingness" of the mystics (Meister Eckhart), and we only reach authenticity when we allow things to reveal themselves according to their own possibilities. It is the end of both instrumental value and anthropocentrism. Later voices, still Heideggerian in spirit, will give us the rallying cry of deep ecology: "Let beings be."

THE ECOLOGICAL
AND THE MONUMENTAL

As early as 1927, in *Being and Time*, Heidegger (1962) had called for an authentic historiography as critique of the present—"a way of painfully detaching oneself from the falling publicness of the 'today' " (p. 449). It is only from the profoundest understanding of our history that we can find the motivating vision of what we can, ourselves, be; and the task of the work of art is to show that picture, monumentalized: what *can be.* Similar themes weave through the machine-aesthetic vision of Le Corbusier's *Vers une Architecture* of the same year. With the fall of the Third Reich, the waning of the *moderne*, and the triumph of the International Style, neither a critical historicity nor a monumentalized picture of possible worlds could find a place in the endeavors of architects of the new orthodoxy.

In 1943, in collaboration with Fernand Léger and José Luis Sert, Sigfried Giedion wrote "Nine Points on Monumentality"; only two years earlier his *Space, Time and Architecture* had been published, based on 1938–1939 lectures at Harvard, and was arguably the most influential text in catalyzing the embrace of "functionalism" and the International Style.[16] Among the "nine points" are the arguments that monuments are creations of men [*sic*], "as symbols for their ideals, for their aims, and for their actions . . . A heritage for future generations . . . they form a link between the past and the future." Monuments are "the expression of man's highest cultural needs. . . . To satisfy the eternal demand of the people for translation of their collective force into symbols"; and the new task of representation in the postwar world may relate to "the organization of community life in the city which has been practically neglected up to date" (quoted in Frampton, 1985a, p. 223). There followed a 1944 symposium on the need for an expression of the monumental, reported as *New Architecture and City Planning*, edited by Paul Zucker (1945); its participants included both Giedion and Louis Kahn. A partial conclusion, therefore, is that the final ascendancy of the universalist, machine-aesthetic, antimonumentalist, antihistoricist, high-modern turn in the production of space and representation of institutions was coincident with the (Heideggerian) discourse reacting to it. Yet there was another voice, not so well heard in that era, warning against Heidegger's exhortation and also implicitly against the celebrators of the machine. Georges Bataille's essay "Against Architecture"— on monuments as our real prison—belongs to the 1980s and 1990s, but was in fact written in 1929: "Thus great monuments rise up like levees, opposing the logic of majesty and authority to any confusion" (Bataille, 1971, p. 171).

By the time of CIAM V (Paris, 1937, the place and time of the emblematic confrontation of the monuments to Third Reich and Soviet Union), there was some tentative resiling from the universalist position and an acknowledgment of the influence of historic fabric and regional context. It was not until 1947 that CIAM convened again, at Bridgwater in England; but even as the CIAM members gathered, to celebrate their own survival of war and Holocaust and the seeming acceptance (appropriation!) of the modern movement voice, Le Corbusier's Unités d'habitation at Marseilles was commencing construction. The Marseilles block is vast—some 337 apartments, shopping streets, hotel, community services, recreational landscape on the roof—and seems to bring together most of the central ideas that Le Corbusier and CIAM had advocated in the prewar era: the tower block in a park, the OSA two-level and crossover apartments, a "rational" recasting of urban life. It also synthesizes elements from the models of rational communal life that had preoccupied Le Corbusier for decades: the monastery and the ocean liner. In its result, it probably comes closest to that other model of such life, the Fourier *phalanstère*. The Unité was meant to be repeated, but in its mode of representation—Le Corbusier's "voice" of that moment—it seems unique, unrepeatable, more sculpture than rational machine, a monument to define a place and time rather than a model for all space and every time.[17] It is a return to the Manichean worldview, the play with opposites. There had always been *two* dominant, self-definitional voices through which Le Corbusier represented the world.[18] One had been the Cartesian voice of a rational social order, most ringingly heard in the Ville contemporaine, the urban design and architecture prior to 1947, and the CIAM utterances; the other was the Nietzschean voice of the wilful, transcending artist, changing the world but remaining unchanged by it, giving form to the paintings and particularly the sculptures. With Marseilles, both are heard.

The outcome was controversy and confusion. For one thing, the Unité was incomplete, part of a city (Ville contemporaine or Ville radieuse) that would never be realized, discontinuous with its context.[19] To many it was irrational, almost a betrayal of the highest, Corbusian principles. The vast, surreal, sculptural landscape of its roof—incorporating an intermediate school, a nursery, open-air theater, gymnasium, and pool—seemed most irrational of all, signifying its discontinuity and difference relative to the real Marseilles—dialectically, ideologically opposed. More was to come.

From 1950 to 1955, Le Corbusier built the church of Notre-Dame-du-Haut at Ronchamp (see Figure 6.4); the Monastery of Notre-Dame de la Tourette followed in 1952–1960; and a series of buildings in India culminated in the government center for the Punjab capital of Chandigarh (for which he also did an overall city design), in the period of 1951–1965. This is an architecture and urban design of opposites, of a purposive heterogeneity of voices. It is many things. It is an architecture to reexpose human life to ecological place, with great scoops to seize the light, roofscapes reclaimed as meadow, symbolic ears turned toward external nature. (Le Corbusier refers to *acoustique paysagiste*, "landscapal acoustic," or perhaps open to sun, light, air, forest, and meadow.) It is a celebration and monumentalizing of the vernacular. It is a redefinition of the role of architecture and urban meaning, as being to establish the place of the mythic in human experience (*espace indicible*—inexpressible or indescribable space—and one with the monumentalizing of dependence-on-nature and of the vernacular and old memory, with listening ears, open hands, archaic dolmens, caves and deep recesses, swathing forms like the hills and the clouds). It thereby redefines the human and, accordingly, the emancipatory task; each building is specific to its cultural and spatial context—thereby unrepeatable—and, accordingly, posing the end of the universalist vision of the modern movement and the International Style at the moment of its seeming achievement.

The parallels with the later Heidegger are unmistakable. An entity (a work of art) always constitutes the clearing—"something that is, in which the openness takes its stand" (1971a, p. 61)—to gather and make manifest "the storm. . . Trees and grass, eagle and bull, snake and cricket" (p. 42), thereby, in turn, the "fourfold" of "mortals, gods, earth and sky": Humans are not at the center. "Releasement towards things and openness to the mystery belong together. They grant us the possibility of dwelling in the world in a totally different way. They promise us a new ground and foundation upon which we can stand and endure in the world of technology without being imperiled by it" (Heidegger, 1966, p. 55).

Hubert Dreyfus (1993) labels this idea in Heidegger as "cultural paradigm," gathering the scattered practices of a group, unifying them into "coherent possibilities for action," as exemplars in terms of which the people can act and relate to each other. "Works of art, when performing this function, are not merely representations or symbols, but actually produce a shared understanding" (p. 298). There will be

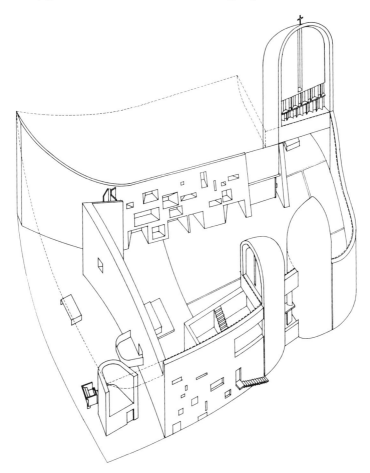

FIGURE 6.4. Le Corbusier: Notre-Dame-du-Haut, Ronchamp, 1950–1955. Drawing by Matt Spinaze, based on *Le Corbusier, 1910–1960* (1960) and Frampton (1985).

new epochs (perhaps "new beginnings") with, following Kuhn, "paradigm shifts" (a modernist notion). Le Corbusier is interesting for having had, seemingly, roles in the two paradigm shifts that marked high modernity.

This part of the account cannot be closed without some comment on Chandigarh. By most criteria it is a disaster. Despite its socialist antecedents in the Ville contemporaine and the Athens Charter, it is zoned for caste and even for class; the motorway grid of the Ville contemporaine is finally achieved, but in a society that cannot afford motor cars; the spaces and distances are those of high-modernist dreams, but not of the intimacy and small scale of Indian urban life. It has often been claimed in Le Corbusier's defense that the ideas for Chandigarh were set before he came on the scene and that the implementation was left to others. But it was always his voice ventriloquated, albeit sometimes from thirty years previously. The extraordinary contradictions of the spatial representation, however, merely reflect the contradictions of what was to be represented: The signified, in 1951, was to be the New India; but here Nehru's vision of a modern industrial state stood against Gandhi's dream of a continuity with a timeless culture above modernist fetish. In the government center, the Capitol, these great uncertainties and paradoxes are explored as part of that autobiographical unfolding of Le Corbusier's doubts that also runs through Ronchamp and La Tourette: The Secretariat, the High Court, and the Assembly are planned on a vast scale, with plain, hills, mountains, and sky drawn into the composition; it has that surreal, mythic, sculptural ambiguity of the Marseilles block or Ronchamp; and like the human condition itself, it leaves one uncertain, unsettled, troubled.

| FRAGMENTATIONS

CIAM VIII was held at Hoddesdon in England in 1951. Its theme was "the urban core" and by most accounts revealed marvelously that the architects and urban planners were utterly bereft of the conceptual insights to address such an issue.[20] CIAM IX, at Aix-en-Provence in 1953, was in part a ritual of worship to Le Corbusier but was also the beginning of the split as the new generation challenged the categories of the Athens Charter (Dwelling, Recreation, Work, Transportation, and Historic Buildings) and turned to questions such as identity, "belonging," neighborhood, and complexity. With the final congress of CIAM in 1956, the spell was broken, the universalist claims abandoned, and the heterogeneity of voices prevailed.

One disparate group would seek the perfection of the modern

movement itself: the glass box reduced to almost nothing but flawless detail (Mies van der Rohe, Philip Johnson), or a mirror in which the chaos of the city would be endlessly reflected back to itself from an object forever alien to it, or—further fragmentation—a play with the language of the modern movement, even parody (Michael Graves, Richard Meier, and a few others in the 1960s and 1970s), one genre of the postmodern. A second tendency was toward an ultimate apotheosis of the machine aesthetic: In Ron Herron's "Walking City" of 1964, it was not the inhabitants who would walk but the buildings; in Peter Cook's "Plug-in City" of the same year, the promise of exchangeable dwelling units inserted and removed from a giant frame, always implicit in Le Corbusier's Marseilles Block, would finally be realized; the Japanese metabolist group was similarly preoccupied with megastructures and plug-in living. What is surprising about virtually all the high-tech, sci-fi utopias of the 1960s is that they were extraordinarily uncritical, even of the limits to the technology they were suggesting, let alone of the social world they might be confronting or for which they might be designing or of the meanings—signifieds—beneath their images. There is nothing of that confrontation of the 1920s avant-garde; rather there is irony, having fun.[21]

A third post-CIAM tendency is best represented in the late work of Louis Kahn (1901–1974). In the 1950s, Kahn designed a series of buildings whose preoccupation was with expressing how things are built (joints, markings of materials, fastenings) and how they work (the pipes and ducts, "served" spaces and "servant" spaces)—with establishing a "social language" of architecture that could permeate and enoble the labor of architect, builder, craftsman, and user. From circa 1957 the concern broadened, from the nature of production to the nature of the thing produced.[22] The attempt was to get back to—to define anew—institutions: to find "the center," "ground-zero," or, in Kahn's terminology, the "existence-will" of things.

> His architecture gives form to what in the contemporary world tends to disappear or not to possess form: the places of worship, taste, culture. But Kahn also created architecture for institutions that are faceless, that the world submerges and annihilates. His architectural works are intent on bringing back a collective memory. (Tafuri and Dal Co, 1986, p. 380)

Although Kahn was the most reflective of architects, and the most preoccupied with the verbal expression and architectural representation of the modern experience of being-in-space, he was in no philosophical camp. The search for existence-will might draw us back to the "first beginnings" of things, perhaps to some Heideggerian,

prereflective sense of being; but Kahn's project differs fundamentally
from Heidegger's in that it posits enduring essences behind all properties and manifestations—"forms" rather than the life-world and the
conditions for disclosedness of things, the separateness of things rather
than their embeddedness. Kahn is still modern; Le Corbusier, on the
other hand, eventually becomes Heideggerian, antiessentialist, attempting to make "the clearing" where entities (nature) are disclosed.
Kahn would "design with nature" (the call of Ian McHarg, his colleague at the University of Pennsylvania); but where Le Corbusier
seizes the light, Kahn guards against it. It is the heterogeneity of spaces
of Nietzsche's insistence that Kahn seems to come closest to (the void,
the sea, distance, etc.); yet there is nothing of Nietzsche's repudiation
of "history"—acceptance, creatively, of the responsibility for the giving
of time. The distinction must be made between a nostalgic return to
origins (Kahn) and a critical, "deconstructive" return oriented to dis-
entangling the links between institutions, space, and power (Benjamin, Foucault). The latter certainly eluded Kahn, and the failure
points up the dilemma of effecting a truly "consciousness-raising criticism" in the sphere of urban and architectural design; but the former
also was problematic. For the return to origins, pursued through such a
tough-minded, rationalist architectural language—architecture almost
as a mathematical puzzle (see Figure 6.5)—led to a stripped monumen-
talism that legions of unthinking acolytes could replicate through the
1970s and 1980s. More interestingly, Kahn's "creative involvement
with the past" prefigured much of the more important work in urban
and architectural design of the ensuing decades by the likes of Aldo
Rossi, James Stirling, and Michael Graves (Lampugnani, 1986, p. 186);
it also in large measure triggered the opposing, antimonumental return
to the world of everyday life championed by another colleague at the
University of Pennsylvania, Robert Venturi.

To complement these accounts of the post-CIAM heterogenity, it
needs to be observed that there was also a much longer-term diversity
within the modern movement itself. Much was serendipitous, related to
"great individuals" (Frank Lloyd Wright, Buckminster Fuller); but
there were also significant regional "schools" and local differences, in
some counteraction to the universalizing intent: local place against
universal space. Among the more notable local languages were the
Scandinavian (especially focused on the architectural personality of
Alvar Aalto), the Brazilian (Lucio Costa, Oscar Niemeyer), an Italian
(extraordinarily vigorous after 1945), the Japanese (from the 1950s);
the list could continue. The post-CIAM differences were accordingly
overlain upon longer running tendencies to diversity. By the 1970s
each was invigorating the other, and the tumult had returned.

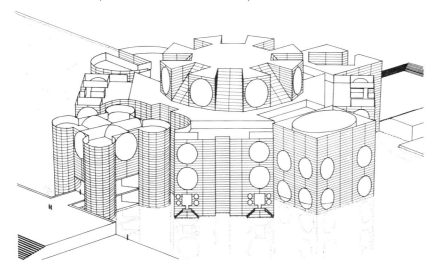

FIGURE 6.5. Louis Kahn: Abstract geometries and first beginnings. National Assembly Building, Dacca. Drawing by Matt Spinaze, based on Ronner and Jhaveri (1987) and Brownlee and De Jong (1992).

OVERACCUMULATION, AND THE IMPERATIVES OF CONSUMPTION

The long boom of the 1950s and 1960s was accompanied by massive overaccumulation of capital: Too much capital was produced in aggregate relative to the available opportunities for its profitable reinvestment. Harvey (1978) traces this phenomenon to (secondary) contradictions embedded in the very structure of the capitalist mode of production. Specifically, there is the contradiction between individual and class interests: Competition between individual capitalists leads to actions inimical to their collective, class interest, with overproduction, falling prices and rates of profit, and other collapses. Second, the need to preserve the rate of profit increases the need to suppress the wages of labor; but this in turn suppresses consumption potential, and overaccumulation is even further exacerbated.

A variety of strategies were involved in attempts to manage the "barrier of underconsumption"; their effect was to exacerbate cleavages and crises in other spheres of social life. For one thing, capital was increasingly switched into *the production of suburbia* in the United States, Canada, Australia, and subsequently Britain and parts of Western Europe. Suburbia in turn enabled successive waves of consump-

tion—of cars, white goods, furniture, fad after fad of electronic gadg-
etry, swimming pools, horticulture, and so forth (Baran and Sweezy,
1966; King, 1987). The institution of suburbia has always been linked
to the gender division of labor. More hidden have been the links
between the space of suburbia at all its levels (the house, the privacy-
reinforcing street, the broader neighborhood and its anonymity), the
power relations thus reproduced (a space for the little woman, a good
place to bring up kids), the environmental and spatial masking of the
consequent repression and self-repression (getting greener, getting better), and the different experiences of women and men (the idyllic,
sylvan world of the suburbs—or is it the world of isolation and the
mortgage trap?—against the "real world" of capitalist production and
bureaucratic guidance). World War II, like World War I, accelerated
the movement of women into that real world, and much of the rhetoric
on "postwar reconstruction" had to do with getting women content-
edly back into the suburbs so that returning servicemen could get
"their" jobs back. The suburban boom, its semiotics, and the successive
waves of commodities were implicated in that project. In those coun-
tries where the 1950s and 1960s were the suburban Golden Age, there
was also an age of radical shifts in gender-related politics and experiences—arguably the most rapid such shifts in the epoch of modernity
and, we will see, possibly triggering its end.

Of a kind with the cultural invasion of suburbia, *innovation in merchandising techniques* became routine. The department store, successor to
the arcades, and the linear shopping strip, typically along the tram and
trolley routes, were developed in the nineteenth century and dominated
until the middle of the twentieth. The first freestanding, drive-in shopping centers date from the 1950s; franchising and its reliance on "signature architecture" also spread rapidly from that time, especially in the
fast-food industry;[23] and "theme" shopping centers and malls proliferated
in the 1970s. The shopping malls and their fantasies especially became
part of women's world, to an extent that was never so for the department
stores (after all they were traditionally associated with the real world of
the city center) or for the shopping strips (along the routes by which the
man of the house returned home each evening). The designed illusions
of the "real world," by contrast, were those of corporate power and
economic progress—not the glitter, exotic impermanence, and historicist themes of the shopping mall, but the power, polished stone, and glass
walls of the office district and industrial "park." The increasing centrality
of merchandising and consumption was also aided by a variety of nonar-
chitectural innovations, including credit cards, debit cards, electronic
banking and retailing, and a seemingly endless array of devices to replace
money with yet further illusion.

Advertising became increasingly important and omnipresent. Whereas it had long tended to generate its own landscape, that too became increasingly ubiquitous. The highways unambiguously signified the machismo world of rods, rigs, and traveling salesmen, and their advertising and marketing were similarly men's world, again in a way that was never so for the old shopping strips. The exhortations to women's consumption were partly through the landscape of the malls, but also through the images of an idealized suburbia of the "lifestyle" magazines and, increasingly, of the television soapies. Both the representation of the world and the media of the representation further differentiated male and female experience.

Yet further strategies were related to *architectural style shifts*, periodically to devalue older investments in the built environment and to trigger demand for newer investments. As the International Style was profoundly implicated in the idea of the "postwar world" after 1945—thereby devaluing the investments of the 1920s and 1930s—by the mid-1960s, a fresh wave of investment was under way, distinguished by a "Late International Style," incorporating the previous "aberrations" represented by Kahn, the high-tech fantasists, and even Le Corbusier. And as we shall see, by the 1980s architectural postmodernism supplied yet a further shift, fortunate indeed from the point of view of investors looking for outlets for overaccumulated capital. While the style shifts of the city center signified economic progress, those of suburbia and the malls were more a medium for representing the goodness of new taste, the latest fad, the fetish of change itself.

All of these forms of strategy involved some form of "spatial fix"; and one of their consequences was to "spatialize" the contradiction they were intended to address and, correspondingly, to shift the contradiction into the sphere of the perception and experience not only of space but also of the power that space seems always to mask.

THE FRAGMENTS MISMATCH: INCOMPATIBLE LANDSCAPES

Contradictions between the value systems represented in different landscapes can be observed ubiquitously: in city versus countryside at the beginning of modernity, as in the feudal era; in "dark satanic mills" versus the countryside and, at the time of the Industrial Revolution, in a capitalist versus a "feudal" (or aristocratic) landownership; and in "production" landscapes versus "consumption" landscapes in the age of industrial predominance. The last opposition had especially been addressed, beginning in the 1920s, by the use of *land-use planning*.

The strategies addressing the always imminent crisis of underconsumption—suburbanization, the proliferation of advertising, increasing innovation in merchandising, and style shifts—vastly complicated
the problem of land-use planning by yielding three new, mutually
exclusive, incompatible landscape types. There was, first, what we
could call *the landscape of the corporate elite: progress and patriarchy*. At its
best—say, Chicago or New York in the 1960s—the central business
district achieved an urbanity and consistency that rivaled that of the
eighteenth century neoclassical city. Mies van der Rohe's Seagram
Plaza or C. F. Murphy's Chicago Civic Center (with help from Picasso)
are models of "high art" urban design, to stand alongside anything from
the past. The corporate elite, in seeking the legitimacy that comes with
sponsorship of high culture, implicated the realm of art in the contradictions that confronted corporate capitalism in the 1970s and 1980s.

In sharpest contrast was always *the landscape of consumerism*. The
landscape of advertising hoardings, neon lights, drive-in merchandising, car lots, McDonald's, Kentucky Fried Chicken, and other franchises is gawdy, frequently tawdry, and inimical to the images and
meanings associated with the landscape of the corporate elite—almost
enough to make you ashamed to be a capitalist! Barbara Rubin (1979)
sees the new conflict partly as history repeating itself:

> In the nineteenth century, the cultural elite and professional taste-
> makers excoriated the corporate monoliths which had begun to
> dominate the urban skyline. Their twentieth century counterparts
> devote their critical faculties to condemnation of the myriad small
> businesses which have filled in the urban interstices and occupy
> now-valuable urban space. (p. 358)

It was more than that, however; for to attack the world of small
entrepreneurs, franchises, and advertisers is also to attack the underlying, legitimizing ideology of "a society committed to the preservation of
individual liberties through free enterprise" (p. 358). (Not all taste-
makers have lashed the landscape of advertising and franchises, however—a point to which we return.)

The third of these incompatible semiotic worlds was *the landscape
of suburbia*. Although the ultrapurism of the modern movement and
International Style has frequently informed the design of the detached,
"suburban" villa (with such exemplars as Le Corbusier's Villa at
Garches and his Villa Savoie of 1927 and 1929–1931, respectively,
Mies's Farnsworth House of 1946–1950, and Philip Johnson's own
house of 1949), the more Romantic exemplars of suburbia have tended
to dominate and, indeed, triumph. The model of low-density, leafy

suburbia owes more to Philip Webb and Norman Shaw in England, and to Frederick Law Olmsted and Frank Lloyd Wright in the United States.

With the incompatibility of these landscape types, and of the first and third with the persisting industrial landscape, land-use planning after 1945 became a thriving industry.

| LATE VOICES

By the 1970s, new eyes were viewing this fragmenting space. Just as new architects were responding to it in the "second" languages of spatial representation (in their case, by abandoning the universalist, internationalist delusion), critiques in the texts of "first" language were mobilized to unmask the instrumentalist nightmare that had been the obverse of the delusions of modernity. Heidegger (1959/1966) insists that our "greatest danger" is that "the approaching tide of technological revolution in the atomic age could so captivate, bewitch, dazzle and beguile man that calculative thinking may someday come to be accepted and practised *as the only way* of thinking" (p. 56).

Certainly, the *space of efficiency* still beguiled, and by the 1980s it seemed that "economic rationalism" and its instrumentalist view of space had triumphed "universally." This could still be emancipatory *in its intention*: "the cornucopia of modernity—equality of abundance at last!" But it was precisely the universalism (equality) of the dream that had been lost. The endeavors to represent a unified human space (in International Style, international law, class politics, etc.) appear now as vain attempts to seize an already fragmenting vessel—voyages against the ebb of modernity.

It is instructive that when, in 1973, David Harvey sought to sensitize geographers and planners to Marxian insights in spatial analysis, he had to deal first with liberal "spatial science" that would oppose ideas of *equity* to *efficiency* and would see the problem of space as residing in its unevenness: Different people get different levels of benefits and opportunities, depending on where they live, work, study, and so on. Both city and countryside might be differentiated, but the focus is always on the pattern rather than the fragments.[24] Harvey's *Social Justice and the City* and Castells's *La Question urbaine*, both from 1973, are commonly identified with "the neo-Marxist revolution," "the new urban studies," "a paradigmatic shift" in the way that space is seen. The "new" focus was on the social production of space (that unevenness is socially produced!), and on the cultural construction of the messages that space carries. Yet there were other, older voices resonating through these various texts of the 1970s. Louis Althusser and Henri Lefevbre (among others) had already "rediscovered" the structuralist metanarrative of Marx's thinking and a geography to match its *historical* materialism. Yet these ideas can be detected even earlier, from Antonio Gramsci's Italian prison cell of the 1930s; Georg Lukács and his followers and colleagues of the Budapest School had lent insights (essentially Marxist) into the fragmentation of bourgeois taste cultures and into the increasing distance between aesthetic judgment and the judgment of taste in a world of collapsing historical consciousness (perceptions *not* echoing through Harvey and Castells). The Frankfurt School—it and the Bauhaus, in retrospect, as if holding mirrors to each other—had turned its critique to the "dialectic of Enlightenment" and to a different (productivist) Marxist aesthetic, marking the fragmenting of Marxist thought itself.

Yet there were other voices: Although Heidegger's confrontation with metaphysical thought might from a later epoch seem continuous with Nietzsche's, it was in fact an explicit reaction against Nietzsche, especially in the "later" writing after 1936; it was far more an engagement with the passion of Kierkegaard (to counter the lack of meaning and seriousness in the modern age, we must pit our own individual, absolute commitment—make thyself!) and with Husserlian phenomenology.[25] At the beginning of the century, in an attempt to escape the "relativism and historicism" of Western thought, Edmund Husserl had proposed a "phenomenological method" that would refocus the eye of the age—on description of the things disclosed in our experience and on description of our experience of them—"back to the things themselves!" Space and time are the fundamental media of all experience, though in Husserl's writing it is time that is privileged; the step with Heidegger is then to *Being and Time*—from the phenomenology of time to the history of the disclosure of being. There is also a step from the unfulfilled promise of a phenomenology of space to the vast, ecological vision of Heidegger. By the 1960s, we get a different reading of Husserl (and of Kierkegaard, Nietzsche, and Heidegger) in the radical subjectivism of the French existentialists; different again is the seminal, 1976 reading by Relph in *Place and Placelessness*: What it is to experience space and how that experience is expressed in landscape is addressed directly.

There is a distinction to be observed between the grand visions (of processes, patterns, forces, classes, etc.) that would structure the texts of economic rationalists, liberal spatial science, and neo-Marxists, on the one hand and, on the other, the erosive turn to the space of real lived experience that weaves through Nietzsche, Heidegger, the phenomenologists, and the existentialists. A final comment: This frag-

mentation of the city and countryside, and of the readings (constructions) to be placed upon it, has been thematized anew in the 1990s.[26]
The fundamental fragmentation is of experiences themselves; and
there is a new, analogous geography of the distances between private
worlds and shared worlds (if there are indeed any such things as the
latter), both as lived by different individuals and as brought into
existence—Heidegger's task for the work of art.

CHAPTER 7

The Space of Signs: 1968, Modernity and Postmodernity

How can we exceed the modern? How can we break with a program that makes a value of crisis (modernism), or progress beyond the era of Progress (modernity), or transgress the ideology of the transgressive (avant-gardism)? . . . [There are concerns with] a critique of Western representation(s) and modern "supreme fictions"; a desire to think in terms sensitive to difference (of others without opposition, of heterogeneity without hierarchy); a skepticism regarding autonomous "spheres" of culture or separate "fields" of experts; an imperative to go beyond formal filiations (of text to text) to trace social affiliations (the institutional "density" of the text in the world); in short, a will to grasp the present nexus of culture and politics and to affirm a practice resistant both to academic modernism and political reaction.

—HAL FOSTER, "Postmodernism: A Preface," in *Postmodern Culture* (1985, pp. ix, xv)

How then to represent a new experience of space as fragmented and time interrupted? Two questions are salient. First, What is to be represented: How is the present experience of space, time, nature, the self, and others "different"? It is certainly not just in the presence of "fragmentation," "transgression," "interruption," or "skepticism," for these have been there throughout modernity. And second, How is the present experience to be represented so that we might understand it and act upon it—the task of an emancipatory art in the context of an emancipatory politics? I will discuss the first question first; though, be warned, the two are ultimately the same: It is through representation, in whatever languages and images, that experience is brought most sharply into consciousness and that paths are defined.

| PARADOX

Since the 1960s, a variety of trends, some long observable, have seem- ingly coalesced to give what many see as a new society and a new age. Some time around 1972, in the advanced economies, the long postwar boom ended though the signs had been there all through the 1960s— most notably in the overaccumulation of the boom and the increasing difficulties in endlessly pushing out the barrier of fixed consumption. The economy that succeeded it seemed more volatile and far more globally integrated: Symptomatic of the new times were the oil price crises of the 1970s and the redistributions of wealth that they entailed, as well as the "new international division of labor" represented in the shifts of manufacturing activities from high-wage to low-wage regions and the consequent breaking up of previously locally integrated proc- esses. In the advanced economies, there was also a marked shift from the production of manufactured commodities to the production of services (to both firms and individuals). In many inner-city areas, old industries collapsed, beaten by decentralized rivals, whether at the periphery, in a "new" region, or offshore; the production of services took over, and the inner cities transformed suddenly and dramatically. Before that, however, the inner cities had in the late 1960s been the focus of urban protests on a scale not seen since the early 1930s. What made the Black revolt in the United States, the anti-Vietnam War rallies, and the 1968 student uprising in France so unique, however, was that they came at the end of a period of great prosperity and, indeed, "progress." Whatever the ostensible causes, those involved in that social unrest seemed to reject a society that was manifestly, stunningly successful. The politics that followed were distinctly different from those preceding—mediatized, based on a marketing "shaped by images alone," as if replacing new progress and grand projects with a recalling of older virtues. Architectural production also apparently moved from the grand program of the International Style and the representation of material advance to a more nostalgic, historicist recalling of local specificities, vernaculars, and older values. In urban planning there was a clear shift from concerns with broader urban morphology, and cer- tainly from any preoccupation with the structure of urban society, toward the incrementalist, ad hoc planning for specific projects, many of them vast in scale, spectacular in design, and speculative in intent, and toward the explicit urban design and improvement of disconnected precincts.[1] Fragmentation replaced comprehensiveness. And there were seemingly parallel shifts, since the 1960s, in literature, music, the graphic arts, cinema, criticism.

These various changes are empirically observable. But what is to be made of them? Mere continuation of long-term shifts, or fundamental change?

In *The Condition of Postmodernity*, David Harvey (1989) argues that since circa 1970 there has been a shift to "a new round of accumulation," of possibly equal significance to that signaled, in the 1910s, in the Fordist introduction of mass production, mass consumption, and a new politics of labor control and management.[2] The Fordist–Keynesian economy by the 1950s and 1960s was decreasingly able to ensure the conditions for economic expansion in a world awash with money or to respond quickly and flexibly to the increasingly frequent crises of the era (the 1973–1974 oil crisis and the end of the Vietnam War were the last straws). Behind the limiting rigidities of the system lay "a rather unwieldy and seemingly fixed configuration of political power and reciprocal relations that bound big labour, big capital, and big government into what increasingly appeared a dysfunctional embrace of such narrowly defined vested interests as to undermine rather than secure capital accumulation" (Harvey, 1989, p. 142).

Corporations were forced into rapid rationalization, restructuring, the circumvention of union power or other means of intensifying labor control, to undermine "the Fordist compromise." The rigidities of Fordism were confronted by new flexibilities—by what Harvey calls "flexible accumulation."[3] This resolution seems to have compelled yet further compression of space and time. Increasingly rapid decision making (also more innovative and "flexible") has depended on new technologies and faster travel (the forces of communication), but also, paradoxically, on greater physical proximity for the armies of new consultants, designers, advertising experts, corporate lawyers, investment analysts, finance packagers, takeover experts, market analysts, and the like—what Bourdieu (1984) terms the *new bourgeoisie*. So there has been both centralization of control and decision making (and a new hierarchy of key "world cities," secondary centers, and so on) and the final dissolution of space in the transmission and execution of those decisions—anything can be manufactured anywhere, so long as it is profitable. Local sentiment and loyalty no longer count. There is a new round of evermore rapid uneven development, both between regions and between sectors: Its manifestations include the various silicon valleys and sunbelts, their opposite in the rustbelts, the extraordinary rise of the service sectors and, correspondingly, the expansion of new class fractions (Bourdieu's *new bourgeoisie* and *new petite bourgeoisie*), the increasing takeover of the inner cities by those new groups, sudden investment in new regions, and, often, their equally sudden abandonment.[4]

We can turn for a moment to Henri Lefebvre's diagnosis of the change, from which Harvey's is in part derived. In late capitalism, Lefebvre argues, the contradiction between the forces and relations of production has been *apparently* resolved by completing the "commodification of all space." There have been two crucially important aspects of this in the post-1945 period. The first has been the opening of new paths to accumulation in building development and speculation: Especially in the context of overaccumulation and increasing rates of inflation in the 1960s and early 1970s, booms of development and speculation provided major new outlets for investment. The second has been the extraordinary expansion of the leisure industries (tourism, entertainment, the media)—surely the most novel phenomenon of the postwar boom. Even the most desolate, untouched, inaccessible wilderness has been instrumentalized to sell holidays, magazines, television advertising time—"We have conquered for leisure the sea, mountains and even deserts" (Lefebvre, 1970, p. 265). Thus, by 1970 Lefebvre could conclude that "capitalism is maintained by the conquest and integration of space" (p. 262). But the resolution was indeed only apparent, and the contradiction merely reemerges in new forms in the production and use of space. Specifically, there is a contradictory (and gendered) relationship between increasing centralization of *capitalist control* and the fragmentation and dispersal to increasingly distant peripheries of the *reproduction of the relations of production*: "The center attracts those elements which constitute it (commodities, capital, information, etc.) but which soon saturate it. It excludes those elements which it dominates (the 'governed,' 'subjects' and 'objects') but which threaten it" (Lefebvre, 1976, p. 18).

As economic and political power centralize, cultural hegemony weakens. A further form of (secondary) contradiction has emerged since the time observed by Lefebvre: Contradiction at the level of space is matched by that in the dimension of time. The property speculation boom of the 1960s and early 1970s in the developed economies was initially a cause and increasingly both cause *and* effect of asset inflation; but inflation cannot feed endlessly on itself, and the bubble burst in 1974–1975. The subsequent devaluation was far from uniform, and new waves of speculation and development began almost immediately, though in quite specific submarkets. Architectural style shifts and new approaches to urban design have been actively employed to attract tenants, customers, or residents to new submarkets and away from old. This process of uneven development has had to occur with ever greater frequency as sources of speculative capital have proliferated; style shifts and urban design ideas have likewise had to speed up. Thus, there is a contradiction in the time spans "necessarily" involved: Investment requires the assurance of long-term stability and rent-flows; but *continuing* investment requires not only the destruction of that stability but also rapid devaluation. The representational task confronts both these spans simultaneously.

Lash and Urry (1987), following Offe (1985), see the transition of the age as one from "organized" to "disorganized" capitalism. But this describes mere surface appearance. Certainly at one level the new regime of "flexible" production and accumulation is very decentralized, as vertical integration is broken down, processes are split up and their components dispersed, and self-employed consultants and outworkers replace in-house experts. All this fluidity is, however, ultimately highly organized, there are strong coordinators in the form of the financial markets, and the key investment and management decisions are more centralized than ever before. If there is *disorganization*, it is in the sphere of the reproduction of the relations of production, identified by Lefebvre—in the loss of cultural hegemony. But here, too, the coordinating mechanism looms, in the essentially *gender-differentiated* and mediatized production of the space of suburbia encountered earlier (with advertising, the women's journals, lifestyles of the rich and famous, the soapies), and deriving its reality as warm and loving counterpoint to the centralized space of corporate power. Whether a coordinated, capital-serving production of that signification can be maintained—or whether control will indeed be lost—is something we cannot yet know.

Some clue to the direction of economic change is therefore likely to emerge from considerations of how the present tensions and contradictions generated in flexible accumulation would seem to be coalescing in the cultural sphere—how that "spectre of a crisis of under-consumption" (Harvey) is having to be managed by increasingly frenetic enticements to consumption. Stated otherwise, it is the question of how the *spatial contradiction* of the dissolution of cultural hegemony (Lefebvre), its *disorganization* (Lash and Urry, Offe), undermines the power of capital over consumption. And it is the question of how the "temporal contradiction," of the destruction of order in the name of order, destabilizes the structure of urban meanings attached to the signs, "spectacle," of the city and, thereby, reproduction of the status quo.[5] Some such clues are hinted at in the work of Jean Baudrillard.

FLEXIBLE ACCUMULATION AND THE PRODUCTION AND CONSUMPTION OF SIGNS

In the present age—Baudrillard calls it the age of "consumer capitalism"—domination is no longer effected through capital (as means of production *and* as commodities produced), but increasingly through appearances and images. We consume no longer products, but signs—of television, of advertising; and the material objects of consumption have value for us precisely as signs—clothes as sign of identity, house or car as sign of status, music or paintings as sign of culture, education or travel or size of office as sign of achievement, and so on (Baudrillard, 1981). It is Baudrillard's argument that the task of domination in "consumer capitalism" shifts to the signifier, and thereby to the media—either through a decoupling from meaning (the world is reduced to spectacle, unreadable, and structures of domination are thus rendered opaque) or through the arbitrary assignment of meanings to signifiers (most notably, in the transformation of products, but also, Baudrillard adds, in the transformation of the relations of production—class is communicated away!).

Given the increasingly necessary dependence of capitalism on flexible accumulation (a dependence of which individual entrepreneurs are all too conscious), these transformations have had to become ever more frenetic: assignment and then devaluation of *exchange* values (to trigger yet a new round of consumption) dependent on ever more frequent assignment and devaluation of *sign* values—*meanings*. Social integration thus rests increasingly on communication—sign value, therefore ideology and the sphere of culture—rather than on simple exchange:

> Marx set forth and denounced the obscenity of the commodity, and this obscenity was linked to its equivalence, to the object principle of free circulation, beyond all use value of the object. . . . The commodity is readable: in opposition to the object, which never completely gives up its secret, the commodity always manifests its visible essence, which is its price. It is the formal place of transcription of all possible objects; through it, objects communicate. Hence, the commodity form is the first great medium of the modern world. But the message that the objects deliver through it is already extremely simplified, and it is always the same: their exchange value. . . . One has only to prolong this Marxist analysis, or push it to the second or third power, to grasp the transparency and obscenity of the universe of communication, which leaves far behind it those relative analyses of the universe of the commodity. All func-

tions abolished in a single dimension, that of communication.
(Baudrillard, 1985, p. 131)

Whereas the universalization of exchange value marked the first
great wave of capitalist modernization, the universalization of sign
value marks the second. And more significantly, capitalist expansion is
now thereby dependent on a cultural sphere over which it has declin-
ing hegemony—the Lefebvre argument! In Althusser's terms, insofar as
relations at the economic level—the *relations of production*—continue
to determine the relations between the economic, political, and ideological levels, those relations of production are presently determining
that dominance slips from the economic to the ideological level
(Althusser, 1969). If we take the conclusion further, and accept the
Castoriadis argument that the idea of "last instance" economic determination was itself historically contingent (and how could we logically
do otherwise?), then we must question whether we may have reached
the moment where the *determining role* of the economic (and our belief
in it!) also finally slips and modernity ends? It is the question for
Chapter 11.

In considering the city, Baudrillard pushes his argument much
further: If everything is reduced to spectacle, there is no spectacle!
Reality becomes a screen, depthless, with ever-changing images without meaning, a world of surface brilliance and indifference—nothing
to distinguish between a desert and a metropolis—a network of highways beginning nowhere in particular and going nowhere in particular
(see especially Baudrillard, 1988).

Thus the body, landscape, time all progressively disappear as scenes.
And the same for the public space: the theatre of the social and the
theatre of politics are both reduced more and more to a large soft
body with many heads. Advertising in its new version—which is no
longer a more or less baroque, utopian or ecstatic scenario of objects
and consumption, but the effects of an omnipresent visibility of
enterprises, brands, social interlocuters and the social virtues of
communication—advertising in its new dimension invades everything, as public space (the street, monument, market, scene) disappears. . . . It is the same for private space. In a subtle way, this loss of
public space occurs contemporaneously with the loss of private
space. The one is no longer a spectacle, the other no longer a secret.
(Baudrillard, 1985, pp. 129–130)

For private space is transformed by television—the endless soapies
that mimic domestic life and suburbia, to be mimicked in turn by
everyday life and suburbia. Population simulates the media, which in

turn hypersimulates the population, until there is no original, but only a world of "simulacra"—*everything* is a copy. So everyday life is "imploded" into the hyperreality of the spectacle, again a world without depth or meaning (Baudrillard, 1983).

Now I would agree with Lash and Urry (1987), against Baudrillard, that domination in present everyday life is "not through the attachment of signifieds, of meanings to images by culture producers, but by the particular strategies of dominant social groups to *refuse* to attach any meanings to such images" (p. 290). (Thus, office buildings are no longer signs of bureaucratic penetration or capitalist control but, when cleverly designed, visual fun.) But herein lies the ultimate contradiction: To continue to push out the barrier of fixed consumption is dependent on the detachment of meanings from commodities and ultimately from space; but the continuing reproduction of the relations of production is dependent on the production of socially motivating meaning. The conditions apparently necessary for consumption and those for reproduction are increasingly opposed. Life means nothing—just endless consumption of ephemera. The contradiction is at the ideological level, to do with meanings. It can be stated otherwise: The cognitive potential represented in the new *means of communication* (revealed so clearly in the instrumentalizing of all of space and all of life) cannot be realized in a higher level of communicative and productive action until the developmental lag in the *relations of communication* is overcome—until "uneven development" in moral–practical consciousness is overcome.[6] But the *relations* of communication (therefore, of production) remain suppressed by the *means* of communication themselves. Again the contradiction is revealed to be at the ideological level.

FLEXIBLE ACCUMULATION, MEDIATIZED POLITICS, POSTMODERN CULTURE

It is easy enough to argue that shifts in the economic and political spheres—toward more flexible relations of production and regime of accumulation, a primacy of sign values over exchange values, a mediatized politics—have conditioned a population to be receptive to new forms of cultural production. Such is certainly the argument of Lash and Urry (1987, especially pp. 287–288) and Harvey (1989), and it also runs through Soja (1989). But there is also an opposite argument, and from the same retrospecting era. Allan Megill's reading of Nietzsche, Heidegger, Foucault, and Derrida finds, not just the world-disclosing role of the work of art, but a *world-creating* role—"the world [as] a work of art that gives birth to itself" (Nietzsche)—bringing worlds into existence, "Towering up within itself, the work opens up a *world* and keeps it abidingly in force" (Heidegger) (see Megill, 1985, p. 3). Modernism's attempt to excavate to Nature, or History, or the Mode of Production, or some other great substratum underlying the ephemera of superficial experience is to be left behind: It is art (language, discourse, the text) that constitutes the billowing "reality" of human experience, and there is no substratum.[7] (No longer modern, but *postmodern*.)

But we have previously confronted this part of the argument, and Nietzsche and Heidegger are already familiar. Foucault is different, for he is also post-1968, straddling that great discontinuity of the Paris uprising and confronting the supreme disillusionment from watching one bourgeois regime seemingly follow another. After 1968, the attention and the voice begin to shift: With Foucault's *Surveiller et punir* (1975), the previous focus on social practices (the expressions of power–knowledge) is slipping; with his *Histoire de la sexualité, 1: La Volonté de savoir* (1976), the question of discourse becomes central, and through discourse all reality is artifactual. Foucault will assault us with Nietzsche's dictum that history must propagate "myths that will be useful in the present" (Megill, 1985, p. 235); such myths will be those that disorder order, demolish what is extant, turn the present into a past (all presents are derelict, all are to be overthrown). It is "an unending task": No motivating visions, for the new vision is merely the next order to be shattered by Foucault's disordering rhetoric ("art"). Not making worlds but shattering them; not bringing worlds into existence but out of it.

For Foucault, like Nietzsche, "the will to a system is a lack of integrity" (Nietzsche, 1968b, "Maxims and Arrows," no. 26). Megill's (1985) summary is that there is no natural order, but only "the certainty of successive regimes of power. Each of these regimes is made to be attacked, for each participates in the perpetual crisis of the present" (p. 254). A distorted, fragmented, postmodern (post-1968) world is to be utterly shattered to demolish the power-knowledge that is masked in the present *illusion* of disintegration and *disorder*. And any aesthetic recreation of the world is itself doomed to be destroyed. To overthrow every present moment is thus the emancipatory task—deconstructive, violent, explicitly against Heidegger's "letting beings be." For this is a new form of text (work of art): Foucault (1972) is building labyrinths—"No, no, I'm not where you are lying in wait for me, but over here, laughing at you" (p. 17).

We will see that architecture, that concretization of all experiential geographies, makes the labyrinth manifest (the new present moment!).

Jacques Derrida (b. 1930) is also post-1968, and the labyrinth is thematic. Derrida is not the artist but the antiartist; he will not by his art (text) make worlds but unmake them.[8] "Il n'y a pas de hors-texte"— there is nothing outside of the text. But the text for Derrida will not shatter *institutions* (in the manner of Foucault's discourse), but *the real*: That binary pair of art–reality, foundational to the philosophical enterprise of Kant, will be deposed. To be deposed also is the ternary dialectic central to Hegel; the three terms of *position*, *negation*, and *negation of the negation* (which becomes the new position) are to be joined by a fourth, the *preface*. The preface, for Derrida, is another text altogether, the "double" of the main text, preceding the opposition and destabilizing it. All of Derrida's books, observes Megill (1985), are as prefaces to another with which he refuses to engage—interminably evading "the maw of the dialectic" (pp. 272–273). We can turn to a different reading: Robert Bernasconi (1992) sees Derrida's project of a "critical reading" (of every text—and remember, there is nothing outside the text) as that of " 'producing' the relationship between what the writer commands and what he [*sic*] does not command of the patterns of language that he uses" (p. 139). "What Rousseau says" is set (in Derrida's *Of Grammatology*, 1976) against "what Rousseau wants to say." Against *every* text is to be set this "supplement"—the task of the preface. Bernasconi (1992) again: "In consequence the text [for Derrida] is to be defined as the history of its various readings" (p. 147).

In these leaps of Nietzsche, Heidegger, Foucault, Derrida, and, as we shall see, Walter Benjamin, the old certainties have fallen away. Derrida would even acclaim the end of the age of representation—of Heidegger's age of the world-as-picture and, therefore, of modernity.[9] How have such assertions of the aesthetic realm as constitutive of our experiential worlds ("determinative in the last instance") been paralleled in the purposive production of that realm itself—in art? Put otherwise, what is the new cultural production that would make new worlds in the present? It would seem to have three distinguishing characteristics. There is, first, a shift in *what* is represented: effectively, a new experience of space without differentiation, difference without hierarchy, and time without progress. (So representation persists, *contra* Derrida. It is just that the picture has disintegrated.) Second, there is a shift in *how* cultural production is represented: without the aura of uniqueness and originality, but multivoicedly, through collage of preexisting images and texts. And third, there is a shift in *to whom* the production is represented—with a purposive shading of the differentiations between previously autonomous fields and between high and low art. While something of these properties ran like threads through the long progress of modernist culture, there seems now, in the few decades since the 1960s, a coalescence. Because some understanding of these properties is essential to the further task of understanding the purposive production of space in the present age, we need to explore each in the sections following. Then, in Chapter 8, we turn expressly to that production.

POSTMODERN CULTURE, 1: SPACE, TIME, AND DIFFERENCE IN THE POSTMODERN EXPERIENCE

Ours is a brand-new world of allatonceness. "Time" has ceased, "space" has vanished. We now live in a global village . . . a simultaneous happening. We are back in acoustic space [acoustic space—acoustique paysagiste (Le Corbusier)]. We have begun again to structure the primordial feeling, the tribal emotions from which a few centuries of literacy divorced us.

—MARSHALL McLUHAN, *The Medium Is the Massage* (1967 p. 63)

The ephemeral and the volatile has been one part of the experience of modernity, to repeat from a previous chapter; the other part has been the search for "the eternal and the immutable." Many things came together in the 1950s and 1960s to tip the balance: the speeding up of the circulation time of capital with the shift to flexible accumulation; the concomitant "mobilization of fashion in mass (as opposed to elite) markets" (Harvey, 1989, p. 285), accelerating the pace of change not only in clothing and visual ornament but also in mass leisure and lifestyles, pop music, cinema; and most dramatically, the all-pervading impact of television—all events, all places reduced to images without context or content, ubiquitously and instantaneously projected, and received vicariously and for the most part without engagement. As "the transient, the fleeting, the contingent" invaded, "the eternal and the immutable" waned: Material progress was attained and sustained; but in precisely those societies where it seemed most sustained—North America, Western Europe, Britain, Australia, latterly Japan—it increasingly seemed a chimera. The sustaining myth of modernity— emancipation through material progress and liberal democracy—was suddenly lost where it had seemed most securely held.

Time without progress, space without content! As part of his project to "respatialize" social theory, Edward Soja has drawn attention to Foucault's attempt to understand the different experiences of space that have progressively unfolded through the history of modernity (Soja, 1989, pp. 16–18). The Middle Ages, argued Michel Foucault, were characterized by an hierarchic "ensemble of places"—the Heavenly Jerusalem, the Earthly counterpart, church, square, lane, house, and so forth. With Galileo (and even more with Descartes) there is the presentation of a new, enveloping "space of emplacement"—space better described by grid references than by hierarchies of places. With modernity, this opens to the endlessly unfolding "space of extension," of material progress and the appropriation of nature. The characteristic spaces of present experience, by contrast, are "heterotopias," the actually lived and socially created spaces of life at its most intense and "real," heterogeneous—the habitus of fragmentary possible worlds and social practices, the state "in which we live, which draws us out of ourselves, in which the erosion of our lives, our time and our history occurs" (Foucault, 1986, p. 23)—church, cemetery, theater, garden, museum, prison, brothel, and other spaces of experience at its most heightened. In their functioning, these heterotopias operate between two extremes: Either they create a space of illusion that effectively unmasks every "real" space ("all the sites inside of which human life is partitioned") as even more illusory and as inadequate against the vision thus conjured up, or they are indeed "real" and more perfect than those other real spaces of everyday life—heterotopias of "compensation" rather than "illusion" (Foucault, 1986, p. 25). Though they may be the spaces of human motivation, they are not utopias—they are real spaces of real life.

The insight here is that these successive experiences of space flow from the social production of meaning—signifieds—layered on to a preexisting world of physical spaces, sites, and the relations between them.[10] Any emancipatory project will in part need to unmask the heterotopias that ensnare us (the prison and asylum to create the illusion that the rest of space is rational, the museum to mask our alienation from aesthetic production); and in part it will need to create new spaces, heterotopias, which will expose the inadequacy of our lives and their spatial settings and propel us to something better—to make something of ourselves. The study of society and space, accordingly, in this Foucauldian conception, is *to deconstruct the social production of heterotopias*. In one sense, it is to lay bare the linkages between space, knowledge (and thus the obfuscations of language), and power and, thereby, to enable resistance on many fronts to the production and constitution of repressive knowledge at the specific sites of such production—the core of Foucault's life work. In a second sense, it is to understand such linkages and their creation so that our own visions can be drawn out, represented, and projected into the physical spaces about us, as new motivating visions of what life can be—heterotopias of resistance and remotivation (an issue for Chapter 12, to follow).

Foucault's argument needs to be taken further, however. Walter Benjamin's *Passagen-Werk* was to trace the social production of a "space of illusion" at the beginning of modernity. The levels of meaning at which it functioned (as a heterotopia?) could be progressively stripped away, and there would be some common sharing of those meanings, and their evolution traceable (Buck-Morss, 1989). A similar deconstructive project characterized Foucault's archaeology of the spatial masking of power in other typical spaces of early modernity—prison, asylum, other sites of incarceration and the "bounding of space and time." But the present, by contrast, is characterized by a social production of space where meanings are not shared (What are the heterotopias of suburbia, for they are certainly there? How do they vary for men and women?) and where the projection of multilayered, ambiguous meanings on to the actual physical spaces of the city ("spaces of dispersion") would seem both frenetic and unstable.

|DERRIDA AND DECONSTRUCTION

The high priest of philosophical deconstruction is Derrida, with whose work the focus shifts more from the experience of space and time (Benjamin, Foucault) to that of the self—of "Being." Because Derrida's ideas will thread through all the chapters that follow, it would be useful at this point to try to define deconstruction. Yet such an endeavor confronts Derrida's own stricture that, rather than being defined, deconstruction is to suspect the question (of definition) itself (Doel, 1992, p. 173). Further, "There is no single monologue possible in Deconstruction . . . there is no single author of any Deconstruction. It is always a multiplicity of voices, gestures. And you can take this as a rule: each time Deconstruction speaks through a single voice, it is *wrong* and not Deconstruction any more" (Derrida, 1989b, p. 75).

Indeed, it is this Bakhtinian multivoicedness that lies at the heart of the deconstructive concern. For Derrida, as for Heidegger before him, the task for philosophy is to express the experience of "Being as presence"—what it is like to be human. But in that task, as John Griffiths (1989) has summarized Derrida's earliest arguments,

> the history of philosophy is the history of philosophers fruitlessly trying to offer in writing (that is, in rational discourse) their experience of the presence of Being. But the wrong medium has been used for this essential task. Only the living, not the written, word can convey that presence. Rational discourse obfuscates the real presence of Being. The living indicates Being by showing the "difference" or distance between the "rational" self, or object, or meaning, and the "unthinkable" thought or self. (p. 94)

So Derrida sets out to deconstruct "mimesis"—the imitation or reproduction of the supposed words of an "other." More specifically, the target is what he labels "mimetologism," the capture of representation by the "logocentrism" of Western philosophy since Plato, whereby the referent is always prior to and privileged over the material sign. Philosophy is privileged over literature—over the text. Writing and all other symbolic systems are reduced to the status of a "vehicle." Thomas McCarthy (1990) observes of Derridean deconstruction that its iconoclasm is seen as "a commitment to bear witness to the other of Western rationalism: to what has been subordinated in hierarchical orderings, excluded in the drawing of boundaries, marginalized in identifying what is central, homogenized or colonized in the name of the universal" (p. 154). To redress this bias—deafness, as it were, to the signifier and the voice that carries it—is the focus of Derrida's *Of Grammatology* (1976): the counter-Enlightenment, in effect. Yet, warns Derrida (1976), the task is not one of *denying* reference: "It is not a question of 'rejecting' these notions. They are necessary and, at least at present, nothing is conceivable for us without them" (p. 14). Rather, the task is to approach reference in an entirely novel way—to interrupt, juxtapose, and superimpose the utterances, words and images of real experience so as to complicate "the boundary that ought to run between the text and what seems to lie beyond its fringes, what is classed as the *real*" (Derrida, 1981a, p. 42).

The method that Derrida would use for this deconstruction of mimesis is *montage*, and Gregory Ulmer's (1985) euphoric approval is worth quoting:

> Derrida is doing for this new mode of representation what Aristotle, in the *Poetics*, did for "mimetologism." In the same way that Aristotle provided at once a theory of tragedy (mimesis) and a method (formal analysis) for the study of all literary modes, Derrida in a text such as *Glas* (identified as the "exemplary" text of poststructuralism [where the "structuralist" link of signified and signifier is no longer privileged]) provides a "theory" of montage (grammatology) and a method (deconstruction) for working with any mode of writing whatsoever. Derrida is the "Aristotle" of montage. (p. 87)

Time will tell! Certainly both the theory and the method are to be found with Walter Benjamin, four decades earlier; and the triggering concern with the utterance and the distinctive voice of its transmission emerges with Mikhail Bakhtin even before that. Most specifically, Derrida's "montage" is the extension of Benjamin's representation by "dialectical images" rather than by dialectical argumentation. What is, however, distinctive in Derrida is the sort of picture of the human condition that unfolds with this deconstruction of mimesis. For beyond the functionalist sterility of our texts—writings, paintings, architecture, the city—there is that "unthinkable" thought or self, *différance* (the "difference that escapes language"), "otherness." This we sense through an "archi-écriture," or aboriginal writing that differs from our present writing (or painting, or representation of space) in that it is freed from the finite condition, from death:

> The pathos, the even tragic note, of Derridean philosophy comes in with its stress on that human finitude which inevitably deprives us of the full presence of Being. We sense full Being as somehow present to us . . . but as obscure, as neutral, as different from our own incomplete, condition-unto-death. We are condemned always to see through a glass darkly, enigmatically. (Griffiths, 1989, p. 94)

The human condition that Derrida finds is one of profound emptiness—the loss of meaning, of identity, of a sustaining myth; the presence of absence.

THE POSTMODERN EXPERIENCE
AND THE TASK OF REPRESENTATION

So how are we to understand this new experience of space, time, and the self (and, therefore, of the city)—what is to be made of it? Some clues emerge from Fredric Jameson's (1985) argument on the interrelated, contextual settings of signifiers in language; it is an argument that applies with equal force to the spatial forms of the environment:

> We don't translate the individual signifiers or words that make up a sentence back into their signifieds on a one-to-one basis. Rather we read the whole sentence, and it is from the interrelationship of its words or signifiers that a more global meaning—now called a "meaning-effect"—is derived. The signified—maybe even the illusion or the mirage of the signified and of meaning in general—is an effect produced by the interrelationship of material signifiers. (p. 119)

For at least one critic, Bakhtin is the originator of the idea that "the most important thing for making sense of meaning is not the sign, but the whole utterance into whose composition the sign enters" (Ivanov, 1974, p. 237).

With the coming of the allegedly new epoch (postindustrial society, postmodern culture, consumer capitalism, etc.), there is a shift in
the way in which meanings are grasped—in what Lash and Urry (1987,
p. 288) call "the semiotics of everyday life"—which is characterized by
a breakdown in the relationship between signifiers. Jameson (1985)
employs insights from Lacan's concept of schizophrenia as a language
disorder, to link this new way of seeing to the postmodern experience
of the end of history:

> The experience of temporality, human time, past, present, memory,
> the persistence of personal identity over months and years—this
> existential or experiential feeling of time itself—is also an effect of
> language. It is because language has a past and a future, because the
> sentence moves in time, that we can have what seems to us a
> concrete or lived experience of time. But since the schizophrenic
> does not know language articulation in that way, he or she does not
> have our experience of temporal continuity either, but is con-
> demned to live in a perpetual present with which the various
> moments of his or her past have little connection and for which
> there is no conceivable future on the horizon. (p. 119)

It is a perpetual present of vividly heightened intensity and sensory energy: To be underscored "is precisely the way in which the
signifier in isolation becomes ever more material—or, better still, *literal*—ever more material in sensory ways, whether the new experience
is attractive or terrifying" (Jameson, 1985, p. 120).

Certainly, this isolation of the signifier is not unique to the present
epoch: It is the nature of signification that signifieds and signifiers
continually break apart, reattaching in new combinations.[11] It is, however, a process that is especially significant to the production of urban
meaning in the present age—to the social production of heterotopias,
to continue the Foucauldian argument. For one thing, there is the
apparently *increasing frequency* of decoupling and recoupling of meanings that seems to come with the speeding up of technological change
and the proliferation of images consequent on new technologies of
communication. The "schizophrenic" loss of contextual interrelation-
ships between signifiers (Derrida's "absence," the loss of motivating
meaning) and the sensory intensification ("the city as spectacle") are
accordingly more likely.

Further, there would seem to be a proliferation of self-conscious,
purposive attempts at denying, or at least obfuscating, meaning. In
postmodernist art there is the turn to the dadaist methods of collage
and photomontage—"To write means to graft. It is the same word"

(Derrida, 1981a, p. 355). It is a turn of special significance to postmodernist architecture, as we shall see. More profoundly the shift is to be seen as an attempt to problematize the very activity of reference rather than to deny it (Ulmer, 1985, p. 95). And contrary to this "deconstruction" of reference, there is a proliferation of purposive attempts at assigning new meanings—new signifieds to signifiers—and at linking both the decoupling and the recoupling to enticements to consumption (part of Baudrillard's argument again).

In so far as the task of cultural production is to represent experience—to help us recognize ourselves and our real condition, as if for the first time—then, in the light of such an "experience of postmodernity," two chores would seem to loom. The first is to represent the tensions and paradoxes of the "end of history"—more specifically, the consequent vacuum of *socially motivating meaning*. Of some primacy among these tensions is the way in which the vacuum will be filled: discursively through self-determination or, as Habermas (1979a) warns, through new administrative processes of motivational control by dominative interests (p. 166). The extraordinary inability to come to grips with this expression of the present experience of time, progress, and history has also been commented on by Jameson, and again it is useful to turn to his arguments. In a discussion of contemporary cinema, Jameson (1985) he can observe the style of nostalgia films (*la mode rétro*) "invading and colonizing" even those films with a contemporary setting,

> as though, for some reason, we were unable today to focus our own present, as though we have become incapable of achieving aesthetic representations of our own current experience. But if that is so, then it is a terrible indictment of consumer capitalism itself—or at the very least, an alarming and pathological symptom of a society that has become incapable of dealing with time and history. (p. 117)

Second, it would seem necessary to represent the dialectical relationship between an increasingly homogeneous, undifferentiated space (everywhere invaded and commodified, everywhere equally accessible through the media image) and the increasing preoccupation with *place*, with *fragmentation* and *reestablished differentiation* (with locational advantage and space economy in investment, nationalism and localism in political life, identity and something akin to Foucault's heterotopias in the world of lived experience). It is the tension between Jameson's (1984) "postmodern hyperspace" and the search for the local, vicariously recalled.

| POSTMODERN CULTURE,
| 2: THE MODE OF REPRESENTATION

So how is this ambiguous and contradiction-ridden experience of the times to be represented so that, through recognition and understanding of it, we can seek emancipation and fulfillment?[12]

What especially distinguished the great age of high modernist representation was the Great Artist—idiosyncratic, exaggerated, producing masterpieces in a highly personal idiom, proclaiming individualism (emancipation through personal expression, as it were—no matter that the path of genius was not open to all!), so that no initiate in a field of high art could ever mistake that this is indeed a Picasso or a Matisse, or a composition by Stravinsky or Schönberg, part of a novel by Faulkiner, or a building by Le Corbusier, Wright, or Mies. Now part of the sport of that age consisted in parodying such *unique*, idiosyncratic, and eccentric styles, often reverentially, often scarcely consciously. The effect of parody is to cast ridicule on the private nature of these mannerisms and eccentricities "with respect to the way people normally speak or write." So, behind all parody is the idea that a linguistic norm persists, against which the style of the great modernist can be mocked. But what, asks Jameson, if one no longer believed in the existence of a "linguistic norm" (or architectural norm, or any other representational norm)?

> Perhaps the immense fragmentation and privatization of modern literature [painting, architecture, urban design?]—its explosion into a host of distinct private styles and mannerisms—foreshadows deeper and more general tendencies in social life as a whole. Supposing that modern art and modernism—far from being a kind of specialized aesthetic activity—actually anticipated social developments along these lines; supposing that in the decades since the emergence of the great modern styles society has itself begun to fragment in this way, each group coming to speak a curious private language of its own, each profession developing its private code or idiolect, and finally each individual coming to be a kind of linguistic island, separate from everyone else? (pp. 113–114)

(But perhaps they *always* spoke in private voices—modernism was nothing but the embracing of a myth!). So the very possibility of any linguistic norm vanishes, and with it, incidentally, the possibility of any Habermasian grounding of validity claims, a point to which we will return. At this moment the very possibility of parody ceases, and *pastiche* appears. This, Jameson argues, is the clearest distinguishing characteristic of postmodern expression.[13] Like parody, pastiche is the imitation of a unique style, the voice of others, but its mimicry is neutral, without parody's satiric purpose—it is "blank parody," the dance of the text.[14]

Jameson links this mimetic shift to the "death of the subject," the end of individualism as such. Now various critics put various constructions on this term. The more modest argument is that once—in the heyday of competitive capitalism, the nuclear family, and the emergence of the hegemony of the bourgeoisie—there *was* such a thing as individualism and the validity of individual expression. But it is no longer possible. So pastiche might indeed be nostalgic for the individualistic representations of another experience of space and time. A more radical argument adds that the bourgeois individual subject was not just a thing of the past but also a myth—it is ideological, to convince people that they had this power of the wilful, autonomous subject. It was Charles Taylor's (1985) "disengaged image of the self"—the flattering, inspiring, Enlightenment-engendered "notion of freedom as the ability to act on one's own, without outside interference or subordination to outside authority" (p. 5)—with the effect of masking from view "the way in which an individual is constituted by language and culture which can only be maintained and renewed in the communities he is part of" (p. 8). So pastiche has a far more serious purpose in this "poststructuralist" conception of the times: to destroy the myth of individual power, to put the cultural sphere back in its place, perhaps to reestablish the salience of class.

If pastiche is the outcome of representation, what are the *means* of its production? Gregory Ulmer's (1985) reading would suggest that there are four "factors" of such production. The first, *collage/montage*, is certainly not novel to postmodernist representation: We have seen its significance to that of high modernism—in Picasso, Braque, Walter Benjamin, the plays of Bertolt Brecht. Collage, argues Ulmer, is the "transfer of materials from one context to another"—quoting, appropriation of the ready-made, "speaking with the voice of others"; montage is the "'dissemination' of these borrowings through the new setting"—as in photomontage. Indeed, photomontage is characteristic of the *postmodernist* use of collage: Reproductive technologies are now so close to perfect that the distinction between original and copy ceases to exist. There are no originals, no copies—everything is a *simulacrum*.

The second is *graft/mime*. Ulmer quotes Derrida (1981b) at length, to the effect that "no element can function as a sign without referring to another element which itself is not simply present" (p. 26). So the interweaving of collage/montage results in each element "being constituted on the basis of the trace within it of the other elements of the chain or system" (Ulmer, 1985, p. 88). But there is always more than one such chain for any sign, and more than one level of meaning. So every sign, linguistic or visual, can be cited, "put between quotation marks," thereby to "break with every given context, engendering an infinity of new contexts in a manner which is absolutely illimitable" (Derrida, 1977, p. 185). The point of this is that collage/montage comprises a deconstruction and reconstruction of *meanings* that are more fundamental and less determinate than those apparently in-tended by a Picasso or a Braque.

Derrida accordingly refers to "grafting": (repeating) "To write means to graft. It's the same word." To graft changes the meanings of both the source and the montage: "Each grafted text continues to radiate back toward the site of its removal, transforming that too, as it affects the new territory" (Derrida, 1981a, p. 355). Cultural production thus needs to "endeavour to create an effect of *superimposing*, of super-imprinting one text on the other" (quoted in Ulmer, 1985, p. 91).[15] The effect is one of *layered signification*. Derrida also invokes the idea of "mime": Montage is to achieve a "new mimesis," in which the text mimes its object of study. Where the traces are in the form of simulacra, representation can also achieve reversible temporality, rather than the irreversible temporality of the sign (see Figures 7.1 and 7.2).

The third "means" of postmodern cultural production is *allegory*. Ulmer would distinguish the "narrative allegory" of postmodernism (favoring "the material of the signifiers over the meanings of the signifieds") from more traditional allegory, preoccupied rather simply and directly with meaning, albeit meaning under the guise of other meanings. So despite the recognition of the indeterminacy and layer-ing of meanings in the material grafted in collage/montage—or, per-haps, because of it—the concern is rather with the material itself. Of course, the material has meanings; but, argues Ulmer, the postmod-ernist artist/critic addresses literal meanings of the material, which are to be reassembled in montage to emphasize *difference* and to create *interruption*.[16] This is close to Schönberg's (high modernist) view of cultural production as a search for knowledge that lies outside the artist, as potential in the material itself. Design as the production of knowledge!

Equivocalness is the fourth means. Postmodernist design and so-called poststructuralist criticism are frequently accused of parasitism—living off a source text as a parasite off a host. More specifically, the accusation is that the "deconstructionist reading of a given work is plainly and simply parasitical on the obvious or univocal reading" (Miller, 1977, p. 439). Ulmer turns the charge: A parasite takes and weakens but it is also a guest, exchanging flattery and praise for food; and it is an interrupter, "noise" in the system, and both part of a

FIGURES 7.1 and 7.2. Modern/postmodern. Architecture as representation of progress, universalism: Le Corbusier, villa at Garches, 1927. Architecture of interrupted time and deconstructed space, a baroque stair in industrial steel, both classicist and cubist composition, the local and the vernacular, discontinuity: Charles Jencks and Terry Farrell, Thematic House, London, 1978–1982. Author's drawings, based on Jencks (1985, 1987).

relation and agent for change in that relation. So postmodernist design and poststructuralist criticism are indeed parasitical, but thereby undermining the possibility of any "univocal reading" by stressing the paradoxical, the equivocal in representation.[17] This is Derrida's double reading (a theme for Chapter 9)—"what Rousseau says" set against "what Rousseau wants to say," with the task of the deconstructive reading being to "produce" the distance between the two (though it is always already there, in the text). It is the role of the preface (that destabilizing fourth term with which Derrida would endlessly interrupt and postpone the dialectic) or the "supplement" (Rousseau's term): "The concept of the supplement . . . should allow us to say the contrary at the same time without contradiction" (Derrida, 1976, p. 179; and see Bernasconi, 1992, p. 144). And the purpose of this parasitism? Play, Nietzsche's cosmic dance transposed to the text. But it is also political: "Derrida's enterprise is perhaps best seen as a clearing-out operation, intended to free a space for the active power of creation in a world that in an illusory way has grown old" (Megill, 1985, p. 313). It is Heidegger's clearing, also transposed.

There is another view on this turn to equivocalness that emerges in the arguments of Soviet psychologist Yuri Lotman (and again drawing on Wertsch's analysis [1991, pp. 73–76]). Texts, claims Lotman, can function in more than one way: to convey meanings adequately and to generate new meanings. The first corresponds to a "transmission model" of communication and is best achieved where the codes of speaker and listener most nearly coincide—for example, where there is an artificial language (chemical equations, mathematical symbols, etc.). The second, "dialogic" function arises in the multivoicedness that preoccupied Bakhtin: There is a difference between the message of the speaker and that received by the listener. Instead of working as a mere passive link, the text becomes a "thinking device," triggering ambiguity, equivocalness, and the evocation of new meaning. The main characteristic of a text in this second function is an *internal heterogeneity of social languages* (again in Bakhtin's sense), and the generation of meaning arises from an interaction between structures. "Their interaction in the closed world of a text becomes an active cultural factor as a working semiotic system. A text of this type is always richer than any particular language and cannot be put together automatically from it. A text is a semiotic space in which languages interact, interfere, and organize themselves hierarchically" (Lotman, 1988, p. 37). But not *always* "hierarchically."

The most useful insight here comes with Lotman's view that both functions occur in any social setting but that one or the other dominates for certain activities and at certain times: The first, univocal function would seem especially important in "providing a common memory for the group, of transforming it from an unstructured crowd into 'une personne morale,' to use Rousseau's expression" (the French Revolution? the Russian Revolution?); it also seems important in non-literate cultures and those with "a dominant mythological conscious-ness" (p. 35). But it would seem that in postmodernist representation there is a purposive suppression of that first function and a shift to the second. And one reading of Derrida's analyses, and certainly of his own "texts," is that, within the context of that second, multivocal function, there is also a shift to suppress Lotman's "hierarchy": The social lan-guages indeed "interact, interfere, and organize themselves," but with-out hierarchy.

It is in this distinction between a univocal function of the text oriented to a shared experience and a multivocal (and equivocal) function characterized by ambivalence and heterogeneity, and in the shift from one to the other, that we find the key to Foucault's observa-tion of a shift in the experience of space from the unambiguous to the heterotopia. The social languages, thereby signifieds, break apart and multiply.

POSTMODERN CULTURE, 3: THE AUDIENCE OF REPRESENTATION

The jargon in the various arguments is appalling, and much of the confusion borders on the self-glorying obscurantism of "experts" trying to score off other "experts." Yet the problem is also in the culture itself: Modernism has not been very good at talking about representation. Something does, however, emerge from these vague assertions, which can be summarized as a series of oppositions (in Table 7.1—note, though, that Derrida would put all oppositions into question). To those associated with the "mode" of representation (aura and personal style in modernism vis-à-vis pastiche in postmodernism) and the "means" of representation, I have added oppositions apparent in the "relations" of representation. Something needs to be said about these relations.

The claim is frequently made that, in the present age, high and popular culture increasingly shade into each other. Certainly the char-acteristics in the right-hand column of Table 7.1 could be recognized in the ubiquitous pop music video clip, just as readily as in a Robert Rauschenberg "painting" (a transformed picture surface able to receive "a vast and heterogeneous array of cultural images and artifacts") (Crimp, 1985, p. 44). Yet no one could pretend that the audiences of these are the same. There seem to be two factors that militate against a

TABLE 7.1. Oppositions: Characteristics of the Modes of Representation in Modernism and Postmodernism

	Modernism	Postmodernism
The mode of representation	Auratic (the aura of the "great artist")	Antiauratic
	Personal, idiosyncratic style	Pastiche
The means of representation	Direct signification (of progress, new technology, the universal)	Collage/montage (of ready-made representations: of nostalgia, vernacular technologies, the local)
	Emphasis on originality	Simulacra, technological reproduction
	Direct, single meanings	Acceptance of indeterminate meanings, ambiguity; superimposition; double coding
	Favoring the meaning of the signified	Favoring the material of the signifier; transformation of reality into images
	Continuity	Difference, interruption, fragmentation of time into a series of perpetual presents
	Claiming a univocal interpretation	Emphasizing paradoxical and equivocal interpretations
The relations of representation	Production controlled by relatively autonomous "great artists"	Production controlled by media capital
	Eschewing commodity status	Celebrating commodity status
	Elitist in the images mobilized	Democratic in the images mobilized

democratized, or participatory, "cultural life" in this age. First, the relations of production are especially exploitative, though in a somewhat peculiar way. There is what Harvey (1989) refers to as the effect of "sheer money power as a means of domination rather than direct control over the means of production and wage labour in the classic sense" (p. 347). These "asymmetrical money relations" are essential to enable creativity and ingenuity to be quickly and flexibly mobilized to devise and market new products and services and, increasingly, to ensure their transformation into spectacle. But, as Harvey goes on to observe, "asymmetrical money power does not necessarily promote class consciousness"; rather, these conditions "shape attitudes different from those that arise out of the conditions of wage labour" (p. 347).

Second, there is a "cultural class" constituting a market for "high art," in postmodernity as in modernity. The identity of the social strata comprising this clientele has varied over the decades. Today, argues Pierre Bourdieu (1984), it is dominated by the "new bourgeoisie," typically private-sector executives and professionals, especially in the expanding services sectors (finance, design, etc.), mobilizing cultural capital in the "classificatory struggle" to establish social space and distinction—"habitus" is Bourdieu's word—vis-à-vis the dominant class, on the one hand (the bourgeoisie and the intellectual gurus), and the working-class fractions, on the other. And to perform its classificatory function, that cultural capital must itself be "distinguished"—in the form of "high art" postmodern film, music, writing and criticism, graphic design, architecture, and the urban design of the residential milieus, shopping precincts, holiday resorts, and the like that the new class would occupy. Different spaces classify differently.

There is, however, an important sense in which the often avowed intention of a democratization of cultural life is indeed pursued: The images stored on film, videotape, or whatever, for instantaneous retrieval and use—whether in nightly television news, video clip, art cinema, advertising, or political propaganda—are increasingly torn ("grafted," in Derrida's parlance) from *the context of everyday life and experience, including the everyday life and experience of "others."* So too, we will see, with the design of city and countryside.

CHAPTER 8 | # "Postmodern"

> Architectural and philosophical concepts do not
> disappear overnight. The once-fashionable
> "epistemological break" notwithstanding, ruptures
> always occur within an old fabric which is
> constantly dismantled and dislocated in such a way
> that its ruptures lead to new concepts or structures.
> In architecture such disjunction implies that at no
> moment can any part become a synthesis or
> self-sufficient totality; each part leads to another,
> and every construction is off-balance, constituted
> by the traces of another construction.
>
> —BERNARD TSCHUMI, "Parc de la Villette,
> Paris" (1988, p. 35)

The mounting skepticism/cynicism that emerged in the 1960s toward the idea of human fulfillment through capitalist progress,
liberal democracy, and the American way, inevitably extended to
its "official style" and material signification in the International Style
and its totalizing, universalizing program. The reaction from critics,
and increasingly from the designers themselves, was to reject that
program (its promise had not been redeemed) and variously to grab at
often-old ideals submerged in the wonderful, confident flood of high
modernism ("learning as suppression"). There are four specific and
interrelated forms of this reaction that especially wove through the
discourses of the decades that followed.

137

REACTIONS, 1:
THE ENVIRONMENTAL MOVEMENT,
AND THE WORLD AS IT MIGHT BE

In part, the environmental movement that seemed so strident in the developed economies in the 1960s was an effect of a new experience of affluence: If things were getting better all the time, why did local spaces manifestly deteriorate (the street, the nearby stream, the beach, etc.)? It was easy to mobilize the affluent, with spare income and spare time, to fight for what Castells has called goods of collective consumption— collectively consumed, that is, by the affluent! There was also, however, a set of concerns over wider issues of the perceived consequences of modernity. Rachel Carson's *Silent Spring* (1962) stands as something of a marker; Ian McHarg's *Design with Nature* (1969) links both levels of concern; there were also issues of nuclear fallout, whales and other endangered species, conservation of rain forests and coastlines, river pollution and the degradation of the North American Great Lakes; the list could go on.

The various concerns arising at these two levels—the local and the global—tended to coalesce in a third, to do with planetary sustainability. This was not just a question of outputs (How long before we poison ourselves?), but also of resource use, especially triggered by the oil crises of the 1970s. And for many it became a question of equity and, hence, of moral–practical judgment more than theoretic–cognitive (or scientific).[1] It was the question of fair shares of resources across society (the problem of space) and across generations (the problem of time).

Finally, there was the (fourth) level of *affective* concern—something of a fight-back of the "participating consciousness" of nature introduced in Chapter 2. Berman's work addresses this redefinition of human experience and the human condition (1984, 1989), though earlier sign-posts are Paul Shepard's (1967, 1973). While all four levels of environmental discourse are significant to the experience of postmodernity, it is the third and the fourth that hold some clue to a resolution to the dilemmas of the times.

REACTIONS, 2:
JANE JACOBS AND THE CITY AS IT IS

Jane Jacobs's *The Death and Life of Great American Cities* (1961/1964) was subtitled "The Failure of Town Planning," and its purpose was to excoriate the planners of modernism from Burnham and Howard to Le

Corbusier and the dream of modernist order: "There is a quality even meaner than outright ugliness or disorder, and this meaner quality is the dishonest mask of pretended order, achieved by ignoring or suppressing the real order that is struggling to exist and to be served" (p. 25).

We had mistaken "organized complexity" for chaos: Planning theory was missing the point, and city planners revealed the extraordinary paradox of an active hatred for cities. Complex neighborhoods, visually and socially cacophonous, worked better than any planned by the planners. So Jacobs advised an urban practice that respected existing neighborhoods and built on their lessons for new ones: Districts, and even their constituent parts, must serve more than one primary function, and preferably more than two; most blocks must be short (plenty of streets and corners); buildings must be of varying ages and conditions; there must be a "sufficiently" dense concentration of people.

Jacobs's appeal was passionate, articulate, and influential, though certainly not isolated. It had two effects. The first was the useful one of knocking the planners' confidence in the stock solutions of land-use planning, zoning, and denial of diversity—the modernist means of resolving the dilemmas of contradictory landscapes of the capitalist city—though it is likely that the gentrification of the inner cities, beginning in the 1960s, was more significant to this shift. The second effect, more fundamental, was to contribute to a change in the way we perceived cities and urban space: Not only was diversity praised, but also forms of visual complexity and "layered signification" (new activities layered on the reminders of old ones), the antithesis of the modernist dream.

It is noteworthy that a decade later this pro-urban (and antiplanning) form of journalism persisted, but its focus had shifted. In a remarkable set of essays that he published in 1974 as *Soft City*, Jonathan Raban saw the vitality of the city less as the expression of *activities*, as insisted upon by Jacobs, than as *expression itself*—as images and signs for a society of individuals, increasingly isolated, and defining themselves through precisely such images and signs (Foucauldian heterotopias?). The city is the "emporium of styles," from which the individual may choose, discard, then choose again, all the time apparently defying simple classification by class position in a mode of production:

> It is an unfortunate assumption that whenever the city evades the rhetoric of class-analysis, then it must be the details, not the nature, of the rhetoric which is at fault. For class-determinism simply does not help us very much when we confront the random

and wilful patterns of personal style and behaviour in the city.
(Raban, 1974, p. 62)[2]

The cacophony, the emporium, also defines us in another, far more
significant way, Raban seems to suggest (p. 14). For it is against the real
city that we shape our dreams of the ideal city and therein find our
motivating meaning of (urban) life. We define ourselves, thereby,
dialectically. It is Augustine's twin cities of God and Man, "wonderfully
and delicately balanced," or, as Buck-Morss (1989) paraphrases Benjamin: "It is the unfulfilled potential for happiness of our own recol-
lected past [the shambles that surround us] that gives us insight into the
Messianic drama of the cosmos" (p. 243). It is also two sides of Lenin's
tripartite contradiction underlying "all" great revolutions. And it is
this that the planners, would-be eradictors of cacophony, fail to understand.

REACTIONS, 3:
ROBERT VENTURI AND AMERICA AS IT IS

Far more radical onslaughts on modernist sensibility were to come. In
Complexity and Contradiction in Architecture (1966), Robert Venturi
argued that architects respect the honky-tonk "landscape of consumption" described in Chapter 6, rather than shun it or wish it away. "The
main justification for honky-tonk elements in architectural order is
their very existence. They are what we have" (Venturi, 1966, p. 48). So
Venturi was led to question whether the banality of Main Street was
not "almost all right" (p. 102). He went further than this tolerance of
the honky-tonk however, to its absolute extolling, in *Learning from Las
Vegas*, which he published in 1972 with Denise Scott-Brown and Steve
Izenour. The context became the exemplar—the evolutionary the
revolutionary. In the earlier book (Venturi, 1966), "our new architecture" was to be characterized by "the multifunctioning building" (the
futurist projects of Sant' Elia are cited), the "double-functioning element" (where there is "nonexact, ambiguous correspondence between
form and function, and form and structure") (p. 40), and "both-and"
signification (the varying levels of meaning that have their source in
contradiction, their basis in hierarchy, and breed ambiguity and tension) (p. 31).

The insistence on double meanings anticipates Charles Jencks's
1977 identification of double coding in postmodernist architecture, but
also Ulmer's "collage/montage" and "equivocalness"; it is roughly coincident with the earliest publications of Derrida.[3] In the later book

(Venturi, 1972), the sources of the elements and one level of their meanings are made far more uncompromisingly explicit: the world so clearly liked by Americans—Main Street, the suburb, Disneyland, and, quintessentially, Las Vegas. But there is here a quite serious, though dangerous, objective. Venturi et al. acknowledge the gross domination, manipulation, and violence of casinos, mafia, and most else about Las Vegas, and likewise acknowledge the role of the images of Las Vegas in masking that violence but, simultaneously, representing it. If, however, this landscape becomes a model for the concealment of the brutality of our environment—the new exemplar—then new signification may indeed force us to confront the outlandish contradiction between violence in domination and fun in signification. Something of this is suggested in the earlier book (Venturi, 1966): An architecture with varying levels of meaning "will be difficult to 'read,' but abstruse architecture is valid when it reflects the complexities and contradictions of content and meaning. Simultaneous perception of a multiplicity of levels involves struggles and hesitations for the observer and makes his perception more vivid" (p. 31).

There is, however, a more depressing possibility. The glorification of violence may merely deaden the sensibilities—the ultimate aestheticization of the sphere of morality.

REACTIONS, 4:
CHRISTOPHER ALEXANDER
AND NOSTALGIA FOR THE PREMODERN

Yet a further response to the alleged totalizing excesses of the International Style was to reassert an altogether earlier vernacular—not the city as it is, whether the layered activities and representations of New York or the kitsch of Las Vegas or suburbia, but the city as it was. Its strongest expression was in the work of Christopher Alexander: In *A Pattern Language* (1977) and *The Timeless Way of Building* (1979), Alexander presented a romantic–utopian vision of a world where ordinary people could take command of the production of their environment. In the past, there was a "pattern language" existing in a culture; the environment was produced according to it, and everybody recognized it. So the pathologies of the present city are to be attributed to a breakdown of the pattern language; and the only path away from present dilemmas is for a community to sit down and find again these patterns for producing and using the built environment. Once again, the parallels are with Derrida (language's "double origin" in melody and image, though this time it is the "originary language" of spatial

meaning that is sought), but also with Heidegger ("authentic origins"—"Man, become essential!"), and ultimately with Nietzsche. The
argument was restated, simplified somewhat, and more explicit links
were drawn to urban design, in A New Theory of Urban Design (Alexander, 1987).

Alexander's vision is ultimately to be rejected as Romantic, prein-
dustrial and, indeed, premodern, imagining that *relations of production*
can be turned back regardless of the technological development of
forces of production. Yet it does focus on those components of the
high-modernist architectural debate—vernacular culture and popular
empowerment—lost in the instrumentalizing onslaught of the International Style. His search for meanings—signifieds to be projected onto
spatial signifiers—locked as they are in some scarcely recognized cultural memory, moreover, confronts Wittgenstein's (1972) warning that
"what confuses us is the uniform appearance of words" (p. 6e). Finally,
a program for a grassroots practice, somewhat akin to Habermas's
communicative action, would seem compellingly attractive to reestablish some tension between presently submerged local-to-global rules
(in the sense implied in Durkheim's "organic" social solidarity) and the
totalizing global-to-local generative rules and practices of late-modern-
ist spatial production (akin to "mechanical" solidarity)—perhaps as a
"training ground" for a more broadly encompassing program of communicative action.[4]

DIFFERENT REPRESENTATIONS

None of these responses to the new skepticism—neither environmental earnestness (Rachel Carson, Ian McHarg), nor pro-city and
antiplanning crusades (Jane Jacobs, Jonathan Raban), nor the extolling of kitsch (Venturi and colleagues), nor the nostalgic search for
value and meaning (Alexander)—succeeded in addressing the central
question of how this shifting experience of space, time, nature, and the
self was to be represented in the production of space. This search for
right representation of the sort of world in which these seemingly new
times might be lived can be traced through those heterogeneous stories
of postmodern movement architecture and urban design begun in
Chapter 6: Their continuation is the present chore.

Two stories, in particular, help us to see the place of many more.
The first is the "ironic shift" in late-modern movement design, espe-
cially emerging in the domestic architecture of a small group of North
Americans, most notably Richard Meier, Michael Graves, and Peter
Eisenman in the late 1960s. In a 1971 critique of Meier's Smith House,

Peter Papademetriou (1971) attacked Meier's debasement of a revolutionary image to a popular one:[5] "Through a softening of the revolutionary overtones of its sources (Le Corbusier, the Heroic Period), it must appear inevitably as another form of packaging . . . The dialectical tensions of Le Corbusier are gone, and the International Style stands before us finally to be recognised as a *décor de la vie*" (p. 24). But the point is missed, countered Peter Eisenman (1971), for "it is precisely because the Smith House is not avant-garde that it is accessible to popular taste . . . In the end, what [Papademetriou] may be objecting to, is that while he aspires to a populism, the Smith House aspires to high art and in the process it may also eventually become popular" (p. 524). The task of architecture, to Eisenman, was to have high art permeate down to transform popular culture—forget the broader, 1920s goals of a transformation of the relations of power inevitably represented in architectural and urban space and imagery. Eisenman (b. 1932) was himself designing private houses in a vein similar to the parodying abstractions of Meier and Graves—for example, his Falk House (House II) at Hardwick, Vermont (1969–1970). With his House III at Lakeville, Connecticut (1971), there is, however, a clear shift: The modernist tendency to abstraction is extended, as Eiseman attempts to create a purely autonomous architecture where form and "meaning" come only from the rules of its own generation (see Figure 8.1). He takes two grids at 45° to each other and within that framework lets spaces and structural elements compose, come apart, and recompose again: The outcome abounds in Corbusian and other 1920s references, but for the observer to work out what is going on, it is necessary to compare the experienced building with the series of diagrams that explain the generation of its highly complex, abstracted geometry. Any understanding is dependent on reading one text onto another; each, as it were, *deconstructs* the meanings locked in the other.

Whereas this first (incomplete) story concerned an acceptance of modernism and the modern movement but an attempt to move beyond them, the second is of a direct rejection of the modern. It returns us to the case of Robert Venturi, who as early as 1959 was incorporating elements of American suburban kitsch into ironic, ambiguity-laden designs, in some anticipation of his 1966 publication of *Complexity and Contradiction* (where, moreover, they were generally reported). His 1960 North Penn Visiting Nurses Association building is arguably the first self-consciously anti-modern movement building: walls at strange angles to acknowledge the exigencies of street and context rather than the functionalist logic of its internal spaces, decorative mouldings to exaggerate windows and a functionless arch to distort the scale of the entrance but also to parody the sorts of geometrics being explored by Louis Kahn, Venturi's colleague at the University of Pennsylvania—"mannerist" in its purposive awkwardness and haphazardly historicist *and suburban* in its references. In subsequent designs, other coding from other American vernaculars, including Las Vegas, were grafted in.

Underlying these various endeavors was the argument that the architecture of modernity is *not* unitary and that the everyday experience of space is similarly heterogeneous. Venturi's concern is accordingly with "other" representations and "taste-cultures"—with "otherness," that is, relative to the high art of the modern movement and its self-preoccupied practitioners. Kitsch elements in unaccustomed settings are to jolt the senses, thereby to compel reflection on what those elements mean to us. (A modernist reading! Alternatively, it is "the play of the text in the world," and the language is floating free—Der-

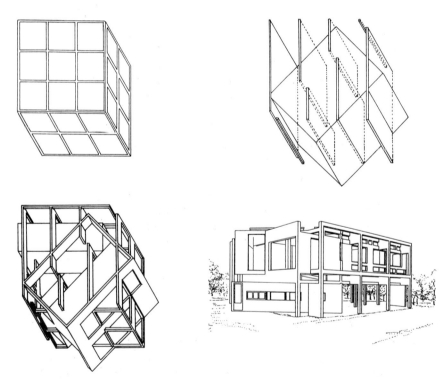

FIGURE 8.1. Peter Eisenman: House III, 1971. Steps 3, 5 and 10 in its generation as text and as built. Drawing by Clare King, based on Jencks (1987) and *Peter Eisenman House of Cards* (1987).

rida.) If those meanings and the values attached to them can be discursively grounded and reflected upon (to continue the modernist reading), then the signifiers are no longer mindless, no longer kitsch. They are effectively deschlocked, even in everyday life, and recognized as symbols—of home, of mindless consumption, of the gender-based divisions of labor and relations of power. The strength of these things is to communicate at a mass level, unlike high art; the present failure is that the meanings are not critically received. To trigger that critical reception seems to be Venturi's still self-consciously modernist project.[6]

Much of North American architectural production in the 1970s can be read as these two stories (and different voices) continuing to unfold, interweaving and, increasingly, interanimating.[7] The first, the forcing of a dead-end modern movement to a new level of abstraction (Meier, Graves, Eisenman), was drawn in the post-1972 houses of Eisenman to the point where the generative rules of modernism "float free" from any utopian or revolutionary agenda and the signifiers are freed from any signifieds outside the now abstracted rules. And the second, the rejection of elitist high art in favor of lifting the everyday world and its signs to the level of self-conscious, critical reflection (Venturi and followers), was pulled toward an eclecticism to provide communicable references to local culture, but *without* critical intent (Moore, Stern, the later Graves). Both attempted a depoliticization of space—one by abstracting representation away from real life, the other by broadening representation to all social languages and genres but wishing away the power relations typically masked by them.

|POSTMODERN ARCHITECTURE

In 1977, Graves designed the Plocek House at Warren, New Jersey; it was built in 1979–1982 (see Figure 8.2). Like the Schulman House of a year earlier, its references are complex and scarcely explicit (they might be to Frank Lloyd Wright, the American Romanesque of nineteenth-century architect H. H. Richardson, small-town beaux arts, Ledoux's giantism of the high Enlightenment, 1930s homely . . . who knows!). It introduces a new element—a giant, functionless arch, albeit with its keystone missing but still implied; and it brings in a new theme—a play with inconsistent senses of scale (helped by the implied arch). These and a few similarly complex, multireferenced buildings from about that time mark something of a maturing of endeavors to find a postmodern movement form of architectural representation (see Figure 8.3); and 1977 also marks the publication of the first edition of Charles Jencks's

FIGURE 8.2. Michael Graves: Plocek House, Warren, New Jersey, 1977.
Displaced columns, missing keystone, and spatial layering. Author's drawing,
based on Wheeler et al. (1983).

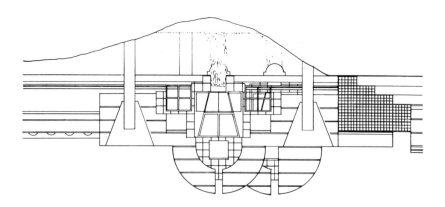

FIGURE 8.3. Michael Graves: Fargo–Moorhead Cultural Centre Bridge,
1977. The clearest references are to Ledoux. Author's drawing, based on
Wheeler et al. (1983).

The Language of Post-Modern Architecture and the conferring of a name on it all.

The vast order (arches, columns) and the concomitant play with scales, generally missing from the modern movement, offered the clue to the next round of stylistic transformations of the city fabric and its significations. In a new cycle of uneven investment and disinvestment after the accumulated crises of 1973–1974, a new "style" was needed (new age, new submarkets!), and the hour of the postmodernist architects had come. Philip Johnson and John Burgee's AT&T Building in New York, of 1978–1983, is the significant exemplar (Johnson had previously teamed with Mies to design the Seagram Building and Plaza of 1958, one of the ultimate icons of the modern movement); it is historicist but oblique in its coding, and ultimately has the monolithic unity of an art deco tombstone. A different variant is found in Helmut Jahn's 1982 project for the Bank of the South West Tower in Houston: no oblique, subtle references here, but a Scheerbartian tower of glass and flashing lights, a crystalline *Stadtkröne*, and a homage to the expressionist, art deco, New York skyscrapers of the 1930s. Laden also with allusions to the past, non-avant-garde styles and icons of the North American city was Michael Graves's 1980–1982 Public Services Building in Portland Oregon. The references are close to those of his Plocek House—the arch of those beaux arts city monuments when the North America city was in its first great, confident boom; municipal kitsch similarly monumentalized; and the soft, warm colors of home. Of interest also is Graves's 1982–1986 Humana Corporation Medical Headquarters in Louisville, even more abstracted in its coding, but "mediating," in both its references and its play with massing and scales, between modernist and nineteenth-century neighbors and reemphasizing the street as "public realm" (see Figure 8.4).

There is a small number of buildings by Graves from circa 1980 that are indeed important. For with their giant orders and ambiguous play with scales (ex-Louis Kahn, -Jefferson, but also -American beaux arts), functionless arches (again Kahn and beaux arts, also Richardsonian Romanesque), missing elements and distorted uses (Venturi, but also the nostalgia for ruins), art deco lattices and high-modernist grids, machine age detailing and precision, the effect is a new and distinctive voice, in a new social language (to revive the Bakhtinian analogy), albeit ventriloquating through a seemingly limitless regression of previous voices from an undifferentiable past—as memory is always in one sense layered and undifferentiable.[8]

Charles Jencks refers to a "New Representational," or "Communicational," mode of architectural and urban design since 1980. The label is clearly intended to embrace these languages (among others) and points to the use of ornament and, more generally, pattern making to represent preexisting architecture of value (*sign* value!) to specific *local* constituencies. The architecture and urban design that Jencks more broadly labels postmodern is characterized by an *immediate communicability* that is supposed to be secured in three main ways, which it is useful to review here. The first is respect for context—for the preexisting world of values and memories: "The failure of modern architecture and planning, very briefly, was its lack of understanding the urban context, its overemphasis on objects rather than the tissue between

FIGURE 8.4. Michael Graves: Humana Corporation Medical Headquarters, Louisville, 1982–1986. Reestablishing the street (compare with Mies and Johnson's Seagram Plaza), mediating between otherwise incompatible neighbors. Author's drawing, based on Jencks (1987).

them, design from the inside-out rather than the exterior space to the inside" (Jencks, 1987b, p. 110).

The second is the active grafting of "traces" of past patterns and uses: The tissue may be gone, but *something* must be left to trigger memory—a remnant element, a street pattern, a bomb crater! The analogy with Derrida's program "of superimposing, of superimprinting one text on the other," is obvious. Third, there is *new* design with the same intent: to take elements that are either simulacra with the past or oblique, even distorted grafts or quotations, and to incorporate these (through *montage*) into new settings and contexts. It is these that we find threading through the designs of Venturi, Moore, Stern, Graves and their myriad colleagues and followers. (Ignore, for now, the problem of *content*. The account here is of the *forms* or *languages* of representation; the question of what is represented is more problematic.)

This grafting, quoting, and montage is to be done with purposive discontinuities—*difference* and *interruption* in the sense of Benjamin and Ulmer. In explicit agreement with Louis Kahn, Oswald Mathias Ungers, and Vincent Scully—postmodernist fathers all—Jencks (1987b) cites Hadrian's Villa (A.D. 118–134) as *the* exemplar: "For some it is the richness of overlapping spatial focii [*sic*] which is the lesson of the villa, for others the eclecticism of sources (Egypt and Greece), the palimpsest of meaning or the mannerism of sharp juxtaposition" (p. 111). He quotes Colin Rowe's comment from *Collage City*:

> For if Versailles may be a sketch for total design in a context of total politics, the Villa Adriana attempts to dissimulate all reference to any single controlling idea. . . . Hadrian, who proposes the reverse of any "totality," seems only to need accumulation of the most various fragments. . . . The Villa Adriana is a miniature Rome. It plausibly reproduces all the collisions of set pieces and all the random empirical happenings which the city so lavishly exhibited. . . . It is better to think of an aggregation of small, and even contradictory set pieces (almost like the products of different regimes) than to entertain fantasies about total and "faultless" solutions which the conditions of politics can only abort. (Rowe and Koetter, 1978)[9]

Herein lies one of the great dilemmas of postmodern architecture. For the designers and polemicists alike decry the absence of a communicative intent in modern movement architecture (mistakenly, even ludicrously—as if "technology," "efficiency," "material progress," and the universalizing project of modernity were not being implied); instead, they have generally claimed to have restored the communicative function to architecture, by actively grafting codes with immediate meanings to ordinary people (again, as if "technology" or "progress" did not have such immediacy!). In fact, the achievement of the postmodern architects has been not so much to reestablish as to shift the focus of codes and meanings: from the universal to the local and from some idea of progress and faith in the new to antecedents and to memories— traces—of the past and of broader culture. The dilemma, however, is in the mode of representation of the local and the past—not by revival or reproduction, but ironically, with detachment from context and, in the postmodernist manner described earlier, with discontinuity, interruption, difference, "eclecticism of sources," and "sharp juxtaposition." So oblique, ironic, and detached is the reference, however, that communication can be eschewed and obscurantism can result. The mode of representation, for the most part, contradicts the communicative intent.[10]

Not for one moment could one claim that *modernist* modes of representation retain validity in the present age of new "forces of communication"; nor can one deny that this dismembered, decontextualized representation can trigger the sorts of profoundly troubling memories of past experiences and actions that can, in turn, compel a questioning of *present* actions and practices—emancipation from present ideological structures and worldviews. Rather, the dilemma is in the random, haphazard nature of postmodernist representation and signification. Like most other aspects of the communicative overload of the age, it ends up being communication for communication's sake. More specifically, the allusions to the past end up being eclectic and historicist rather than critically historical (indeed, the "end of history"!).

NEORATIONALISM, LA TENDENZA, THE THIRD TYPOLOGY

This account of postmodern movement representations of the space of "the postmodern condition" (Lyotard) has to now been restricted to North American events and arguments. To turn to the European is to add to the story a further layer that is distinctive in its characteristics despite the inevitable intersections.

A sensitivity to local context and the play with historical allusions had never really been absent from the Italian modern movement. When Carlo Aymonino built his housing project in the Gallaratese quarter of Milan between 1967 and 1973, the greater part of it was vast in scale, overarticulated, even expressionist, and aggressively confrontationist to any context or historical reference (unless it be Sant'Elia's futurism). Inserted into it, however, was a block by Aldo Rossi—a minimalist, stripped, classical abstraction, expressing no function; a Boulléean play with geometric forms and their shadows; and the exact antithesis to Aymonino's crest-of-the-wave modernism.[11]

Aldo Rossi published *L'Architettura della città* in 1966; Giorgio Grassi's *La Costruzione logica dell'architettura* appeared in 1967. Both authors sought to counter all-pervasive consumerism and its urban manifestation in an instrumentalized landscape, by insisting on a return to the true realm of architecture (free of capitalist penetration and appropriation and where form does *not* follow function) and to the true realm of urban design (seen as the design of the *public* realm).[12] Rossi would have us return to the tough, rational principles of the Enlightenment—in a sense, to seek "the completion of the project of modernity," by transcending those principles in an architecture that reestablishes the morphology and meanings of the city. This is to be achieved by bestowing a pure, architectural autonomy on certain building types most significant to social life and cultural memory—school, hospital, prison, monument, cemetery.[13] A modern movement language is rejected, and instead the needed "pure architecture" is sought in an abstracted vernacular—what Rossi calls an "analogical architecture" that lies somewhere between "inventory" and "memory"—to trigger the cultural memory and, hence, the rereading of the city and, thereby, of society. His often quoted 1971 project for the Modena Cemetery does just that: Both building typology and forms of construction are abstracted from traditional buildings of the region (ossuary, farm, factory), and the final imagery is formal and classicist (see Figure 8.5). (Another neorationalist, Demetri Porphyrios [1982, p. 51] proclaims that all classicism is "the mimetic elaboration of vernacular.")

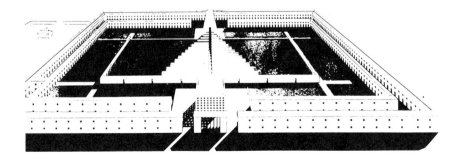

FIGURE 8.5. Aldo Rossi: The Modena Cemetery, 1971. Copyright 1971 by Aldo Rossi. Reprinted by permission.

The neorationalists, also self-identified as "La Tendenza," have had considerable influence in Europe where their program has tended to prevail over the more eclectic and historicist proclivities of North America, and of Britain for that matter. Within the neorationalist tradition—though in some contrast with the ideas and practices of Rossi and his colleagues—is the work of Leon and Robert Krier. Whereas Rossi would reestablish the morphology and integrity of the city by "correcting" the signification of building types crucial to the cultural memory of urban society, Leon Krier would do it by creating completely new (new/old!) spatial types that will weave their path through the junk of the commercialized city, reestablishing a "public realm" and knitting together the presently disparate bits—a new "order" to be layered on to the urban detritus (see Figure 8.6). So his 1970 project for the Luxembourgeois city of Echternach comprised a single, pitched roof building of endlessly repeated bays, reminiscent of Haussmann's Paris and of the gallery of Fourier's *phalanstère*, accommodating shops, apartments and a school, and weaving together medieval, baroque, and modern elements. His Royal Mint Square Housing Project of 1974 maintained traditional street lines, but quite arbitrarily bisected the site with a new diagonal building—a quite formalist "public room."

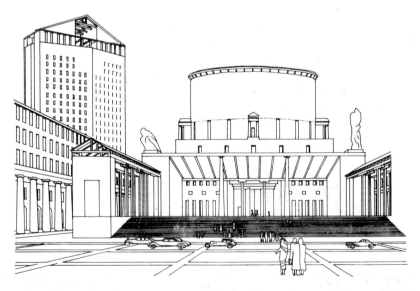

FIGURE 8.6. Leon Krier: Place du parlement Européen, Luxembourg, 1978. The public realm reestablished. Author's drawing based on "Luxemborg, the New European Quarters, 1978" (1984) and Economakis (1992).

Jencks's (1987b) summary is that

the Post-Modernists, Culot, the Krier brothers, Conrad Jameson for
instance, take a different view of city life [from that of the Modern
Movement] and stress the active, valuative aspect. The planner,
architect or market researcher *intervenes* to bring about those values
he supports, but he does this within a democratic, political context
where his values can be made explicit and debated. The proper
place for much that now happens as architecture and planning,
Jameson contends, is the political forum—the neighbourhood
meeting or the meeting of political representatives. While no ade-
quate city forum exists to express or guarantee this process, Post-
Modernists insist on its desirability. Basically this is a return to an
old and never perfect institution, the public realm—the agora, the
assembly area, mosque or gymnasium that acted as a space for people
to debate their varying views of the good life or assert their commu-
nality. (p. 108)

If Rossi's model is based on nineteenth-century *building types*,
Krier's goes back further to the eighteenth-century neoclassical *spatial
ensembles*—neoclassical Bath, Berlin, St. Petersburg. And if Rossi's is
concerned with articulation of uses and elements (in the best modernist fashion?), Krier would mix activities and uses—to resist monofunc-
tional zoning in the interests of more "ecological" urban living, less
wasteful of time, energy, and land. Both are totally at odds with North
American eclectic postmodernist design, and even more with Venturi's
celebration of Las Vegas (though, it might be noted, Vegas and suburbia are as much a vernacular as the rationalists' sources).

There are regional and local variations in the European neorationalist endeavors. A rationalist tradition had thrived in Madrid since the
1930s, and the intersection of this with the neorationalism of a
younger generation in Spain, and a new political and cultural diversity
after 1975 has yielded a distinctive representational language. A group
of architects in the Swiss Ticino region has explicitly followed the ideas
of Rossi, but here again there had been an underlying rationalist
tradition for some decades, with links to the prewar Italian rationalist
movement, and again a distinctive school has arisen (Frampton,
1985a, pp. 295–296). Similar stories can be traced in France and
Germany. It is the German architect O. M. Ungers (b. 1926) who
warrants some special mention: His odyssey took him from ambivalent
modernist (a 1963 student hostel for Berlin would have tried, like
Hadrian's Villa, to resolve the perpetual tension between monument
and context), to teaching and writing at Cornell from 1967 to 1974
(and an increasing conviction that the future task in urban design will

have far more to do with urban *contraction* than with expansion or renewal), to a return and radically different practice in Germany in 1975. It was in Germany that his concern shifted toward *themes* (an idea, perhaps a fantasy, or something abstracted from the urban and cultural context) and their *transformations* (the analogy is variations on a theme in musical composition). Sometimes they are called *topological transformations.* Although the context and the site will yield the themes for these variations and interweavings, the rules of the transformations are autonomous and are, indeed, the architecture itself. And what are these themes? They are an institute of navigation at Bremerhaven that is abstracted from an image of a ship; a Marburg housing scheme that puts a basic, four-story housing type of that town through progressively more radical transformations; a further transformation of the basic Berlin apartment type to the point where the facades actually look like musical notations; and the list could continue.

Whereas Ungers's themes tend to relate to context ("meanings") and local building types (vernaculars, certainly), the rules of transformation have a lot to do with Cartesian grids, and the effect is one of references back to the Bauhaus and earlier German traditions. Ungers has been influential, especially among the deconstructonists. Before turning to their work—transformations to the point where the themes may be annihilated—we need to consider the most extraordinary of all effusions of the neorationalist tendency.

THE NEOCLASSICIST TURN

Another long-thriving, local rationalist variant was to be found in Barcelona; among its younger architects in 1960 was Ricardo Bofill (b. 1939), who that year founded the Taller de Arquitectura. Bofill and the Taller's early work took on the common neorationalist task of representing the relationship between public realm and contextual background; by the 1970s, however, in a series of bizarre public housing schemes on the outskirts of Paris, that representation had shifted to an entirely new form of response to the experience of postmodernity.

In *Les Arcades du Lac* at Saint-Quentin-en-Yvelines near Versailles, of 1974–1981, the spaces of the public realm are as grand—and as uncompromisingly classicist—as anything from the eighteenth century, but it is all mass produced and high-tech, and explicitly so. Whereas *Les Arcades* were generally four stories, and a sort of in-scale, socialist counterpoint to Versailles, with *Les Espaces d'Abraxas* at Marne-la-Vallé (1979–1983), the classicist, human-centered vision is seized in the way that Le Roi Soleil would himself have grabbed it if he had lived in Bofill's time (and if he had been a communist). Because modern precasting technology enables orders far vaster than those of the past, and modern services greater heights, there is an Arc de Triomphe ten-stories high, a classical theater the same height, and a palace over nineteen stories. And lost into the bases, columns, pediments, and arcades of these gigantic monuments is mass housing. The most extraordinarily original is the concave face of the theater: Faceted glass columns rise over nine stories, interrupted by triple entablatures (actually superimposed planter boxes), each column surmounted by a cypress tree in a lawned roof garden—you live in a theater for giants and heroes made of glass flowerpots (see Figure 8.7).

Both the program—what is built and represented—and the mode of representation need comment. It turns history around: As in

FIGURE 8.7. Ricardo Bofill: Theatre, *Les Espaces d'Abraxas*, Marne-la-Vallée, 1979–1983. Drawing by Matt Spinaze, based on Futagawa (1985) and Jencks (1987).

Fourier's phalanstère, the vision of grandeur is revived, *la Gloire*, but given to a mass proletariat. Unlike the phalanstère, it is not however a vision of a new everyday life—new mode of production and communication. The inhabitants of this new heroic world, like everyone else in these French new towns, are commuters—the palaces, theater, triumphal arch do not even have their own shopping. In its mode of representation though, it is indeed important. Though every bit as totalitarian (and totalizing) as Le Corbusier's Ville contemporaine (and Versailles for that matter)—and, thereby, modern rather than postmodern—nevertheless, in demonstrating that modern technologies of production do not necessarily imply the machine aesthetic of modernism, it signals the end of the modern mode of representation. Michelangelesque orders, glass flowerpots—anything—are as consistent with the present means of production as the high-modernist curtain-walled boxes of Chicago or New York: The aesthetic underpinnings of the modern movement and the rationale for that built space of modernity are shot away forever.

There are other, far less histrionic versions of this return to the classicist viewpoint. Arata Isozaki (b. 1931) has developed a language wherein can be traced the *architecture parlante* of Ledoux, voices of the Japanese vernacular, and a gridded space that is as much traditional Japanese as it is Cartesian rationalist and high modern. Into this has more recently been grafted both classical motifs (arches, barrel vaults, rusticated orders) and axial modes of planning. A very explicit, free-form classicism informs Charles Jenck's house in London (1978–1983)—symmetrical, historicist elements overlain (asymmetrically) on other symmetrical elements. Equally explicit is the classicism that runs through virtually all of the Kriers' recent work; and finally classicist traces arise in much North American architecture and urban design, albeit derived from different sources and serving a different agenda (of Philip Johnson, Michael Graves, Charles Moore, Robert Stern, Robert Venturi). The lists could go on.

|AFTERWORD

The world (space—even more, *time*) is "but a shop of images and signs" (Baudelaire); the past, for its part, can only ever be real as we "seize its images and signs"—"seize hold of a memory as it flashes up in a moment of danger" (Benjamin). The danger of modernity was recognized long ago: "May God us keep / From single vision and Newton's sleep!" was the prayer of William Blake; deliverance from technological thinking was Heidegger's. The very concretization of "global civilization" (Ricoeur), single vision, and technological thinking was in that space that the International Style would represent. The fragmentation of languages, the wonderful profusion of stories and texts (merely alluded to in the stories above), and the seizing of a thousand memories (no holds barred) reveals the emancipatory endeavor of the postmoderns: The postmodern space would be ironic, Nietzsche's "play of the world," the joy of the text, fun. To be a postmodernist architect could be to play the clown (and what a humorless world was that from which we would escape—totalizing visions of space to be confronted by the space of laughter).

CHAPTER 9

Space
and Deconstruction:
Map as Myth

*It is the incessantly reawakened drive of play that
calls new worlds to life.*

—FRIEDRICH NIETZSCHE, quoted in Haar
(1992, p. 64)

Repeating: Western metaphysics is built on the dualisms and distinctions of opposed terms and on the contradictions and hierarchies that gather round them. But what if we call into question the initial distinction on which choice is founded—if, into the "trinitary horizon" of the dialectic (position, negation, negation of the negation), we throw a fourth term (Rousseau's "supplement," Derrida's preface), so that we lose the comfort of decidability? If we allow the other part of language—play, poetry, song—to soar? Such is the task of deconstruction: It must, "by means of a double gesture, a double science, a double writing, practise a *reversal* of the classical opposition *and* a general *displacement* of the system" (Derrida, 1982, p. 329). Derrida will typically illuminate the supposed contradictions within the texts that he will comment upon, associating them with the fissured structure of Western philosophy.

| ARCHITECTURE

The disjunctive force can only be put in the architectural work at the moment where, by some secret or denied synergy, it can be integrated into the order of a narrative [récit], whatever the dimension, in an uninterrupted history between the beginning and the end, the founding sub-foundation and the top of the house, the cellar and the roof, the ground and the point of the pyramid.

—Jacques Derrida, "Fifty-two Aphorisms for a Foreword" (aphorism 40) (1989a, p. 69)[1]

If one pole in the attempts to represent a postmodern experience is revealed in the search for refound and reexplored cultural memories presently locked in the institutions and morphology of the city (the Foucauldian agenda, so to speak, most clearly seen in the work of Rossi) and if another is to put the proletariat and everyday life in the symbolic seat of grandeur reserved for the deity in premodernity, the state in early modernity and capital in high modernity (the Nietzschean vision, albeit trapped in an irresolvable contradiction with mass culture, and at its most problematic with Bofill) and if yet another response is that search for a spatial language that can represent different experiences, ease in the presence of otherness, and a belief in human development that is not dependent on material progress and the privileging of present over past (the Heideggerian or postmodern, the historical eclecticism of Graves, Stern, Venturi, and the "mainstream" in which they seem to move), then the last pole, and in many ways the most troubling, is deconstruction. If it is to be identified with a philosophical trait, then it is that of Derrida. This, the fourth pole, can only really be understood through the stories of some of its pursuers: The first is the continuation of one introduced earlier—Eisenman's progressive autonomization and abstraction of the rules of architectural generation.[2]

In House III of 1971, we have seen, Peter Eisenman opposed two three-dimensional grids at 45° to each other, so that elements and spaces collide, interrupt, superimpose, come apart and recompose again; in this house experienced space only makes sense if it is read against another text that explains the abstracted, autonomous rules of its own generation. Houses IV and VI continue these transformations. So in House VI of 1972–1976, as example, the architecture is against the idea of making function thematic—it is almost antifunctionalist, and certainly avowedly *post*functionalist: There is a stair that does not work, a window in the bedroom floor, a column in the middle of the bedroom so that you cannot put a bed in it. "My work attacks the concept of occupation as given," declares Eisenman (1989). "It is against the traditional notion of how you occupy a house" (p. 142). In this case, the "other text" to be read against the experienced space is in our own assumptions about the nature of space and of its occupation. With House X, designed in 1975–1977 but never built, Eisenman concluded his allegedly "structuralist" period (though Jencks has found it more "poststructuralist") and began his "deconstructionist" work. The design method is more decomposition: Elements and space are taken away rather than added ("composed"), so that spaces are decentered, scales distorted, and functions rotated, inverted, then opposed. "Rooms" end up upside down. But are there rooms? Are there norms for what spaces should be?

From there, Eisenman's project was to pursue *uncertainty* (all assumptions and givens will be destroyed), *distancing* (process becomes the object; it is architecture about architecture rather than about things or functions; it is scaleless, like a Malevich painting), and *decentering* (what is being represented is a "positive absence"; cubes are eroded and distorted until they are akin to logic-defying mind puzzles). House 11a, designed in 1978 but again not built, is mirror-imaged and then excavated into the ground: One of the texts against which it is to be read is presented to us as the "archaelogy of knowledge" of its own generation (see Figure 9.1). In its turn, it generates yet further distortions—not so much transformations as logic-free interruptions of itself. So House El Even Odd (a play on 11a), of 1980, is an axonometric projection of its former self, making no sense except from a single viewpoint. All assumptions about architecture itself, space and the self are to be stripped away, laid bare. (The constructed model of the house is, in its abstract geometry, clearly reminiscent of the early "experimental" period of Russian constructivism: House El Even Odd seems to have arrived at a representation that was for the constructivists the starting point. There is however a great difference in what is represented: in the case of the house, the hypothesized active experience of absence and uncertainty in postmodernity.)

The deconstruction of House 11a goes still further. Around 1978, it seems, Eisenman underwent something of a sea change: House X came to nought, he went to Venice to work on the Cannaregio urban design project, became preoccupied with philosophical deconstruction and its decentering thrust, and began to undergo psychoanalysis, as excavation into the subsconscious, to be paralleled in architecture as the archaeology of knowledge. The Cannaregio, a large and somewhat ill-defined public place, would use House 11a three times, at three different scales:

[The project for Cannaregio would take House 11a and build it] as three differently scaled objects. One of the objects is about four feet high, it sits in the square and is the model of a house. You can look at it and think "well, that is not a house; it is the model of House 11a." Then you take the same object and put it in House 11a; you build House 11a at human scale—and you put this same model of it inside. . . . Once the model inside is memorialized, it is no longer the model of an object; it has been transformed . . . into a real thing. As a consequence, the larger house, the one at anthropomorphic scale, no longer functions as a house.

Then there is a third object, which is larger than the other two, larger than "reality," larger than anthropomorphic necessity. . . . It becomes a museum of all these things. (Eisenman, 1981; quoted in Jencks, 1988a, p. 27)

It is an urban design of absences and self-referentiality. It ignores both the space and time (history) of Venice, countering the contextual preoccupations of the neorationalists; its most significant traces are of the *nonbuilt* hospital that Le Corbusier designed for Venice and whose

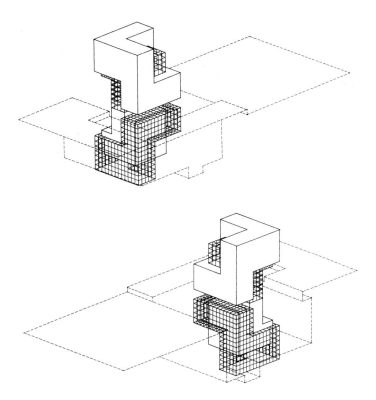

FIGURE 9.1. Architecture as archaeology of knowledge: Peter Eisenman, House 11a, 1980. Drawing by Matt Spinaze, based on Eisenman (1989).

grid it adopts; by denying scale, it denies the significance of the user. The Cannaregio also marks Eisenman's avowed shift toward the larger, urban scale. This continued with his 1982–1987 social housing project for South Friedrichstadt, Berlin, which he designed with Jaquelin Robertson: Alongside the Berlin Wall, the eighteenth-, nineteenth- and twentieth-century street grids are memorialized in an idealized, Bauhaus-reminiscent grid at 3.3° to the "real" pattern of streets and retained buildings and fragments (see Figure 9.2). So the "real" is destroyed by its own memorial, elevated (layered) above it; and the agenda is to produce an "artificial excavation": "In the conscious act of forgetting, one cannot help but remember."

> Our strategy for developing [this] site was twofold. The first inten-
> tion was to expose the particular history of the site; that is, to render
> visible its specific memories, to acknowledge that it once was spe-
> cial, was *some place*. The second was to acknowledge that Berlin
> today belongs to the world in the largest sense, that its specificity
> and identity have been sacrificed on the altar of modern history,
> that it is now the crossroads of *every place* and *no place*. In the process
> of materialising this duality the architecture attempts to erect the
> structure of both somewhere and nowhere, of here and not here: to
> memorialise a place and to deny the efficacy of that memory. (Eisen-
> man and Robertson, 1983, p. 26)

So they write of "antimemory"—neither demanding nor seeking a past (nor a future!), but rather obscuring the memory of a past that renders present space *no place*—denying the present reality of the Berlin Wall and thereby the division of the human race, by the turn to nostalgic, sentimental memory. The purpose of antimemory is to reveal to us what the past is doing *now* (Benjamin's "to seize hold of a memory as it flashes up in a moment of danger")[3] and what the myth of human progress is doing to us *now*, so that the present with its oppressions and divisions (the moment of danger) can be accepted and confronted for what it is and so that out of the present we can create *some place* (a new geography?). "In this way memory and anti-memory work oppositely but in collusion to produce a suspended object, a frozen fragment of no past and no future, a *place*. Let us say it is of its own time" (Eisenman and Robertson, 1983, p. 26).

As constructed, the street facades represent their "own time" by a green and white gridded wall, the eighteenth century foundation of the Friedrichstadt is represented by another grid at 3.3° to the first, with each intersecting and interrupting the other, and the link to the world and the geopolitics of the Berlin Wall by the (imagined) Mercator grid.

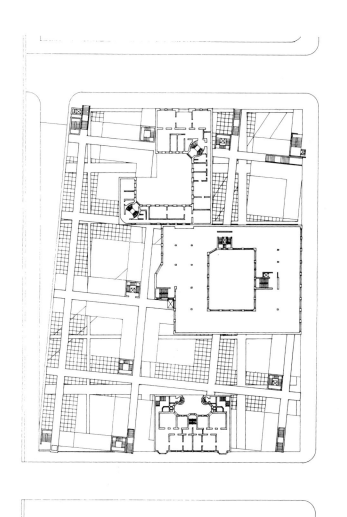

FIGURE 9.2. Urban design as excavation: Peter Eisenman, social housing project for South Friedrichstadt, Berlin, 1982–1987. For its strata, and thereby its derivation, see Eisenman (1994, p. 79). Drawing by Matt Spinaze, based on Eisenman and Robertson (1983) and Bédard (1994).

Though scarcely obsessed with dull habitability, the block does succeed in endowing something on its streetscapes, with lots of interest and tension from its skews and tilts and interruptions. But to get its meanings, one again needs another text: The building and "the book" need to be read onto each other and then onto that further text of our own (individual) assumptions and experiences of space, time, and power. We need both the map and the Baedeker, as we do for the city itself: architecture as metaphor for our reading the city.

The Wexner Center for the Visual Arts at the Ohio State University, Columbus, was first published as a project in 1985 and completed 1990 (see Figure 9.3). As with South Friedrichstadt, it is a linking of existing buildings and of nonexisting (*absent*) buildings: There are excavations to the foundations of an armory that once occupied the site and, then, offset, an ensemble of sloping red walls and quasitowers as a "ghost" of the long-departed armory. Linking both buildings and postbuildings are *two* three-dimensional Mercator grids (scaffolding rather than buildings) at 12.5° to each other, tracing the grids of the

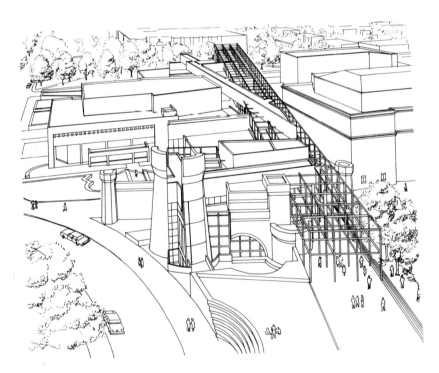

FIGURE 9.3. Peter Eisenman: Arts Center, Columbus, Ohio, 1985. Author's drawing, based on "The OSU Center for Visual Arts, Columbus, Ohio, 1985" (1985).

campus and the city, which are similarly skewed to each other, so that the various intersections of grid with grid and grid with building and postbuilding yield accidents, collisions, and disturbances along a scaffolded, galleried "street" (a Cartesian Fourier, deconstructed!). The site is used, says Eisenman, as a palimpsest—"a place to write, erase, and rewrite," a metaphor of the city again.

| OTHER DECONSTRUCTIONS

We will turn to Eisenman again (indeed recurrently in the pages that remain); but it is important to note other voices in this challenge to the ways in which we represent our shifting experience of space to ourselves. If the starting point for Eisenman is language (progressing from Chomsky and structuralism, through poststructuralism, to Derrida and deconstruction) and the multivoicedness of all texts, then for Frank Gehry it is dadaism, Duchamp and ready-mades, and the early Russian avant-garde; and for OMA (Office for Metropolitan Architecture), Arquitectonica, and Zaha Hadid, it is overwhelmingly the Russian constructivist tradition.

Frank O. Gehry (b. 1929) takes deconstruction quite literally. His later buildings (say, from his own house of 1978) tend to look as if bombs had hit them—broken walls, bits pulled off and strewn around, crumpled bits often in cheap industrial materials, beams and columns seemingly in the wrong places (see Figure 9.4). His Wosk House additions of 1982–1984, placed atop an apartment in Beverly Hills, California, adopts the aesthetic of a junk village of bad-taste urban detritus to subvert the good-taste base on which it sits: There is a baby-blue classicist dome to offend Michael Graves, bits of an aircraft hangar, some modernist gridded glazed wall, a corrugated shed. Slightly earlier, from 1981, and decidedly more restrained was his complex for Loyola Law School, also in Los Angeles: a public space with three broken, "deconstructed" temples (columns without base, entasis, or capital—again a tilt at the postmodern classicists), a broken palazzo (but with obvious homage to Adolf Loos and Le Corbusier's Pavillon Suisse), a belfry without a bell, baroque stairways without balusters, and everywhere missing elements. All the set pieces of classicism appropriate to a law school are there, except that they all imply discontinuity, difference; and they all sow doubt. The genre—and, therefore, possibly what it stands for (education, norms, and the law itself) are brought into question (see Figure 9.5).

As the keystone or its absence is Graves's emblematic referent, and the Cartesian grid is Eisenman's, so the fish is Gehry's: friendly, fun,

laden with Christian–Freudian symbolism, and Jewish. He has designed fish restaurants in Japan, a fish skyscraper for New York, and fish
lampshades for the fashionable galleries. Charles Jencks (1988a) draws
attention to the Neitzschean argument of an arbitrary base in all
cultural form: Architects can never prove a rational foundation to their
choice of style, so Gehry's choice serves to "deconstruct all our assumptions" about style, ornament, classicism, the modern movement, and
especially Graves's emergent language of postmodernism (p. 18; see
also Jencks, 1988b). Why copy Greece and Rome when you can just as
easily copy fish!

For Frank Gehry, one suspects, the golden age, the dreamtime, was
somewhere around 1918: The dadaists were in full outrage toward both
popular and high taste, Duchamp was still finding ready-mades, and the
flying-apart aesthetic of the early Proletkult, protoconstructivist kiosks
was taking over the streets and squares of Moscow—and soon, one could
dream, the world. These are overwhelmingly the voices through which
Gehry proclaimed in the 1980s. The iconography tended to be early
constructivist; the ironic tone, the send-up, was dadaist. With OMA,
founded in 1975 in New York but with a more Europe-oriented practice,
there has been a progression from an explicit neoconstructivist urban

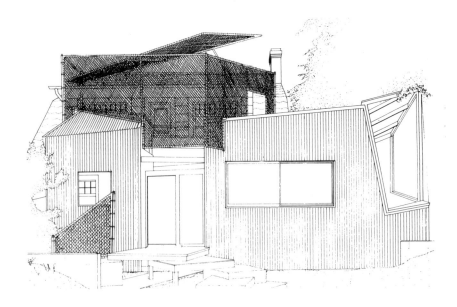

FIGURE 9.4. Urban detritus as architecture: Frank Gehry, own house, 1978.
Drawing by Matt Spinaze, based on Arnell and Bickford (1985).

design (with Leonidov as the admired model) toward a method of superimposition or layering of urban typologies—text on text—that is deconstructionist in its effect of unmasking differences, interruptions, and discontinuities (with Leonidov and his defenders still as model). OMA's approach has also had a lot to do with O. M. Ungers's ideas of *themes* and their *transformations*—Rem Koolhaas (b. 1944), the principal founder of OMA, had collaborated with Ungers since about 1972. The name of the firm is in part a pun on Ungers's name.

Another version of the deconstructionist intent informs the work of Zaha Hadid (b. 1950), who was with OMA briefly in 1977–1979 and who also takes Leonidov—but also the very different voice of Malevich—as source. The principal expression of her ideas has been in drawings and paintings, rather than in executed projects, and reveals a world of exploding elements, beams that fly out into space, tilted and cantilevered planes—a world that is, for the most part, scaleless. If there is a second text on which this one is to be overlain, to throw it into question and new reading, then it is the text of the site and of conventional expectations (of what a club or an office building, or whatever, "should be")—the very opposite of Rossi. But Hadid's neoconstructivist

FIGURE 9.5. Deconstruction: Frank Gehry, Loyola Law School, Los Angeles, 1981. Author's drawing, based on Jencks (1988a) and Arnell and Bickford (1985).

text itself is quite unlike anything of Eisenman's in that it remains impossible to decode: There is nothing like Eisenman's program or Book of Genesis, but just the ventriloquated voice of a 1920s revolutionary avant-garde. So why a revolutionary trace in the 1980s, and why *that* avant-garde?

DECONSTRUCTION AND CONSTRUCTIVISM

The beautiful *Deconstruction Omnibus Volume* (Papadakis, Cooke, and Benjamin, 1989) begins with an essay by Catherine Cooke entitled "Russian Precursors." Its siting in the book, and the weight placed on Cooke's ideas in the pages of the journal *Architectural Design*, reflect the preeminence accorded the constructivists and their ideas and imagery in contemporary accounts of architectural and urban deconstruction— at the risk, one should add, of suppressing the significance of dada, the high modernist grid, and the idea of deconstruction as an extension (and transformation) of the modern. The argument is important and needs to be opened here.

   Constructivism "denotes a mode of thinking, a certain ordering of the processes of thought"; constructivist design, in turn, is to *represent* this new mode or ordering.[4] (If the processes of thought can be represented rightly, they can presumably be changed, and a new social order— and experience of space, time, and the self—can come about.) But, adds Cooke, the basic paradigm of logical thinking in that era was one akin to mechanical engineering, and the space of social progress and its social production were represented accordingly. It was the "First Machine Age." But now is the Second Machine Age, the age of information technology and of space measured by time; the appropriate paradigm is no longer of Cartesian atomizing and of things that move other things but of how information is understood and exchanged *now*. Cooke (1989) quotes with approval Fritjof Capra's (1983, pp. 66, 70) description of this difference; it is worth repeating:

> In contrast to the mechanistic, Cartesian view of the world, the world view emerging from modern physics can be characterised by words like organic, holistic, and ecological. It might also be called a systems view, in the sense of general systems theory. The universe is no longer seen as a machine, made up of a multitude of objects, but has to be pictured as one indivisible, dynamic whole whose parts are essentially inter-related and can be understood only as patterns of a cosmic process. . . . In quantum theory you never end up with

"things"; you always deal with interconnections. . . . It shows that we cannot decompose the world into independently existing small-est units. (p. 14)

And even more tellingly, "the world thus appears as a complicated tissue of events, in which connections of different kind alternate or overlap or combine and thereby determine the texture of the whole" (Cooke, 1989, p. 14). This time it is Cooke quoting Capra, who in turn is quoting Werner Heisenberg.

So to extend the argument: The task of understanding is, there-fore, not to break down and atomize the mechanisms, but to reveal the connections, overlays, and textures of the events that constitute real life and experience. It is a task of unmasking; and the task of aesthetic activity is to represent *that* task, so that it becomes omnipresent and inescapable. Now the best of the urban designers and architects cer-tainly understand this, so why do they turn back to that other paradigm of representation, in the constructivists?

There are three possible reasons. First, there is a nostalgia for the revolutionary intent of it all: Nowhere else in history is there such a clear example of the endeavor to represent a new world in a new aesthetic of space. If we are to find a way of representing our times to ourselves so that we can seek a path out of the seeming impasse of consumer capitalism, and if we believe that that path must be "so new as not to contain even a grain of the old" (Lenin), then where else are we to look? Second, there is the sheer clarity of expression of the constructivist vision: Regardless of any nostalgia for a revolutionary time and mission, there was in the 1980s an admiration for an urban space uncompromised by having to be built. Third, the constructivists are a source of fascination for the present because already in the 1920s there were some who were attempting to explore the representation of that new worldview of postmodernity. So Cooke draws attention to the writings of Soviet sociologist Mikhail Okhitovich, in the constructivists' journal *Sovremannaia Arkhitektura* in 1929, to the effect that the "rapid growth in the means of communica-tion" deposes all reigning ideas about society and space:

If one talks about the essence, then this new complex will be called not a point, not a place nor a city, but a process, and this process will be called Disurbanisation. Disurbanisation is the process of centrifugal force and repulsion. It is based on just such a centrifugal tendency in technology . . . which reverses all the former assumptions. Proximity is henceforth a function of dis-tance, and community a function of separateness. (Okhitovich, quoted in Cooke, 1989, p. 17)

The disburbanists' preoccupations with rhythms and textures of space anticipate similar concerns of the deconstructionists in the 1980s; and it is little wonder that the representations of the former find explicit reference in the urban projects of the deconstructionists. There were similarly attempts to represent, in a constructivist language, the suprematist vision of a four-dimensional space, where the fourth dimension (of an experiential time) is the disintegrator "which explodes the material into the spiritual" (Cooke, 1989, p. 18). This attempted synthesis of essentially opposed ideas of space is found in the work of Chernikhov, Lissitzky, and especially Leonidov; and it is these three—and especially Leonidov—whose voices sound most clearly through the drawings, paintings and urban projects of the deconstructionists. More than anything else, the event that brought into focus this search for an appropriate representation of the experience of postmodernity—as well as the voices through which the representation might be effected—was the early 1980s competition for the Parc de la Villette in Paris.

|LE PARC DE LA VILLETTE

In *Joyce's Garden* of 1976–1977, painter and urban designer Bernard Tschumi took a literary text (James Joyce's *Finnegan's Wake*) as a program for decoding an "architectural" text of urban meanings (the urban fabric of London from Covent Garden down to the Thames), where the point grid—homage to Le Corbusier?—was used as mediator between the two. The superimposition of heterogeneous texts is an explicit lifting of the Derridean approach to textual deconstruction. With *The Manhattan Transcripts* of 1976–1981, Tschumi used the point grid as a device for breaking apart the texture (text) of the city so that its superimpositions and disjunctures came into consciousness (Tschumi, 1981). While Tschumi was speaking in part through the voice of the Russian disurbanists (as Catherine Cooke demonstrates), and partly through that of Derrida of a half-century later, the effect was to represent something of that "tissue of events" and the "alternating, overlapping or combining connections" that determine the texture of life and space in Capra's characterization (of 1983) as well as the multivoicedness that fascinated the Russians of the 1920s.

With Tschumi's 1982 winning competition masterplan for Paris's Parc de la Villette, published in 1983, and with its subsequent implementation, we get the first large-scale urban design parading under the deconstructionist banner, as well as a new focus for the debates on an appropriate representation of the contemporary experience of space and time (see Figure 9.6). Proclaimed as a "park of the twenty-first century," it operates at a number of levels both literally and figuratively. It is a deconstructionist superimposition of points, lines, and surfaces, reflecting Klee's and Kandinsky's 1920s (Bauhaus) aesthetics; but these three types of elements are of different, disjointed orders of reality. The surfaces, it seems, are gardens and buildings, an abstract pattern that most resembles an aerial photograph, or perhaps a land-use map, of "any city," as Charles Jencks calls it.[5] The lines are the superimposed avenues and crescents of grand landscape design, the landscape de-signer's conventional wares. But they also include a three-kilometer twisting gallery, like photographic film randomly thrown down on the

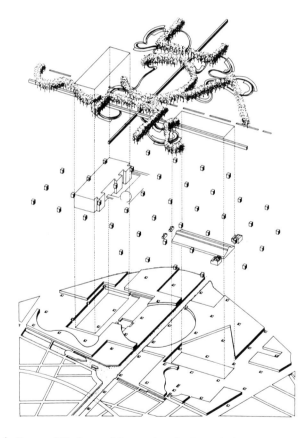

FIGURE 9.6. Bernard Tschumi: Masterplan for Parc de la Villette, Paris, 1983. Surfaces, points, lines. Author's drawing, based on "Concours International pour le Parc de la Villette" (1983, June), Wilson (1983, July), and Tschumi (1988).

site, a "cinematic promenade" as a montage of images: Photographic film, after all, is seen by Ulmer (1985) as the ideal model of Derrida's notion of mime: grafted images, representing through discontinuities, disjunctions, and *différance*, and with reversible temporality.[6] The points comprise some forty *folies*, on a 120-meter grid, each a fire-engine red construction of enameled steel and each serving some pleasure or educational activity (see Figures 9.7 and 9.8).

It is laden with references: The point grid evokes Le Corbusier's method of planning (grids of freestanding columns, with screens and walls twisting and winding and bearing no seeming relationship with them); the lines pay homage to the Russian suprematist tradition and to the essays in urban design of Iakov Chernikhov, while the abstracted geometries of the freestanding *folies* are closest to late-constructivist architectural projects with more distant references to the street tribunes and kiosks of early constructivism. At another textual level, Tschumi's *folies* evoke those other "folies": of the eighteenth century English landscape garden; "folie" in the sense of that which contradicts Reason and Enlightenment, as Foucault's deconstruction of the ideological underpinnings of modernity; and "folie" as the stupidity of a government that had previously misplanned La Villette as a never-used meat market. The most powerful allusions of all, however, seem to be to that ultimate disurbanist vision of a new, disintegrated space and time: Barshch and Ginzburg's 1930 "Green City" plan for the "social reconstruction of Moscow" (Kopp, 1970, pp. 173–178). Yet all these references are pulled apart, deconstructed, just as the references to the suburban sprawl of "any city"—to Jameson's "postmodern hyperspace"—are deconstructed.[7] Derrida's (1986b) comments on La Villette are illuminating: "These *folies* destabilise meaning, the meaning of meaning, the signifying potential of this powerful architectonics. They put in question, dislocate, destabilise or deconstruct the edifice of this configuration" (p. 69).

However the effect is not a negative one; rather, "the *folies* affirm." So, Derrida asks, what is a deconstructive/reconstructive architecture to be? "Deconstructions would be feeble if they were negative, if they did not construct, and above all if they did not first measure themselves against institutions in their solidarity, *at the place of their greatest resistance*: political structures, levers of economic decision" (Derrida, 1986b, p. 70; for more on Derrida and Tschumi, see A. Benjamin, 1988).

Yet the *promise* of deconstruction/reconstruction—the reconstructive bit—remains unredeemed. The point grid and the random sprawl are to be interpreted as emptiness, "the kind of urban reality already created by Modernism, industrialisation and the 'dispersion' of contemporary life" (Jencks, 1988a, p. 24; see also Tschumi, 1986, p. 3). In Tschumi's (1988) words,

> The Park calls into question the fundamental or primary signified of architecture—its tendency (as Derrida remarks in *La Case Vide*) to be "in *service*, and at *service*", obeying an economy of meaning premised on functional use. In contrast, La Villette promotes programmatic instability, functional *Folie*. Not a plenitude, but instead "empty" form: *les cases sont vides* . . . an architecture that means nothing, an architecture of the signifier rather than the signified. (p. 39)

Deconstructive, certainly; perhaps even subversive (though it is too intellectualized and self-indulgent by far for any effective demolition of presently prevailing ideological underpinnings to an instrumentalized everyday life, an issue to which we must return). But where is the reconstruction? Tschumi's (1988) answer is that the reconstruction will be the task of the individual observer who "will project his own interpretation, resulting in an account that will again be interpreted . . . and so on" (p. 39).

There is another, very beautiful representation of a postmodern space of different, overlain stories that emerged from the La Villette competition. It is the entry by Rem Koolhaas and his OMA group (see Figure 9.9). It comprised a long series of lateral strips—ribbons of different sorts of plantings and activities—over which were superimposed a layer of small elements and activities as if randomly dropped on to the site, a layer of larger elements, then layers of small elements and connections. It is multilayered, discontinuous, characterized by seeming random juxtapositions and sudden breaks and absences, and indeterminate. In other words, it is like the (post)modern city and *unlike* the modernist totalizing *vision* of the city. Like Tschumi's vision, it compels a rereading of the text of the contemporary city.

| DERRIDA AND EISENMAN

The point of these several preceding pages is that an architectural and urban design practice has been transformed since the 1960s by a sudden opening of its discourse to the central insights of contemporary semiotics: that every utterance, linguistic or otherwise, resonates with the answering words (or images) of the receiver; that those answering words or images will have come from a context or experience that is different for every individual; and that there can accordingly be no

FIGURES 9.7 and 9.8. Bernard Tschumi: *Folies P6/P7*, La Villette. Author's drawing, based on Jencks (1988a).

single, unique correspondence of signifier with signified and no universalizing potential in architectural meaning. The promise of the modern movement was a chimera.

In the context of this opening (to multivoicedness, uncertainty, a skepticism toward shared meanings) has been a progressive shift, by Eisenman, Tschumi, and a small group of followers, toward the post-

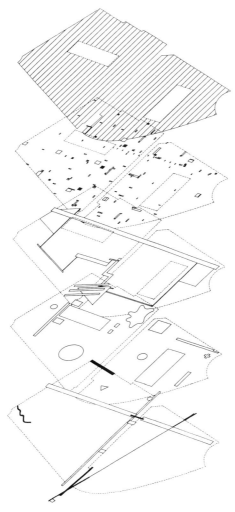

FIGURE 9.9. Rem Koolhaas: Parc de la Villette, c. 1982. Bands of successive landscapes; random activities, elements, connections. Drawing by Matt Spinaze, based on "Concours International pour le Parc de la Villette" (1983, February and June).

structuralist, deconstructionist insistences of Jacques Derrida. Although Derrida sees philosophy and literature as two opposed poles (the search for universal meaning vs. the multivoicedness of real presence), with neither able to be isolated from or privileged over the other, he would seem, nevertheless, to give precedence to literature—the realm of art and the text. (Perhaps to counteract the continued location of his own work in the world of philosophical endeavor!) So Eisenman has similarly moved toward the idea of an architecture that "writes different texts," to stand against that hitherto privileged pole of a single "anthropocentric" text that he sees underlying all previous architectural theories and practices. He set out to disrupt that presently prevailing text by subverting such notions as classicist human focus, human scale, and representation, including the modern movement's pretended abstinence from representation. Central to Derrida's project is the notion of *différance*, which, with its connotations of time, origin, change, and movement, is intended to supplant the ahistorical, Saussurian model of the sign. This too is taken up by Eisenman: The "different texts" to be written in architecture will be about architectural multivalence, matching the multivoicedness of its receivers, and about the origins and temporality of that multivalence—How do different experiences of space arise, where do they originate? Architecture will be a visual exploration of the production of space and of its transformation in the different experiences of different people—not just resonating with the answering words or images of the receiver, but *transforming* with them. So architecture is seen by Eisenman as "a second language" (from which, presumably, there can evolve writing, text, and literature, as Derrida argues that writing and text and literature evolve, via the "trace," from the "first" language).[8]

All this is prefigured in the houses and the development of ideas that they represent (and already reviewed); it also runs through his larger, urban-context-dependent projects.[9] Eisenman's first explicit essay in architecture-as-text (to find this "second language") was his entry for the 1985 Venice Biennale. The site was to be Verona, and the story that of Romeo and Juliet (see Figure 9.10). This story was first written about two castles, but through its various rewritings—Da Porto, Bandello, Shakespeare—was translated to Verona; there the fiction assumed materiality so that today you can "actually" visit the "house of Juliet" ("the point of their division"), the "church where they were married" ("the point of their union"), and the "tomb where they were buried" ("the ultimate point of their dialectical relationship of togetherness and apartness") (Eisenman, 1986, p. 7). So, Eisenman adds, the intent of his project was "to reimprint the castles in what we called a 'hyper-fiction'—that is, a fiction of a fiction" (p. 7), to refictionalize the house, church, and tomb. Eisenman produces a new text (in the "first language") by superimpositions of the three original texts; the visual representation (the "second language") similarly works by superimpositions and rescalings. So he describes the first superimposition, of the two castles on the city of Verona, to reveal apartness and absence:

> The first scaling involves the transposition of place and superposition of scales in time to reveal aspects of the structure of the textual narrative. The castle (which is analogous to Romeo) attempts to unite a Verona divided between the Capuletti and the Montecchi. The Adige River which both joins and fractures the city of Verona also acts upon the castle of Romeo so that it becomes, in its left hand segment, a presence and, in its right hand segment, part memory—the absence of its former presence—and part trace—the presence of an absence—an immanent castle. The castle of Romeo is thus a palimpsest and a quarry, where the stones which are removed from the actual walls of the castle form the grid of the city of Verona. (Eisenman, 1986, p. 7)

The second superimposition (of the castle of Juliet as an active trace at the actual church) is supposed to reveal the idea of union. The third (the castle of Juliet as an active presence over the tomb) is to reveal the dialectical relationship between union and division. Then there is a "labyrinth," created by superimposing three scalings as re-presentations of the concepts of division, union, and their dialectical relationship.

Much of Romeo and Juliet, as urban representation, is not surprising and continues preoccupations previously in Eisenman's work: the palimpsest, quarry, transpositions, superimpositions, rescaling, active representation of absence. At least analogously they are also themes running through the thought of Foucault and Derrida (and, half a century earlier, both Heidegger and Walter Benjamin). The one thing that is new here, however, is the pursuit of a textual architecture.

In 1985 Tschumi invited Eisenman and Derrida to collaborate on the design of gardens for three sites in the Parc de la Villette. To their discussions Eisenman brought his Romeo and Juliet project and the quest for architecture-as-text and the "second language"; Derrida brought his manuscript on Chora, introduced in Plato's Timaeus (Chora: place, residence, habitat, the openness or void that permits things to take place—Heidegger's clearing, which "grants and guarantees . . . a passage to those entities that we ourselves are not"—and that receives all things as an imprint). In the event Eisenman pro-

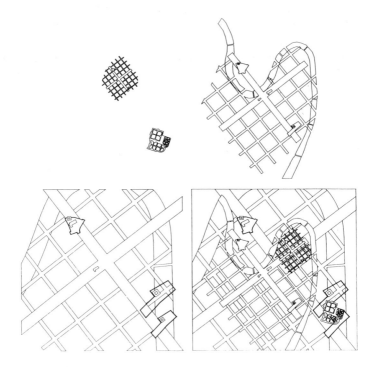

FIGURE 9.10. Peter Eisenman: Romeo and Juliet, 1985. The first superimposition: The city as labyrinth; space as the representation of time. Drawing by Matt Spinaze, based on Whiteman (1986).

duced and transformed the material images, while Derrida contributed, first, the interpretation of the Platonic Chora that gave the work its program and, second, a text entitled "Why Peter Eisenman Writes Such Good Books?" to explore his experience in working on the project and to reflect his interest in architecture (building, garden, city) as reading.[10] To the project they attached the name *Choral Works* (see Figure 9.11).

Eisenman has claimed that Tschumi's La Villette was derived from his own gridded Cannaregio project for Venice of 1973, which in turn referred to Le Corbusier's 1965 hospital for Venice—also a regular grid superimposed, in a typically Corbusian opposition, on the irregular fabric of Venice. To evoke these two unbuilt projects as memories, Eisenman would superimpose the grid of their project on that of Cannaregio and on that of Tschumi, with shifts in scale and density; the diagonal that had been used to interrupt the grid of Cannaregio (to indicate the fourth dimension of unknown past and unknown future) was in turn layered on Tschumi's diagonal; and some elements marking these grids were excavated into the ground (past), others were at ground level (present), while others were elevated (future). There are three texts: Tschumi's, which may or may not be seen as a text on Eisenman's Cannaregio, itself written in part through the voice of Le Corbusier; and Eisenman's, in turn to be seen as a text on Derrida's; and finally Derrida's, which is a text on Plato's *Timaeus*. With these super-impositions on superimpositions and texts on texts, there is also something of a slippage between languages—"first" (of literature) and "second" (of architecture and urban meaning), to and fro. It is, they declare, a *text-in-between:* "What this attempts to do is to undercut the notion of originality and authority, in other words that no one can take credit for it or for who came first" (Eisenman, 1989, p. 145).

It may well be objected that this textual play is at an extraordinary level of abstraction from the world of most people's everyday experience and that urban design to such a program runs the risk of leaving reality (a city that works for people) far behind. It will instead fill books for other deconstructionist aficionados. Nevertheless, two defending arguments must be put. For one thing, Eisenman and Derrida, and Tschumi in his La Villette master plan, were self-consciously attempting just that—to leave "reality" behind by critiquing all assumptions about functionality, anthropocentrism, and aestheticism. La Villette *is* a park, and it is surely the place of a park to represent another nature and another experience to us—to vex, agitate, disturb, interrupt (as

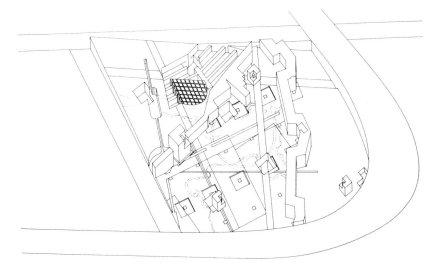

FIGURE 9.11. Peter Eisenman, Jacques Derrida: *Choral Works* garden, La Villette. Drawing by Matt Spinaze, based on Bédard (1994).

Versailles vexed the experience of a still-medieval landscape, and Birkenhead Park that of the Industrial Revolution). So the transcript of one of the Derrida–Eisenman meetings on the project (of April 3, 1986) has Eisenman declaring: "I do not think it matters that ordinary Parisians understand everything, but they must realize that they are in the presence of a textual activity, a simulation. . . . This is the important thing—the dislocation from the ordinary expectation of what is garden. It will be like reading Finnegan's Wake for the first time." Derrida's response: "You have to be amazed by it" (reported in Koukoutsi, 1989, p. 47). It must, for its effect, stand *against* the real: When it becomes "the real," it no longer works.

The second defense is that La Villette, Romeo and Juliet, Cannaregio, the Manhattan Transcripts, and Joyce's Garden before it are to be seen as attempts to represent the experience of the times. It is certainly to be argued that this is nearer to the real experience of the city of the present than anything (the zoned city, modern movement architecture) still paying lip service to the dream of modernist progress and order. Derrida and Eisenman in their textual landscape, and Tschumi and Koolhaas in their respective master plans for La Villette, seem to confront that modernist memory ("false consciousness") with the city as unknowable past, a present of "otherness," and an unknowable future.

|DERRIDA'S GEOGRAPHY

This chapter has not been about architecture but geography. Once again: Derrida would intrude a fourth term into the "trinitary horizon" of the dialectic—the destabilizing preface (Rousseau's "supplement") into "first language" texts, to break the Hegelian chains of the dialectic. But if there is also a "second language" wherein we represent our experience of being-in-space—writing of a landscape "graphically visible" in space, as it is "narratively visible" in time—then how might those graphical texts of experiential geographies similarly be destabilized? How might the preface, in second language, intrude into the "writing" of spatial worlds? One answer, Derrida seems to suggest, is *new architecture*. Almost a description of La Villette gardens (though it comes from Derrida's *Of Grammatology*, originally written in 1967) is: "The logic of supplementarity, which would have it that the outside be inside, that the other and the lack come to add themselves as a plus that replaces a minus, that what adds itself to something takes the place of a default in the thing, that the default, as the outside of the inside, should be already within the inside, etc." (Derrida, 1976, p. 215).[11] For

Eisenman, by contrast, the intrusion seems to be the myth represented in the map—distorted scale, superimposable, all reality flattened.

Into the *Choral Works* garden would be interposed a labyrinth, but it is simultaneously Nietzsche's old–new spatial representation of the experience of modernity (the death of God and the birth of our being thrown back on to self-making—an impossible task for *men*) in the abyss. For, Derrida writes (1978), "the labyrinth . . . is an abyss; we plunge into the horizontality of a pure surface, which itself represents itself from detour to detour" (p. 69).[12] Space as map, again. The Chora resurrects Heidegger's clearing, where entities can be gathered into a coherent whole and where their being is thereby manifested— "dwelling," "insistent caring"—both the palimpsest and the ground of the "play of time–space" ("play that calls new worlds to life"— Nietzsche).

Therefore, I present a conclusion (more appositely, a preface to a conclusion): These last several chapters, from this perspective, have addressed not so much architecture as geography—the architectural representation of progress (the International Style), destabilizing a world preoccupied with its own decadence and destruction; the postmodern, finding the fissures in the space of a successful, totalizing worldview; and deconstruction, intruding the idea that all space, and the repressions and hierarchies that it masks, is a text unstable and endlessly written and rewritten, in languages both of images and of metaphor.

Table 9.1 would attempt to bring these forms of intrusion into some differentiating focus. It lists a series of oppositions, akin to those of Table 7.1, to contrast the modes of production and representation in the modern movement with those of the main body of postmodernist architecture and urban design and to contrast each in turn with the deconstructionist thrust. Table 9.1 is in fact an extension of Table 7.1 and should be read in conjunction with it. No exalted status is to be accorded these generalities—there would be no shortage of specific cases to cast doubt on the validity of each and every item. The point is that there are real differences between these three bodies of practice and their sustaining ideas: They are not on some sequential progression, from modern movement, to postmodernism, to deconstruction; rather, all three coexist in the present, and each stands in intended opposition to the others. Though, be warned, if deconstruction is to disrupt all dialectical and binary oppositions, as Doel (1992) summarizes its intentions (p. 173), then it can scarcely itself stand as one term in an opposition: It affirms, rather, the interruption to all other terms.

TABLE 9.1. Oppositions: Characteristics of the Modern Movement, Postmodernism, and the Deconstructionist Intent in Architecture and Urban Design

	Modern movement	Postmodernism	Deconstruction
The mode of production	Auratic (the aura of the "great designer")	Antiauratic; designers frequently sharing the design task	Multivoiced; authorship and authority denied
	Personal, idiosyncratic style	Eclecticism	
The object of representation	The idea of progress, the radical break	Ahistoricism; refusal to privilege present over past	Subversion of orthodoxy; the presence of absence; *différence/différance*
		Past and present as spectacle	Past as origin, future as unknown
	Selective attitude to context	Variously: celebration of context (Venturi, Graves) and eschewing of context (neorationalists, classicism)	Unmasking of context
The means of representation	Direct signification (of progress, new technology, the universal)	Double coding, ambiguity, irony	Text against text; a counterposing of languages
	Favoring the meaning of the signified	Favoring the material of the signifier	No favoring, privileging, or hierarchy

	Modern movement	Postmodernism	Deconstruction
The means of representation (*cont.*)	Preoccupied with the universal; eschewing the vernacular, the local	Frequently celebrating the vernacular	
	Preoccupied with space	Preoccupied with surface; spectacle	Preoccupied with spatial representation of time
	Continuity	Sharp juxtaposition, interruption	Dislocation
	Design from the inside out	Design from the exterior space to the inside	Design by subtraction
	Preoccupied with simplicity	Preoccupied with complexity	
	Differentiation and articulation of functions; zoning	Mixing, overlapping of functions	
The relations of representation	Design controlled by relatively autonomous "great designers"	Design controlled/conditioned by market research, marketing consultants	Undermining all assumptions about author–reader relations
	Universalist coding	Popular, democratic coding	Elitist; dependent on a "first" text; double reading

CHAPTER 10

Conclusion: New Geography

All the visible universe is nothing but a shop
of images and signs.

> —CHARLES BAUDELAIRE, quoted
> in Walter Benjamin,
> Gessamelte Schriften:
> Das Passagen-Werk
> (Vol. 5, 1982, p. 313)

The Paris of Baudelaire's poems is a submerged city,
more submarine than subterranean. The chthonic
elements of the city—its topographical formation, the
old deserted bed of the Seine—doubtless left their
impression on his work. Yet what is decisive in
Baudelaire's "deathly idyll" of the city is a social,
modern substratum. Modernity is the main accent in
his poetry. . . . It is precisely modernity that is
always quoting primeval history. This happens here
through the ambiguity attending the social
relationships and products of this epoch. Ambiguity is
the pictorial image of dialectics, the law of dialectics
seen at a standstill.

> —WALTER BENJAMIN, Reflections:
> Essays, Aphorisms,
> Autobiographical Writings
> (1978, p. 157)

Method of this work: literary montage. I have
nothing to say, only to show.

> —WALTER BENJAMIN, Gessamelte
> Schriften: Das Passagen-Werk
> (Vol. 5, 1982, p. 574)

Geography is concerned with the reading and picturing of space. A "postmodern," nontotalizing geography is going to acknowledge its task as the breaking open of that reading for each person—to enable each to see space through the eyes of others, however darkly. One part of the reading of space is critical and analytical; the other part is affective. The experience of space is of both kinds, variously counterposed and intermingled. And just as geography is about that reading of the experience of space, so architectural and urban design is about its representation (as, frequently, is painting, poetry, song, etc.).

The book will have two conclusions, of which this is the first. It is to ask, How are we to approach the (geographical) reading of space when not only the voices are counterposed and intermingled (Derrida's philosophical and poetic–rational discourse and literary, creative discourse), but also the languages (the "first" of ordinary speech and writing, as well as Eisenman's "second" of architectural expression and architecture-as-text)? More specifically, How are we to open the reading of space to the insights, expressions, and conscious counterpositions of space of the architects and urban designers? And, How do we show the geographers that architecture and urban design are a proper object of their work? (Painting and poetry are certainly no less so, but that must be for another time.)

The task is to be viewed as one of exposing text to text, at both the level of "different voices" and that of "different languages." Certainly there is something of a model in the Eisenman–Derrida use of texts to erode each other: the concern with origins, exposure of the commodity nature of space, the textual landscape. This "method" of deconstruction is occasionally referred to as "design by analysis rather than synthesis." But as analysis, what the deconstructionists are doing is political in only the most abstracted way, in clear contradistinction to the explicit political consciousness of the constructivists, who stand as apparent models. With Eisenman and company, the "second language" fails to invoke a political critique beyond the "end of progress": We are left to wonder what a feminist deconstructive design—and, hence, the contours of a feminist space—might be like or what might be a space to unmask racist assumptions and practices or how any such endeavors might be represented.

There is an earlier and far more politically savage approach to viewing space as multivoiced cacophony, layered images, a "complicated tissue of events," in the work of Walter Benjamin. The never-completed *Passagen-Werk*, the Arcades Project, was to address ways of seeing—reading—the historical space of the streets and passages of Paris in the nineteenth century (the "arcades" that we entered for a moment in Chapter 3). The method was to be a juxtaposition of "dialectical images" ("I have nothing to say, only to show"); and because of it, Benjamin has become something of a cult figure for grand-theory-eschewing postmodernists. However, Susan Buck-Morss argues that there were clear "centers of gravity" intended in the massive collection that Benjamin left as the raw material for these images and that these imply a very sharp theoretical focus indeed: certainly surrealist in its method, but not postmodern in the sense of eschewing metanarratives!

It seems from the *Passagen-Werk* collection, meticulously edited by Rolf Tiedemann and eventually published in 1982, that the projected book would be in six parts, each juxtaposing a historical individual (as representative of some ruptural break in the way of viewing nineteenth-century "reality"), with a historically novel phenomenon and its images. So there were "Fourier or the Arcades" (the too-early, anticipatory images of modern architecture), "Daguerre or the Dioramas" (the too-early anticipations of photography, film, and television), "Grandville or the World Expositions" (the too-early precursors of the commodity's slippage to pure image), "Louis Philippe or the Interior" (the dust of the bourgeois era obscuring the traces of its own origins, even of revolution), "Baudelaire or the Streets of Paris" (the prefigurement of the loss of meaning—the desert—of modernity), "Haussmann or the Barricades" (the dialectical tension between obliterating the past and actualizing its potential).

However, in *The Dialectics of Seeing: Walter Benjamin and the Arcades Project* (1989), Buck-Morss suggests that there are four more fundamental "ways of seeing" the city, consistent with Benjamin's approach to this enterprise and underlying the six dialectical oppositions of ideas and images. These ways of seeing are "image spheres" that arise from the intersections of *myth*, *nature*, and *history*. The first image is "Natural History: Fossil," the world of industrial objects viewed as fossils, the trace of living history that can be read from the surface of the surviving objects. It is the image in which the origin of the present can be found. Then there is "Mythic History: Fetish," or progress as fetish, a reading to unmask "progress" as the fetishization of the modern experience of time. The third is "Mythic Nature: Wish Image," where the reading is of the city as a text that records the dialectic and the collision (in what Benjamin calls "collective wish images") of past dreams and new technological potential. It is the dangerous field of architectural and urban visions. Fourth is "Historical Nature: Ruin," or the city as ruin, the counterpart (even antidote) to all visions and utopias.

The intention at this point is to take these four ways of critically reading the cacophony of the city (the "shop of images and signs") and, through them, to see again the insights into the present experience of space, time, and the self that were reviewed in the previous two chapters—from the postmodernists, the neorationalists, the deconstructionists, and their various antagonists. That reviewing, through an analytical framework explicitly oriented to political consciousness, may yield something akin to the "second language" text that can stand against the "first language" text of already existing critical geography.

1: THE IMAGE IN WHICH THE ORIGIN OF THE PRESENT IS TO BE READ (NATURAL HISTORY)

When Benjamin spoke of the transient historical objects of the nineteenth century as ur-phenomena he meant that they exhibit visibly—and metaphysically as an "authentic synthesis"—their developmental, conceptual essence
—SUSAN BUCK-MORSS, *The Dialectics of Seeing* (1989, p. 73)

The montage of "dialectical images" that the *Passagen-Werk* was to comprise would have appeared like the city itself: image on image, untheorized. The signifieds were to leap immediately from the signifiers, as Goethe's "ur-phenomena": "The highest thing would be to grasp that everything factual is already theory. The blue of the sky reveals to us the fundamental law of chromatics. One would never search for anything behind the phenomena; they themselves are the theory" (Buck-Morss, 1989, p. 72, quoting Simmel, quoting Goethe).[1]

It sounds like textbook geography at its worst—"just let the facts speak!"—and certainly Adorno was wary of the enterprise. But it seems that the text of the *Passagen-Werk* was to be read in a quite special way; "the axiom of the way to avoid mythic thinking," Benjamin informs us, is "no historical category without natural substance; no natural substance without its historical filter" (Benjamin, 1982, p. 1034; Buck-Morss, 1989, p. 59). It is a method whereby pairs of signs from opposite linguistic categories (nature/history in this first "image sphere") are juxtaposed with material referents from the "real world" (butterfly and Hitler, in a photomontage by Marxist–dadaist John Heartfield, admired by Benjamin), and then the switches are crossed (butterfly to history, Hitler to nature). Pairs of linguistic signs and pairs of visual images, juxtaposed but reswitched: The languages are mixed but interrupted, and Nazism is seen to emerge, "naturally," from the accommodations of bourgeois politics.

The *Passagen-Werk* was to help us "read" the city (of the 1930s, as of the 1850s) in this way—to switch the signs across languages, so that space stands as a "fossil," with traces of past economic epochs running through the world of the present. The old arcades, from the very beginning of the bourgeois age, when the *ancien régime* was still a recent memory, had indeed been Aladdin's caves of new, unheard-of commodities (the first great wave of industrial and merchandising innovation), glowing light (the first gaslight), new culinary exotica, and every new fashion at its moment of emergence. By midcentury, the time of Baudelaire, the arcades were already old, decaying, bypassed, haunts variously of an economic marginalia and the demimonde. Buck-Morss (1989) strings Benjamin's notes together as Heartfield-like titles and captions to these and other images: "In the dying arcades, the early industrial commodities have created an antedeluvian landscape, an 'ur-landscape of consumption,' bearing witness to the 'decline of an economic epoch' which the 'dreaming collective' mistakes for 'the decline of the world itself' " (p. 65). The switches are crossed to make the real point: "Benjamin calls the early bourgeois consumers 'the last dinosaurs of Europe,' grown extinct due to the 'natural' evolution of that industrial capitalism which the bourgeoisie itself unleashed" (p. 65). Natural history!

There is a still darker reading of the city as fossil. Denis Hollier (1989) begins his *Against Architecture: The Writings of Georges Bataille* (*La Prise de la Concorde* in its original French version) with an opposition between two ways of seeing the Enlightenment city and architecture—the world of a generation or so before the arcades. The first way of seeing is Foucault's: With *Histoire de la folie*, it is architecture that bears the responsibility for the invention and then the production of madness; and in *Surveiller et punir*, criminality is similarly invented through the design of architectural space. The second way is Bataille's, an architecture of public authority, "orders and interdictions," rather than subtle intervention; it is a reading wherein "great monuments rise up like levees, opposing the logic of majesty and authority to any confusion: Church and State in the form of cathedrals and palaces speak to the multitudes, or silence them." The storming of the Bastille can only be understood as "the people's animosity (animus) against the monuments that are its real masters" (Bataille, 1971, pp. 171–172). All architecture is a prison, but our evolution (natural history!) is to be traced in two ways:

> Bataille's prison derives from an ostentatious, spectacular architecture, an architecture to be seen; whereas Foucault's prison is the embodiment of an architecture that sees, observes and spies, a

vigilant architecture. Bataille's architecture—convex, frontal, ex-
trovert—an architecture that is externally imposing, shares practically no element with that of Foucault, with its insinuating concav-
ity that surrounds, frames, contains and confines for therapeutic or
disciplinary ends. Both are equally effective, but one works because
it draws attention to itself and the other because it does not. (Hollier, 1989, p. x)

The arcades might be seen as more Foucauldian, enticing the
nineteenth century into the new prison of the commodity; but the real
point is that all architecture is both simultaneously: Foucault's insidious space in which the individual is to be transformed *and* Bataille's
emblems of authority (of church, state, capital, the male, etc.). In such
a reading, Benjamin's crossed switches, of nature with history, are to
deconstruct the formation (production, constitution) of the human
through the mediation of a prison that we ourselves constantly reproduce, operating at two distinct levels.

Georges Bataille (1897–1961) died before structuralism attained
philosophical fashion, yet he is today admired as archetypically poststructuralist. He took part, in the late 1920s, in the dadaist enterprise
of producing an antidictionary: Whereas the function of an orthodox
dictionary is to stabilize language and meaning, the antidictionary was
intended to destabilize language and meaning, to reveal the link between signifier and signified as indeed arbitrary. For the "Dictionnaire
critique," appearing in the journal *Documents* from 1929, Bataille wrote
the entry "Abattoir": The slaughterhouse derives from the temple but
is today cursed and quarantined, hidden away from fine people whose
sensitivities cannot abide their own "unseemliness corresponding . . .
to a pathological need for cleanliness." The photo images juxtaposed
with this "natural history" were of the Abattoir of La Villette. Bataille
also wrote the entry "Musée": The movement is the exact opposite, as
people flee the now-relegated ugliness of slaughterhouses for the redemptive world of museums and their saturating beauty. The image this
time is the Louvre, converted from palace to museum, to replace (with
the help of the slaughter of the guillotine) the king. Each image in a
sense stands to critique the other. Yet they are not just opposite poles—
the monument of attraction and that of repulsion; for what is also
important, suggests Hollier (1989), following Bataille, is the space
between the images; and the ideological problem of this space is the
problem of city planning and of urban design (p. xiii).[2]

To write the "first language" text that can stand against this
space—and thereby unmask the forms of its prison (i.e., of its architecture), the instability of its meanings (the constant slippage within

language and between the "first language" of metaphor and the verbal
utterance, on the one hand, and the "second language" of the visual
and architecture, on the other), and the ideological nature of the space
in-between (urban design)—is the task of geography. But there is
another exploration to be made: to determine whether a *nonimprisoning*
architecture and city space is possible. Hollier (1989) observes that, for
Foucault, architectural devices produce subjects, individualizing personal identities. So why cannot the architectural enterprise be reversed,

> leading against the grain to some space before the constitution of
> the subject, before the institutionalization of subjectivity? An archi-
> tecture that, instead of localizing madness, would open up a space
> anterior to the division between madness and reason; . . . a space
> from before the subject, from before meaning; the subjective, ase-
> mantic space of an unedifying architecture, an architecture that
> would not allow space for the time needed to become a subject. (p.
> xi)

So can there be an architecture against architecture (as distinct
from a form of "critical geography against architecture")—Tschumi's
"architecture against itself"? There is a delicious irony in the fact that
the site of Tschumi's assault—architecture storming itself to dismantle
the very idea of "meaning," as Bataille's mob storming the Bastille
would dismantle the very idea of monument—turns out to be the very
site of Bataille's Abattoir de la Villette.[3] That is also to be the site of
Eisenman's intended reinvention of architecture in the *Choral Works*
garden, as it was the site of Ledoux's Enlightenment reinvention of
architecture in the *Barrage de la Villette*.

There are various present forms of an architecture that would
storm the imprisoning realm of architecture itself. So we have the
purposively dialetical intent in that Foucauldian neorationalism of
Aldo Rossi: the search for a space of heightened recognition of the
origins of cultural rootedness and meaning. (The anomaly is that Rossi
always ends up replacing a prison of envelopment—the world of commodities—with one of monuments.) With Eisenman and the turn to
excavation as urban design (though excavation that reveals the *absence*
of the past rather than its presence—the fossil revealed as imaginary,
fictional) we have more a concern with a postmodern *loss* of meaning
than with Rossi's still-modernist meaning. But the present lesson from
both Rossi and Eisenman is that another, first language text is necessary to comprehend the second: Just as the arcades, great exhibitions,
and Haussmann's boulevards most tellingly yield up their fossil nature

when eroded by Baudelaire's poetry, Rossi's "analogical architecture" needs Foucault's history, and Eisenman only makes sense against a variety of first-language texts (both his own and Derrida's—and, in a sense, Jencks's skeptical demolitions of Eisenman's). A critical, con-sciousness-raising exploration of space in architecture and urban de-sign would seem to be dependent on an equally critical, politically aware countertext that is both analytical ("philosophical," in that earlier, Derridean antinomy) and poetic ("literary") in its voices. That countertext would seem the proper focus of the critical, geographical study of society and space.

2: PROGRESS AS FETISH, MODERNITY AS HELL (MYTHIC HISTORY)

> On the face of that oversize head called earth precisely what is newest doesn't change; . . . this "newest" in all its pieces keeps remaining the same. It constitutes the eternity of Hell and its sadistic craving for innovation. To determine the totality of features in which this "modernity" imprints itself would mean to represent Hell"
>
> —WALTER BENJAMIN, Gessemelte Schriften: Das Passagen-Werk (Vol. 5, 1982, p. 1011)

If the first reading of the city makes the arcades (or abandoned factories or the towers of Manhattan) seem ancient, it is because of the rapidity of technological change—innovation, new commodities, new ways of producing and marketing them, Baudelaire's "transient, the fleeting, the contingent," and new forms of consumption. A second reading reveals that all this "change" is but the surface shifts on the unchanging fetishization of change itself—"hellish repetition" (Buck-Morss, 1989, p. 108). It is the city as phantasmagoria, a world where fashion is the "measure of time," for "fashions are the medicament that is to compen-sate for the fateful effects of forgetting, on a collective scale" (Buck-Morss, 1989, pp. 97–98). "Monotony is nourished by the new" (Ben-jamin); to which Buck-Morss adds: "Hellishly repetitive time—eternal waiting punctuated by a 'discontinuous' sequence of 'interruptions'—constitute the particularly modern form of boredom" (p. 104).

Thus, there are these two images of the space of the city: natural history unmasked as delusion (to Eisenman, as empty!), on the one hand, and modernity and its progress as Hell, on the other. Both images, suggests Buck-Morss (1989), "criticize a mythical assumption as to the nature of history . . . that rapid change is historical progress; the other is the conclusion that the modern is *no* progress" (p.108)—

the myth of the eternal return, nihilism (of Baudelaire, Blanqui, and Nietzsche).[4] These two conceptions of time and history are complementary; they are inescapable oppositions whose critique, we are told, must be directed to yield the "dialectical conception of historical time." Each image of the city, as natural history and as mythic history, is to erode the other. Only through space is time to be understood.

The modern movement in architecture and urban design has been the spatial representation of that belief in progress: The universalization of the fetish is there to be read in the global space of the Corbusian (Miesian, Bauhaus) conquest. With Ronchamp, however—discontinuous, dislocating, "irrational" (the poetic against the philosophical or scientific), and feminine against the masculinity of the modern movement—Le Corbusier breaks the spell, which is why it has always been so disturbing to the architectural imagination. The spell also breaks with Kahn's turn to the mythic in the late 1950s.

The real shift from the fetish, however, comes with the ironic play with fashion itself in postmodern architecture—prototypically with Venturi in the late 1950s, then as a veritable derisive explosion with Graves, Moore, Stern, Jahn, and followers. So, in this (second) reading of the city as the image of fetishized progress, the pastiche of fashion is to be seen as critical of the Hell of fashion. Monotony—the feeling that, however "new," the work has been seen before—is now the very intent of cultural production. This reading also however reveals the paradox of postmodern architecture: Though fashion is mocked, the architects revel in the notoriety of becoming fashionable.

3: PAST AND FUTURE
AS WISH IMAGE (MYTHIC NATURE)

In the dream in which every epoch sees in images the epoch which is to succeed it, the latter appears coupled with elements of pre-history—that is to say of a classless society. The experiences of this society, which have their store-place in the collective unconscious, interact with the new to give birth to the utopias which leave their traces in a thousand configurations of life, from permanent buildings to ephemeral fashions.

—WALTER BENJAMIN, "Paris: The Capital of the Nineteenth Century" (1973, p. 159)

Charles Darwin had undermined the simple opposition between a linear, nonrecurring time of "history" and a cyclical, eternally returning time of nature (and it is this new understanding of "natural history" that directs the gaze to the first of these four images of space). Benjamin constantly was able to view the sphere of culture—of historical phenomena—as if it were nature; and whereas the origin of the present in the traces of "old nature" should be unmasked in that first image (of the natural history of space), the place of "new nature"—our now-possible relationships and responsibilities to external phenomena and technology—is to be sought in the third. It is an image that must, however, critique (erode, deconstruct) the prevailing world of images. For new nature is chronically cloaked in the imagery of the old: Though the arcades were the first architecture in iron and glass (the first artificial materials), they mimicked the cathedrals; photography mimicked painting; industrially produced commodities were made to look hand-made; wrought iron in art nouveau was made to resemble leaves and branches. In our time, production for television mimicked that for the cinema.

Thus, observes Buck-Morss (1989), under archaic masks the potential of *new* nature remained unrecognized: "At the same time these masks express the desire to 'return' to a mythic time when human beings were reconciled with the natural world" (pp. 111–114). Benjamin's claim here is surprising: "To the form of the new means of production that in the beginning is still dominated by the old one (Marx), there correspond in the societal superstructure wish images in which the new is intermingled with the old in fantastic ways" (1982, pp. 1224–1225).[5]

"New nature" is held in its mythic stage, "held back by conventional imagination" and the failure of representation. It seems that here is where the revolutionary rupture is to be sought: How are the images of conventional imagination to be broken open, deconstructed, and new nature given sway? Buck-Morss (1989) makes a distinction: "In nature, the new is mythic, because its potential is not yet realized; in consciousness, the old is mythic, because its desires never were fulfilled" (p. 116). It is the intersection of mythic nature and mythic consciousness that yields the "collective wish images" able to power the revolutionary break. Though "every epoch dreams the one that follows it" (Benjamin, 1973, p. 159, quoting Michelet), this "dream future" is only revolutionary "when dialectically mediated by the material, 'new' nature, the as-yet unimagined forms of which alone have the potential to actualise the collective dream" (Buck-Morss, 1989, p. 117)—*pro*-visions for radical (revolutionary) social practice rather than *pre*-visions of postrevolutionary society.

Although Benjamin (1982) dismisses the nineteenth century's representations of dream futures—"Fashion, like architecture, . . .

stands in the darkness of the lived moment" (p. 497, quoting Ernst Bloch)—presaging a future not yet foreseen, the ruptural break did come, most saliently in the cultural production of Benjamin's own time. While Scheerbart's *Glasarchitektur* of 1914 was seen as still lost in the world of utopias, Le Corbusier in the same year is on the other side of the break—Le Corbusier is master of that dialectical thinking that enables mythic nature and mythic consciousness to intersect and erode each other. Buck-Morss (Benjamin?) juxtaposes the image of the nineteenth-century bourgeois interior ("closed off, draped and dark, musty, and, above all, private") with the sharp, transparent, light-flooded Villa Savoye of Le Corbusier; and Eiffel's wildly decorated iron and glass Paris Exhibition Hall of 1878 is juxtaposed with Gropius and Meyer's Dessau Bauhaus (Buck-Morss, 1989, pp. 297–303).

We can return to the theme of Chapter 5. With both Le Corbusier and the Bauhaus, there is the revolutionary break: We witness the crucible where mythic past comes together with mythic nature ("new nature" held back in conventional imagination), to yield an altogether new language of spatial representation. The myths are demolished before our eyes: The past as dreamworld is revealed for what it is—a classless world, old art and craft, desires never fulfilled; and the dream future is finally seen as the disabling fantasy of either glorified technology or of new technology to mimic the old. But the demolition also shows that the dreamworld of the past was always masking the collective desire for a genuinely better and specifiable—representable—future and that in "new nature" are the now-possible relationships to external phenomena and technology to enable that desire to be realized, by yielding the requisite new languages in which new spatial experience (*achievable* dreams) is to be represented.

Benjamin's is a subtler idea of dialectical oppositions in revolutionary rupture than that suggested by Lenin—"between that which is old, that which is directed at the destruction of what is old and a striving of the most abstract kind for that which is new, which must be so new as not to contain even a grain of the old." Against Lenin, "that which is new" is forged out of "mythic dream states" (the unrealized past, and containing a great deal of the old—albeit the old suppressed by the power relations of the present, the dreamed past against the "real" past) and "mythic new nature" (which must somehow be excavated from the myths and ideological baggage of the present and the most recent past).

The space of the city holds, as residue within it, the images of past dreams and of mythic nature, as well as the images of the forging of these to new reality—the evidence of the revolutionary breaks themselves (early Le Corbusier, the Dessau Bauhaus, the early houses of

Frank Lloyd Wright, etc.), which may in turn lodge in the imagination as the still-unfulfilled dreams of yet a further generation, to await yet another intersection with yet another state of new nature, and thus the forging of the *next* new image of a possible space of human life. To read these interplays of images is the focus of the geographical imagination; the layerings (Eisenman, Derrida) are not to be arbitrary.

There is another lesson to be drawn from Lenin's observation of the birth of "great revolutions": Whereas the defense of the old, the first term in the contradiction, may be located in the sphere of economic relations (as the defense of prevailing material interests) and whereas the endeavor to destroy what is old (the second term) can similarly be attributed to the economic societal base, at least in capitalism, the forging of the idea of the new is clearly to be viewed as occurring in the superstructural realm of cultural practices and relations. Benjamin, for his part, describes a dialectical process in the cultural superstructure separate from that in the economic base and declares that it is *this* process that makes possible "the transition to a socialist society"—so much for "last instance" determinism of the economic! That dialectic, we have seen, is the play between the imagination (of the collective? of the forging, radical individual?) and the productive potential of still-uncomprehended new nature. And as Buck-Morss comments (1989), it is a dialectic that develops not by attempting to *bury* a dead past, but by reenervating it: "For if future history is not determined and thus its forms are still unknown, if consciousness cannot transcend the horizons of its sociohistorical context, then where else *but* to the dead past can imagination turn in order to conceptualize a world that is 'not-yet?'" (1989, p. 124). It is to redeem the old rather than to respect it or yearn for it.

The curious historicism of the 1980s and 1990s is instructive if we accept the Benjamin lessons as hypothesis. Thus, Venturi, Graves, Moore, Stern, and assorted colleagues are not yet postmodern (representing the experience that follows the death of the modern) but *anticipatory of the postmodern*. The forms are of the past, albeit in shifted contexts. It is hard to recognize new nature in this—new relationships and responsibilities to external phenomena and technology. One of the files of the *Passagen-Werk* material is titled "Daumier"; it collects images that unmask the neoclassicism of the nineteenth century—and, by implication, all neoclassicisms—as a peculiarly bourgeois form of pretension (such an unmasking being the savage objective of artist Honoré Daumier). It seems as if Graves and company, with virtually all the "leading" practitioners of Charles Jenck's preferred postmodern classicism, are ultimately supportive of presently prevailing relations of power and are therefore bourgeois, even though they may well be attempting to represent some aspects of a "new" experience of space, time, and self.[6] With the deconstructionists, the citing is more distanced from the sources; and for the most part, the forms, the textures, and the preoccupations with dislocation, discontinuity, absence, and intertextuality are more of an affront to bourgeois susceptibilities. By the time we get to Koolhaas (certainly in his La Villette entry), Tschumi, and Eisenman, there are images of a possible space to challenge myths about both past and future. With Eisenman there is also the representation of *the city as ruin.*

4: COMMODITY SOCIETY CAPTURED IN THE IMAGE OF THE RUIN (HISTORICAL NATURE)

History, in everything it displays that was from the beginning untimely, sorrowful, unsuccessful, expresses itself in a face—no, in a skull . . . it articulates as a riddle, the nature not only of human existence pure and simple, but of the biological historicity of an individual in this, the figure of its greatest natural decay.

—WALTER BENJAMIN, *The Origin of German Tragic Drama* (1977, p. 343)

The ruin is antidote to the dream. One of the most powerful of the *Passagen-Werk* images is a picture by Paul Klee (and owned by Benjamin) of "Angelus Novus." To Benjamin it is the "Angel of History" rather than of the new: He seems to stare horrified toward the past (us, the readers) and to recoil, moving backward into the future.[7] So what does he see? Instead of the chain of progress, it is "one single catastrophe which relentlessly piles wreckage upon wreckage, and hurls them before his feet." It is a storm from the Paradise of dreams and past wish-images, which "drives him irresistibly into the future to which his back is turned, while the pile of debris before him grows toward the sky. That which we call progress is this storm" (Benjamin, 1972, pp. 697–698).

Buck-Morss quotes the angel to illuminate the fetish of progress—the second of the images to be read from the city. But it equally critiques the fourth: Those ruins piled all around are the traces of past dreams. History is to be seen, not as progress, but as the destruction of material nature.

Benjamin was preoccupied with the idea of baroque allegory, wherein failed, decaying, chaotic nature—entropic and melancholic—

stands as "emblem" (a "montage of visual image and linguistic sign") for history.[8] Nature is the representation of all human failure and of the inevitability of human death and destruction. To Benjamin, the quintessential poet of modernity was Charles Baudelaire; and Baudelaire was paradoxically an allegorical poet, reviving an antique representational mode. This grafting of old onto new was problematic, and it is symptomatic of the difficulty that over twenty percent of the *Passagen-Werk* material constitutes the file on Baudelaire. For allegory was a mode of representation peculiar to periods of prolonged war and destruction—a turning away in horror from the world of chaos and decay and, instead, the search for redemption in "the text" (books are not subject to such ruin as cities and nature) and in the human soul (to "rise above base nature"); but Baudelaire's was not such a time of destruction and despair but one of hope, material abundance, and indeed "progress." So there is something of a discontinuity or interruption to be explained.

Baudelaire's text *(Les Fleurs du mal)* reveals the interweaving of the image of women commodified (in prostitution, decoration, fashion), traces of the final emptiness of death, and the streets in which these erosions take place. Observes Benjamin (1978), "What is unique in Baudelaire's poetry is that the image[s] of women and death are permeated by a third, that of Paris" (p. 157). It is an altogether new experience of "destruction and despair," a world of ruins: "The devaluation of the world of objects within allegory is outdone within the world of objects itself by the commodity" (Benjamin, 1972, p. 660).

What is destroyed by the commodity is the use-value of objects (Marx); the human labor in the objects' production for use-value is obliterated by their becoming mere signs: Objects no longer count for themselves but for how they are priced. The poems describe the city as values lost and dreams destroyed, and the human experience is one of despair and emptiness—the loss of meaning. The nineteenth-century city of which Baudelaire wrote represented the seeming climactic commodification of everyday life: the final ruin and destruction of a world once rich with meaning and value—and, hence, the melancholy of modernity, the hollowness of the commodity. Baudelaire's text is set the task to deconstruct this world: "All the visible universe is nothing but a shop of images and signs" (a century and more before Baudrillard!).[9]

It would seem that Benjamin's reading of the space of the city as allegory was, however, colored through another filter—that of dadaism as a rejection of the commodity form. In the dadaist "provocations, demonstrations and defiances," the deconstructing image was neither the skull as emblem of death and destruction nor the prostitute as emblem of the commodity, but the everyday object out of context, its meaning (like the gaze of the prostitute) hollowed out. If Graves and company present the dream as still backward looking and if Koolhaas, Tschumi, Eisenman, and colleagues confront with something that may be nearer to the revolutionary break (both representations of that third image sphere—past and future as wish image), then it is in the dadaist junk-as-architecture of Gehry that the antidote is presented (the fourth image). The melancholic element of allegory is, however, more likely to be found in the positive representation of absence—in the hollowed-out *space* of deconstructionists like Hadid and Eisenman or in the "architecture against itself" of Tschumi.

| THE GEOGRAPHICAL IMAGINATION

Although Buck-Morss's schema of "image spheres" has been used here, the point to be made is independent of it. For the idea of *dialectical images* emerges equally clearly from Benjamin's projected work *and* from Buck-Morss's ventriloquation of Benjamin's voice. The idea illuminates the significance of architectural production as residing in its two possible roles: Either it augments the obfuscating cacophony of images pervading everyday life, as it reinforces the instrumentalizing, commodity-dominated, man's world of modernity, or it stands against those images. The latter—an architecture to stand against the space of everyday experience—would show us, as if for the first time, the origins of the present (preeminent in all of Benjamin's intended chapter groupings), the fetish of progress and the destruction of "old nature" ("Grandville or the World Expositions"), the intersections of an unfulfilled past with the "new nature" of emergent technologies and new responsibilities to the external world ("Fourier or the Arcades," "Daguerre or the Dioramas"), and the erosion of real life by the commodity ("Baudelaire or the Streets of Paris").

The attempts in architecture and urban design to find this space of erosion are profoundly revealing of its opposite: the vast diversity of spaces that constitute the prisons of the present, both Foucault's enveloping space and Bataille's monuments of attraction and repulsion—the spatial worlds of both ourselves and unknowable "others." The search also reveals the resistance of the prisons and of the practices that continually reconstitute them. It would seem that the task of a critical, deconstructive, postmodern geography is twofold: first, to stand against this dialectical mounting of images, as a "first language" countertext to the "second (architectural) language" texts of the prison and its intended deconstruction; second, to record the processes of mutual erosion of images—the masking, unmasking, remasking, and so on, of origins, of the fetish of progress and destruction of nature, of "new nature" intersecting the dreams of an unfulfilled past, and of the corroding nature of the commodity form. Benjamin's work may have been the appropriate model for such an enterprise. But it was never written.

CHAPTER 11 | # The Philosophical Discourse of Modernity versus Postmodernity

The project of modernity formulated in the 18th century by the philosophers of the Enlightenment consisted in their efforts to develop objective science, universal morality and law, and autonomous art according to their inner logic. At the same time, this project intended to release the cognitive potentials of each of these domains from their esoteric forms . . . to utilize this accumulation of specialized culture for the enrichment of everyday life—that is to say for the rational organization of everyday social life.

—JÜRGEN HABERMAS, "Modernity: An Incomplete Project" (1985b, p. 9)

The present chapter will take the form of three essays, albeit interweaving, on the rational (modernity), the dilemma of the prerational (postmodernity), and nature. Where is emancipation to be found? Certainly *not* in Habermas's extolled rationality, responds Jean-François Lyotard (1984): Rather, "The answer is: Let us wage a war on totality; let us be witnesses to the unpresentable; let us activate the differences and save the honor of the name" (p. 82).

Rorty (1985) summarizes a celebrated debate: "For Habermas, the problem posed by 'incredulity towards metanarratives' [Lyotard] is that unmasking only makes sense if we 'preserve at least one standard for

[the] explanation of the corruption of *all* reasonable standards' " (p. 161).

Much of the present philosophical discourse comes down to that question of emancipation, whether the focus of philosophy is to be the perfection of human *reason*, or the experience of *being*—what it is like to be human. (In the last analysis, Derridean deconstruction is about the mutually illuminating juxtaposition of these two experiences of the human.) All critical social theory concerns the choice of emancipatory path (Marx), and here the dilemma of philosophy translates to a more specific debate. Simply stated, Is human emancipation and fulfillment to be achieved through the triumph of Enlightenment reason or through the acceptance of being, ease in the presence of diversity and the experience of others, and the poetic imagination? It is Habermas's "completion of the project of modernity" versus Lyotard's war on totalizing visions, his "incredulity towards metanarratives."[1]

The debate on the design of space (postmodern vs. deconstruction vs. late modern, in all their transformations) is in turn swept up in this broader question of emancipatory paths. So much so, in fact, that the philosophical and architectural discourses are now virtually inseparable—observe, for example, their seemingly necessary interlacing in Margaret Rose's 1991 exploration entitled *The Post-Modern and the Post-Industrial*. Nevertheless, in the next several pages the debates will be prized apart, to privilege the philosophical as context for considering the architectural realm in the emancipatory enterprise. It is a privileging that will subsequently need to be relaxed. The architectural realm, it seems, is equally context for the philosophical.

HABERMAS, AND THE PROJECT OF MODERNITY

To return to a theme of Chapter 1: Habermas characterizes the Enlightenment—the birth of the modern age—as the revolutionary advance of reason in the world of human action. That advance occurred on two levels. The first was the cultural, where the separation of that previously undifferentiated "substantive reason expressed in religion and metaphysics" into the increasingly autonomous fields of "objective science, universal morality and law, and autonomous art" enabled the progress of modern specialization—the explosive "release of the cognitive potentials"! The downside of this extraordinary advance was, however, the separation of the realms of experts from everyday life, as well as from each other. Human emancipation will have something to do with reappropriating these fields of experts—consigning the academics!

The other level at which rationalization has transformed society, in the course of modernity, has been institutional, to do with the ways in which the different actions of people are integrated. Habermas argues that modern societies have "uncoupled" a variety of aspects of material reproduction from the realm of everyday life and have handed them over to two specialized institutions: the "formal" economy and the state. There is, however, a great difference in the ways in which these realms—of everyday life and of economy and state—are integrated. The former, that world of everyday experience (the "life-world"), Habermas sees as *socially integrated*, whereby the various agents (e.g., members of a family) coordinate their actions according to some intersubjective consensus about norms or values or motives. It is a consensus that may be implicit—"normatively regulated," perhaps hidden, masked—or explicitly negotiated through "communicative action." On the other hand, the "system-world," of formal economy and legal–bureaucratic state, is *system integrated*, whereby actions are coordinated by the functional interdependence of their consequences, even though each individual act is determined by the self-interest of the actor. Here, too, Habermas distinguishes between two forms of action, though both come under the category of instrumental action. The first is "teleological action": There is a goal to achieve some given end by a wise choice of means; and "the central concept is that of a *decision* among alternative choices of action, with a view to a realization of an end, guided by maxims, and based on an interpretation of the situation" (Habermas, 1984, p. 85). The second is "dramaturgical action," oriented to achieve a goal through the projection of an image or impression of the actor, "more or less purposefully disclosing his subjectivity"; it is not so much "spontaneous expressive behaviour [as] stylizing the expression of one's own experience with a view to the audience" (p. 36). (And it is the form of action that would seem to characterize artistic production in architecture and urban design.)

So the progressive uncoupling of aspects of *material* reproduction, from life-world to formal economy and legal–bureaucratic state in modernity (education, health, conflict resolution, etc., and, increasingly, the production of the environment of everyday life), has marked an explosive expansion of instrumental rationality and action in the world, in an invasive capitalist economy, in bureaucratic organization, and in professionalized empirical science. It is what Habermas refers to as the system-world colonization of the world of everyday lived experience. That latter realm, however, remains the locale for *symbolic* reproduction—maintaining the linguistic and related norms in which are founded individual and social identity, motivation and meaning, and worldview (they are, in the final analysis, the same thing), as well as the linguistic skills of communicative rationality and action. But here, too, universalizing, instrumental rationality invades, as the world of the commodity, and its architectural expression in the language of the International Style and succeeding variants, erodes local culture. Rather than a utopia of rationality, modernity seems to have promised Weber's "iron cage"; it is what Horkheimer and Adorno (1972) termed the "dialectic of Enlightenment."[2]

However, the iron cage was never inevitable, and deliverance is possible. Observes Albrecht Wellmer, following Habermas, the paradox is only apparent: It does not express any internal *logic* (or necessity) of rationalization processes, if we understand rationalization in the broad sense argued by Habermas.[3] Rather, Wellmer (1981) insists that we speak of *selective* rationalization, where "the selective character of this process may be *explained* by the peculiar restrictions put upon communicative rationalisation by the boundary conditions and the dynamics of a capitalist process of production" (p. 56; Wellmer refers to Habermas, 1981, p. 485).

There was no logical or historical *necessity* for systemic imperatives to destroy the life-world: There *are* alternatives. Indeed, Bernstein (1985) sees this conclusion of the *selectivity* of rationalization processes as the real payoff of Habermas's reconstruction of social theory grounded in a theory of rationality and as Habermas's "most important substantive sociological claim" (p. 23). Again, Wellmer's (1985) excellent summary can be quoted.

> It is precisely in this sense that Habermas reinterprets Marx's idea of an emancipated society: in an emancipated society the life-world would no longer be subjected to the imperatives of system maintenance; a rationalised life-world would rather subject the systemic mechanisms to the needs of the associated individuals. Only then, to put it in Marx's terms, would the dependence of the "superstructure" on the "base"—i.e. the dependence of the life-world on the system—come to an end. (p. 57)

Or, in Althusser's terms, the economic level of social interaction would cease to be determinative, even "in the last instance." To Habermas, accordingly, the path to human emancipation must embrace a reinvestment in the richness of everyday life—in communicative rationality and action to counteract an instrumental rationality "gone rogue"; as corollaries, to redress the uneven development between the forces and relations of production and between the forces and relations of communication. The project of Enlightenment rationality—that is, of modernity—is to be completed. It is an exhortation, however, that has been far from universally echoed, and two critiques of it especially demand attention. One forces a reformulation of the argument; the other would compel its rejection. First, the reformulation.

| THE GENDER QUESTION

In "What's Critical about Critical Theory? The Case of Habermas and Gender," Nancy Fraser (1991) seeks to unmask the "unthematized gender subtext" that lies beneath the more explicit text of Habermas's theory. Crucially, from a feminist perspective, that idea of the world of everyday experience (home, neighborhood) as the realm of socially integrated action, while the system-world of formal economy and state is the domain of system integrated, instrumentally rational action, just does not ring true. The real world is not so black and white. For one thing, the archetypal institution of the sphere of the everyday, the nuclear family, is *not* simply a domain of consensually regulated behavior but is permeated with money economy, commodification, power and coercion. It is *not* (yet?) the model of communicative rationality and action to motivate an emancipatory vision.

The first step to uncovering that subtext is to return, more carefully, to Habermas's account of the institutional fracturing of modernity. In the sphere of the life-world, that antique mélange of tribe, clan, and extended family slowly gave way to two new institutions that specialize in symbolic reproduction and that are socially integrated: the "private" nuclear family and the "public" space of political deliberation (a focus of the Kriers' resought public realm). These stand opposite, as it were, to the system-world institutions of "private" official economy and "public" state. These institutions of the life-world are connected to those of the system through the media of the four roles that humans must play in modern society: the roles of *worker* and *consumer*, linking family to formal economic sphere, and *citizen* and (more recently) *client*, linking our political life to the state and its practices. And it is via these roles that various aspects of material reproduction (and, somewhat pathologically, alleges Habermas, of symbolic reproduction as well) have been hived off from life-world to system.[4] Meanwhile, whereas the direction of change in the life-world has been toward greater differentiation between nuclear family and public political life, in the system-world the drift has been toward increasing overlap between economy and state, with each swept up in the crises of the other.

We have, therefore, a model that can represent *two* distinct but interrelated private/public separations—one at the level of everyday life (family and the space of political participation) and the other at that of "systems" (the official, private-sector, capitalist economy, and the state)—and that can highlight the linking social roles through which the iron cage descends and, counteractively, through which emancipation would presumably be sought (see Figure 11.1).

However, suggests Fraser, the real explanatory power of the model only looms when those four roles are unmasked and the gender subtext is laid bare. Take the role of worker. It is masculine, in male-dominated capitalist societies. This masculine-oriented role underlies the long struggle for a "family wage," conceived not as a payment for labor but as the "necessary" payment to a male worker to support his economically dependent wife and children. In turn, such a role legitimizes wage inequality for women and men. And it is, profoundly, spatially reinforced: The man departs each day for the place of paid work, the tough

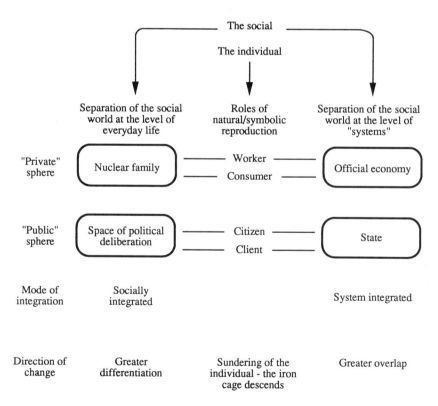

FIGURE 11.1. The fracturing of the social world and the fracturing of the individual (after Habermas, 1984; Fraser, 1991).

"real" world, to return each evening to the comfort and tranquility that is his due and to the good woman whose pleasure it is to give it to him. Fraser (1991) quotes Carol Pateman to the effect that "it is not that women are absent from the paid workplace; it's rather that they are present differently"—as "service workers" (feminized and often sexualized), in the "helping professions," as part-time workers, "working wives" or "working mothers" or "supplementary earners" (p. 261).

In contrast, the role of consumer is feminine in its subtext: The work of purchasing and production of goods and services for household consumption is "rightly" that of women; when men do it, it is newsworthy. It is *unpaid* work; and although the goods and services produced are traded (you can also eat in restaurants, sleep in hotels), they are for the most part unrecognized in the accounting of a nation's production. Again, it is a subtext written partly in the language of urban meaning. The department store, for the most part, directs its appeal to women; the shopping mall entirely so. It is Baudelaire's universe become "but a shop of images and signs," Buck-Morss's fourth image sphere, of commodity society as ruin, Baudrillard's further view of that society corrupted to the "obscenity" of the universe of communication without message. Even more pervasive is its endless writing and rewriting in the home and its hypersimulations in advertising, soapies, and lifestyles of the rich and famous. (But this question of the space of the consumption role goes well beyond Fraser's argument. We will need to return to it.)

Also gendered is the subtext underlying the role of citizen, which links the public life-world sphere of political participation to the public system of the bureaucratic state. The late enfranchisement of women, states Fraser, is merely a symptom of the profoundest of political oppressions: the persistent invalidation of the "voice" of women, in the Bakhtinian sense. Habermas's argument is that citizenship entails participation in political debate and in the formation of public opinion and depends on the ability to have one's voice heard and consent acknowledged. But these are systematically denied to women: In too many cultures women are legally subject to their husbands; the male speaks for the family; and a woman's "no" can be misread, even in law, as a "yes" (witness the ambivalence of the legal tests of rape!). And if women insist that their voices be heard as "male" voices, they are labeled as unfeminine and as not representative of women's "real" views.

Fraser adds another aspect to this citizenship role: Soldiering—the defense of those who allegedly cannot defend themselves (women, children, the elderly) *and* of capital and the state—is clearly written into our assumptions of masculinity. The effect is for the dissonance between femininity and citizenship to be even further reinforced—

here Fraser is quoting Judith Stiehm. Omitted from these arguments however is the mythic (and pathological) extension of this role; for soldiering legitimizes violence and equates it with "being a man." Both city and countryside are progressively appropriated and brutalized, leaving little more than the home and the shopping mall as the domain of women, until violence in the home leaves only the last.

If the role of citizen is masculine, then the newer, still-emerging role of client—that other link between life-world and state—is overwhelmingly feminine in its subtext. Welfare systems tend to be internally gendered to comprise distinctive programs: "masculine" ones oriented to workforce participation and compensation for unemployment; and "feminine" ones designed to support "defective" households (notably those without a male breadwinner—almost exclusively women and their children). Those persons in the latter programs, alleges Fraser (1991), are typically stigmatized, subjected to surveillance, bureaucratically harassed, and excluded from markets both as workers and as consumers (p. 267).

There is an interim conclusion from this rereading of Habermas that is pivotal to the debate on emancipatory paths:

> A gender-sensitive reading of these [linking roles] reveals the thoroughly multidirectional character of social motion in classical capitalism. It gives the lie to the orthodox marxist assumption that all or most significant causal influence runs from the (official) economy to the family and not vice versa. It shows that gender norms structure paid work, state administration and political participation. (Fraser, 1991, p. 264)

Putting aside the narrow equating of the economic sphere of human interaction with the "official" economy, Fraser's point stands. Economic relations, including the relations of production, are as much structured in gender conflict as in economic conflict; whereas the progressive commodification and mediatization of all of life may well be "directed," as it were, by (typically male) entrepreneurs, propelled by the imperative of maintaining the rate of profit, functioning for the most part in the "official" economy (so the Marxists are right), yet *what* the entrepreneurs direct and how they direct it is mediated by their understanding of a thoroughly gender-differentiated realm of everyday life (Will it *really* appeal to women? How does it play on ruling fantasies and myths? Can it shift the fashion?), and the Marxists are less than right. Similarly there would seem to be no aspect of political participation that is not constrained by gender relations and the "necessity" of their maintenance.

THE CULTURAL PRODUCTION
OF THE ECONOMIC,
THE POLITICAL, AND THE CULTURAL

At many points in the preceding chapters it has been necessary to suggest the centrality of worldviews to the "trajectory of history" (if such a modernist concept will be allowed). Likewise, there have been conclusions that the coteries of economic relations are sliding into those of signs—the world of the referent (the commodity, the primacy of price) slips into that of the signifier (Baudrillard); the "modern" problem of the exchange of society with external nature (economy) loses preeminence, in postmodernity, to that of society with our own internal nature (meaning, motivation) (Habermas). What Fraser's rereading of Habermas's *Theory of Communicative Action* does is to unmask something of how the economic and political relations of society are socially constructed—more accurately, how the text of worldviews, meanings, and motivations is constantly rewritten—and how that slippage toward the ever-greater centrality of the cultural comes about.

It happens, in short, in Habermas's sphere of symbolic reproduction. And the mechanism is indeed the constant inscription of a text in which gender relations form the most fundamental of subtexts. (Other subtexts relate to the primacy of the instrumental—the goodness of greed—and to the privileging of an atomizing rationality that suppresses other ideas of the true.) So why is the gender subtext so important?

Symbolic reproduction, in modernity, has come to mean the reproduction (and reinforcement) of different voices whose utterances are increasingly, fundamentally dissonant. "At times when I can't go to sleep," says the self-made man Lopahin in *The Cherry Orchard*, "I think: Lord, thou gavest us immense forests, unbounded fields and the widest horizons, and living in the midst of them we should indeed be giants." Madame Ranevskaya rejoins, "You feel the need for giants—They are good only in fairy tales, anywhere else they only frighten us." Carol Gilligan invokes this exchange to begin her exploration of such dissonances, *In a Different Voice* (1982). The old fairy tales, so often, are allegories of the self-making of the giants and heroes: The prince finally achieves separation (typically from the father, sometimes the mother), finds his true identity *as a man*, and so can save and woo the princess. However, fairy tales also tell of female adolescence: The girl's first bleeding is followed by a time of utter passivity; nothing seems ever to happen, until she is awakened from her sleep, "not to conquer the world, but to marry the prince." However, Gilligan (1982) quotes

Bettelheim: In that profound sleep of Sleeping Beauty there is the inner concentration that is the necessary counterpart to the activity of adventure—where the identity of the prince is defined by separation (and only then can he turn to intimacy), the identity of the princess is inwardly and interpersonally defined (p. 13). But this is merely to see the identity of the princess as an adjunct to that of the prince (no more than the superimpositions of Eisenman's Romeo and Juliet manage to represent!), unless of course the inwardness of the feminine can be seen to equal the "real world" of the hero.[5]

Gilligan turns to an argument of Matina Horner: To the two components most logically constituting "achievement motivation"—a motive to approach success and a motive to avoid failure—there might, improbably, be a third: to avoid success. For *women* appear to have a problem with competitive success. This might have something to do with a perceived conflict between success and femininity (a circularity!); but Gilligan suggests that women may instead experience "a heightened perception of the 'other side' of competitive success, that is, the great emotional costs at which success achieved through competition is often gained" (Sassen quoted in Gilligan, 1982, p. 15). For the child who is awakening to the realization that she can eventually bear and nurture another human being, the value of interpersonal bonding and intimacy must surely be different from that of the child to whom that experience will forever be unknown; and competitive success (and the prince's achievement of separation—masculinity) must be at the expense of the real potential of this moral bonding and fulfillment— the other dimension of maturity. "We might on those grounds begin to ask, not why women have conflicts about competitive success, but why men show such readiness to adopt and celebrate a rather narrow vision of success" (Gilligan, 1982, p. 16).

Habermas's instrumental rationality and action begins to look decidedly gender differentiated. But so does communicative action. For Gilligan's argument is at its most disturbing in a reading of the responses of two eleven-year-olds, Jake and Amy, to a posed moral dilemma (from Kohlberg). A man named Heinz considers whether to steal a drug that he cannot afford but without which his wife will die. The two children exhibit fundamentally different approaches to the dilemma. To Jake it is a question of balancing abstract (but opposed) rules and rights; of course Heinz should steal the drug because the higher right should prevail; it is, in Jake's words, "sort of like a math problem with humans" (quoted in Gilligan, 1982, p. 26). It all conforms comfortably with Piaget's theories of developmental psychology, with Kohlberg's trajectory of moral development, and with Habermas's theory of communicative action: Moral–practical action is to be communicatively grounded in universalistic norms. There *is* moral right. Amy, by contrast, seems merely confused, "evasive and unsure": "If he stole the drug," she equivocates, "he might save his wife then, but if he did, he might have to go to jail, and then his wife might get sicker again, and he couldn't get more of the drug" (quoted in Gilligan, 1982, p. 28). No, they really should "just talk it out." Or expose the druggist to the full consequences of the dilemma—after all, isn't his failure of response the initial cause? The interviewer is frustrated by Amy's inability to confront the problem—the equivocation is typically female, and just an instance of the different rates of moral development in males and females.

But Amy's voice, interposes Gilligan, has not been heard. She constructs the dilemma not as a self-contained problem in moral logic, but as one of the development of human relationships, extending through time.

> Both children thus recognize the need for agreement but see it as mediated in different ways—he impersonally through systems of logic and law, she personally through communication in relationship. Just as he relies on the conventions of logic to deduce the solution to this dilemma, assuming these conventions to be shared, so she relies on a process of communication, assuming connection and believing that her voice will be heard. (Gilligan, 1982, p. 29)

The idea of different voices appeals as intuitively plausible (though this is not to assert that a "feminine voice" characterizes the utterances of all women, nor a "masculine voice" those of all men—indeed, it is going to be argued that an emancipatory path lies somewhere "between voices"). It seems too that both forms of moral reasoning can be invoked (*are* invoked!) to communicatively ground the search for moral right—in communicative rationality and action, in Habermas's terms, though only the "masculine" search for universalistic, abstract norms conforms to Habermas's restrictive definition of the project. Moreover, both voices are subvertible—the feminine into inconsequential waffling and Mills and Boon sentimentality, the masculine into unreflective, closed, normative rigidity. Only the masculine ever receives a glow of respectability, however.

It seems that the differences in voices arise in the first years of life (Gilligan gives special weight to the ideas of Nancy Chodorow, 1978). The differences relate overwhelmingly to the fact that women, universally, are responsible for early child nurturing and care. Female identity formation occurs in the context of an ongoing relationship as "mothers tend to experience their daughters as more like, and continuous with, themselves," while sons are experienced more as the "male opposite" and boys define themselves through separation—the fairy tales again (Gilligan, 1982, pp. 7–8). It also seems that these differences underpin that gender subtext (Fraser) that "explains" the roles linking the level of everyday life and that of "systems" (Habermas) and through which the iron cage encloses and, correspondingly, emancipation is to be sought. But it is not just to be sought in the way in which the privileging of one mode of instrumental rationality (seeking success, avoiding failure) and one mode of communicative rationality (the search for universalistic principles) runs through all the roles and processes of present society—suppressing one half of human experience, as it were—hidden behind the masks of everyday speech and writing. For there is also Eisenman's "second language," of architecture the prison (Bataille, Foucault). And whereas in the first language we can just discern the different voices, where do we find them in the second?

DIFFERENT VOICES, DIFFERENT LANGUAGES

What then is this passion [flânerie] which, become a doctrine, has acquired such notable converts, this charterless institution which has formed such a lofty caste of men? Above all, it is a burning need for individuality, contained within the outermost boundaries of social convention. It is a sort of cult of the self, the self that can survive that search for happiness that we seek in others, in women for example; which can even survive that which we call illusions.

—CHARLES BAUDELAIRE, "The Painter of
Contemporary Life" (1860; in P. Pia,
Baudelaire, 1961, pp. 68–69)

If the man who loiters is the flâneur, the loitering woman is a street-walker, "la grande horizontale," the "landscape," signifier of the "virgin forest" of the city, the body of nature.

—SIMON PUGH, "Loitering with Intent: From
Arcadia to the Arcades" (1990, p. 155)

The spaces of modernity are gendered spaces. We need to turn again, as so often, to Paris of the nineteenth century, though to the painters as much as Baudelaire. In those expanding cities of the West—Paris quintessentially—there was throughout the nineteenth century the progressive definition and differentiation of the private and the pub-

lic; and to the former, the private realm of suburb and home, as
Doreen Massey (1991) observes, women were confined ideologically
if not always in practice. The boulevards and cafés, bars and brothels
were for men. But the art of the nineteenth century (that seminal
art—we have come to ignore the jottings and scratchings of women)
was made from the public space, representing the world of that
space—Baudelaire, Manet, Renoir, Toulouse-Lautrec, and the rest.
Massey quotes Pollock (1988) on Manet's *Olympia* and *A Bar in the
Folies-Bergères*:

> How can a woman relate to the viewing positions proposed by
> either of these paintings? Can a woman be offered, in order to be
> denied, imaginary possession of Olympia or the barmaid? Would a
> woman of Manet's class have a familiarity with either of these spaces
> and its exchanges which could be evoked so that the painting's
> modernist job of negation and disruption could be effective. (Pol-
> lock, quoted in Massey, 1991, p. 47)

The experience of modernity, represented to us in the art of modernism, was a male experience.

Massey argues that the city of modernism has been gendered in a
second sense. For this experience of Baudelaire, Manet, and the avant-
garde was essentially the experience of the *flâneur*, the dandy, "the
stroller in the crowd, observing but not observed" (Massey, 1991, p.
47). The idea of the *flâneuse* was impossible: "Respectable" women
could not roam public spaces—both socially constructed propriety and
male violence (that extension of the gendered citizen role) invalidated
it. Moreover, suggests Massey, it was impossible precisely because of the
unidirectionality of the gaze. "The fundamental event of the modern
age," Martin Heidegger declared in 1938, "is the conquest of the world
as picture." In that mastery through representation, "man contends for
the position in which he can be that particular being who gives the
measure and draws up the guidelines for everything that is." Craig
Owens (1985) cites these aphorisms (p. 66) in constructing the argument that, in modernity, vision is the privileged means of access to
certainty and truth. But it is the vision of the flâneur, detached,
objectifying, that dominates the accepted, seminal images of modernism; in turn, the rest of humanity has come to see Western modernity,
for the greater part, through that same eye. Certainly, women painted
and wrote in the modern age, but their paintings typically were of a
different space: home and domestic life, the garden—or in the public
realm, places of family life. And the eye is more immersed than distanced in what is being represented.

There is a third sense, argues Massey, in which that space of the modern city was gendered: The gaze of the flâneur was frequently erotic, and such a reading of space has permeated the present age as "normal."[6] Massey's argument needs, however, to be taken further. For what is represented to us is a *commodified* eroticism (the shift to "the sexual") in those courtesans, whores, barmaids, and questionable figures in the urban landscape. That which defines the very identity of the female—intimacy, relationship, warmth, empathy—is presented as readily accessible in the commodity form. (If that, then everything: Gendering precedes universal commodification.) Simon Pugh (1990) likens the flâneur to the pastoralist, that equally indolent, gentry relict, translating productive countryside as picturesque "landscape" and "sacrificing duty to the love of ease":

> Both attempted to privatise social space by arguing that passive and aloof observation was adequate for a knowledge of social reality, rhapsodising their illusory view of life. Constructed images of paradise or Arcadia purport to offer a subversive reading of capitalism by protesting with "ostentatious composure" (Benjamin) against the production process and against social control. (p. 157)

Both pastoralism and *flânerie* (Arcadia and the arcades), and their celebration and propagation in the art of the avant-garde, harbored a critical, emancipatory intent. But, adds Pugh (1990), "Arcadian idleness is a mockery rather than a critique of exploitative labour and redundancy, both of which are a necessary feature of capitalism. It seems absence of work is offered as the purpose of capitalism, the *promesse de bonheur*, while it is instead the threat that keeps people under control" (p. 157). Modernism, at this level, is a lie, supporting what it purports to critique. The lie is masked because the underpinning subtext—of the (gendered) commodification of nature itself, in Arcadia as in the arcades—is so appealing to men and so accepted by all.

Now the problem is that the purposive production of space, in modernist architecture and urban design, was infused with this vision; and the discourse that arose around it was informed from its viewpoint (but how could it be otherwise!). That the boulevards, plazas, transport interchanges, and "intimate places" of the modern city were designed by men, to be viewed by the latter-day flâneur, now cruising in the cars that destroyed the pedestrian world of his nineteenth-century predecessors, seems a natural enough regression. But the most significant shift in the history of modern architecture relates not to the public but the private realm: Self-conscious, purposive design, and the production

of architectural knowledge at its most reflective have progressively
penetrated from the grandest mansion to the pokiest condominium,
suburbia, the public housing project, local school and library, neighborhood park and shopping mall. That increasingly differentiated and
redefined space, of Habermas's world of everyday life and Massey's
ideological relegation and confinement of women, has had the most
loving of architectural care and most vituperative of debates lavished
upon it. And again it has been fashioned to a vision seen through a
masculine eye, though it is the obverse of the voyeuristic vision of the
flâneur: The idealized woman is to be safely secluded away from the
profane, prying gaze of the public realm, in a space that can seem its
opposite, enveloping and protecting. Architecture as prison: this time
the Foucauldian.

Symbolic reproduction—the reproduction of socially motivating
meaning (Habermas), self-definition (Gilligan), the vision of the good
(Taylor)—occurs through discourse that is actively shaped by two
languages and many voices: We must be able to utter, in the language
of everyday speech, what it is that we live for; and, in that "architectural" language of the representation of self–other–environment relationships, we must be able to imagine, visualize, what life is and can be.
Those meanings are today, in large measure and seemingly increasingly,
normatively secured rather than communicatively negotiated. If we are
to find emancipation, in the Habermasian sense, we must replace
normativity with communicative negotiation. But in what voice are
we to negotiate—by reference to universal principles (lower norms
replaced by higher, more abstract and more universal ones!) or through
that form of intersubjectivity oriented to the construction of meaning
and identity "in relationship" (Waugh, 1989)—the "male" or the "female"? Clearly, through both (though the implications of such an
enterprise are deferred for the moment), for to do otherwise is to deny
one half of what it is to be human. Now in first language there is
somewhere to start: We have discerned something of the difference
between the feminine and the masculine—in the ways in which success is defined and the moral is explicated. In second language there is
only the masculine. We look seemingly in vain for instances of
women's voices and eyes in the production of architectural knowledge;
the briefly heard dialogues of the age of the Russian Revolution show
the rest of history as poignant silence. Perhaps there is a hint of the
"other" viewpoint in women's painting and in "word pictures" in
women's writing. But "mainstream" art criticism has so privileged the
male viewpoint that its complement remains devalued and, thereby,
lost, and its translation to active spatial design remains seemingly
unexplored.

|THE POSTMODERN AS INCREDULITY

> *The strongest, in the epoque of complete nihilism, will not be the most violent, but the person who knows, with the most moderation, how to live the vastest possible multiplicity of positions.*
>
> —Martin Heidegger, quoted in Gianni Vattimo, quoted in Richard Bellamy, "Post-Modernism and the End of History" (1987, p. 730)[7]

From the viewpoint of that skepticism attributed to the "experience of postmodernity"—Lyotard's "incredulity towards metanarratives"—the arguments above would have to appear as irredeemably locked in totalizing, universalistic delusion. Habermas's appeal to universal principles would only be replaced, in feminist theory, by recourse to other, equally universalist arguments (Fraser) or by consensus otherwise secured (Waugh).

The main characteristics of philosophical postmodernism have been sketched in Chapter 1 and further alluded to in the discussion of present culture and society in Chapter 7. There is first the dehistoricizing of experience. There is no longer novelty in novelty, and attention shifts from a linear progression of past-to-present to a multifaceted, ever-changing, ungeneralizable present—the "end of history."[8] Second, the era is marked by that increasing incredulity toward metanarratives—toward the overarching stories, like modernist progress or Marxist economic determinism or the unfolding of reason, that are called down to give meaning to the accounts or "narratives" of human activity with which we are constantly presented and that describe our own day-to-day lives.[9]

The third and most radical trait of philosophical postmodernism has been the rejection of universalistic foundations for human knowledge. Lyotard in particular rejects any idea of universal, rational rules for accepting "the better argument" in disputes over truth, morality, or subjective expressions. Any such validity claim will be internal to a particular discourse and ultimately dependent for its dominance over rival claims on its function relative to prevailing power relations. There can be no external appeal to higher truth or reason; nor should we feel the need to seek it. As well as the "end of history," the new era is therefore also characterized by the experience of the "end of philosophy."

While the "postmodern philosophers" (to Vattimo a contradiction) might reject the (modernist) idea of human emancipation through the unfolding of rationality—the completion of the Enlightenment project, communicative rationality eroding an instrumentalized world—the question of emancipation remains central to the post-modernist discourse. Rather than through the perfection of human reason, emancipation will be achieved through ease in the presence of diversity and "the experience of others" and through the acceptance of being itself. So Lyotard urges an escape from reliance on metanarratives, toward acceptance, instead, of the primary narratives of "real life" on their own terms. We are to "go beyond" that realm of objective universal criteria for truth or morality or aesthetic expressiveness (Habermas)—to "go beyond" metaphysics, replacing it with what Vattimo refers to as a "weak ontology" appropriate to the postmodern world, where being is linked to life, time, and the rhythm of birth and death rather than to those vaster themes of traditional metaphysics. Bellamy (1987) summarizes the Vattimo argument,

> This new ontology is sustained by "weak" categories of thought in contrast to the "strong" categories of dialectics, such as good and evil, master and slave. It seeks no final synthesis to resolve the conflict between opposites, but rather "disarms" (depotenzia) the subject of these violent metaphysical qualities. . . . There can be no final resolution of the subject with its true essence, no final appeal to external referents—the "bare facts" of natural science. All one can do is to refer back to the innumerable narratives or languages within which being is disclosed to us. (p. 730)

Included would be those "architectural" narratives, languages, and voices in which the spatial setting of being—in postmodernity, the Derridean "presence of absence," the Foucauldian "spaces of dispersion"—is represented and disclosed.

The postmodernist critique of modernist rationality has in turn faced the reciprocating onslaught. To continue Richard Bellamy's argument: Regardless of ease with diversity and the experiences of others, material interests will continue to arise and to conflict; so if we cannot appeal to the "force of the better argument," how are we to proceed? There would seem to be only two ways. The first is to turn to some other principle of resolution (the candidate that Bellamy suggests is Rawls's "equality of respect," but it could equally well be some idea of ecological sustainability)—one universalistic form of appeal merely replaces another. The second is to withdraw into a Heideggerian quietism, abjuring any evaluation between different narratives. Though we might be experiencing the "end of history," we cannot however unlearn its lesson that the tolerance of diversity in values and lifestyles is unlikely to be shared by currently dominant interests. For such a tolerance to be shared would again require appeal to some higher interest; and again the medium for such an appeal would seem to be some form of Habermasian communicative action. So we have Rorty's comment that introduced this chapter: Unmasking, for Habermas, does not work unless at least *one* principle of argumentation is preserved by which to explicate the corruption of all others.

The modernist counteroffensive seems, however, to confuse the argument it would reject and to mistake the experience that underlies it.

THE POSTMODERN AND EMANCIPATION

Nothing is fundamental: this is what is interesting in the analysis of society.

—MICHEL FOUCAULT, "Interview with Michel
Foucault on Space, Knowledge
and Power" (1982, p. 18)

But this is not to say that the resolute, unending struggles to unmask and counter all hierarchies and dominations will not be "principled." It is just that principles will not be "fundamental," *essential*—based on the *essence* of human rationality with that finality that Habermas would have. Something of the tough ("antiquietist") thrust of this endeavor is captured in Grosz's (1989) excellent summary of Derridean deconstruction:

> Western metaphysics is structured in terms of binary oppositions or dichotomies. Within this structure the opposed terms are not equally valued: one term occupies the structurally dominant position and takes on the power of defining its opposite or other. The dominant and subordinated terms are simply positive and negative versions of each other, the dominant defining its other by negation. Binary pairs such as good/bad, presence/absence, mind/matter, being/non-being, identity/difference, culture/nature, signifier/signified, speech/writing and man/woman mark virtually all the texts of philosophy, and provide a methodological validation for knowledges in the West. The first term is given the privilege of defining itself and of relegating to the other all that is *not it.* (p. 27)

Deconstruction is the overthrow of all such privileging—the dehierarchizing of all discourses. It is the refusal (to repeat from earlier) to privilege philosophy over literature—over the text—and the referent over the material sign. It is, accordingly, an emancipatory practice, oriented to freeing us from the ultimate prison: the definition of self and of what is knowledge. Continuing Grosz's (1989) summary, "To recognise that identity depends on difference, and that presence relies on absence is to disturb the very structure of knowledges" (p. 27).[10]

To rehear the voice(s) of Vattimo/Bellamy: The deconstructive enterprise may well seek to "disarm" the subject of "violent metaphysical qualities" that would privilege, albeit sometimes unreflectively, good over bad, presence over absence, the masculine over the feminine. Yet the new self-recognition (emancipation) is not attained without "violence": Foucault's endeavors to unmask the links between space, language, and the production of knowledge (the multifarious prisons of modernity and, at another level, the privileging of time over space in understanding the world) inflict the gravest disturbance— and, indeed, violence—on human knowledge itself.

This is why the struggles of feminism are such a fine elucidation of the wider postmodernist enterprise, though nothing is further from the present intention than to see feminist critique as just another facet of the wider struggle—or worse, as some sort of analogy for it. Postmodernism, indeed, can be as male-centered as modernism ever was (see, e.g., Hartsock, 1987; Bondi and Domosh, 1992). The task of asserting the value of the "other experiences" of motivation (to avoid the alienating effect of success, as much as to approach success and to avoid failure), of morality (communicatively in interpersonal relationship, as much as impersonally through systems of logic and law), and of identity (inwardly and interpersonally defined, as equal to being defined through separation) does *not* disarm us of either human motivation, morality, or the search for self-definition. Rather, it reveals (asserts!) the catastrophically simplistic nature of all previous (male-centered) dominant understandings of motivation, morality, and the self. It reasserts communicative rationality, though scarcely as Habermas would have it.

BETWEEN VOICES, BETWEEN LANGUAGES

In *The Archaeology of Knowledge* (1972), Foucault seems to suggest that social life be viewed as played out in "spaces of dispersion," chaotically and heterogeneously, akin to the "systems of dispersion" in which discourse might similarly be analyzed. When, less radically, he adopts a "levels model" to describe the social world, the levels appear as almost arbitrarily named (not the economic, political, and ideological/cultural of Althusser's conception); and any order in the dispersion, like hierarchy, or "last instance" determination, remains still to be discovered. Indeed, as Philo (1992) demonstrates, Foucault does envisage some pattern of places and events—"not chaos but the connectedness of an order that is transient"—and the task of all enquiry is to reveal "the 'local, changing rules' that in particular times and places govern, and in a sense simply *are*, the observable relationships between the many things under study" (p. 150). But these local changing rules are as far as we can go.

It is at the risk of seeming to slip from this tough, Foucauldian, poststructuralist vision, back to an easier, essentializing, grand-theory structuralism (the "Althusserian") that we have to turn to a conclusion clearly reminiscent of the latter; that, for the heterogeneous texts that describe our lives in modernity, there is that underlying *gender* subtext that Nancy Fraser pinpointed. Taking the risk needs defending, and there are three grounds for doing so. First, the conclusion seems every-where to emerge (certainly since the bourgeois revolution of 1789 smashed an effete ancien régime and replaced it with a masculine discourse of virile politics and soldierly virtues, to the tightening exclu-sion of women); so, though "local and changing," the "rules" seem to operate in all locales and at all times in modernity and in postmoder-nity. Second, it is surely inconsistent with a Foucauldian–Derridean position to deny the mind's turn to this rationalist abstraction: That turn is one part of how the human mind works. The task is not to reject it, but to deny it privilege. And third, when the mind does post such an idea—to temporarily organize thought, to focus the deconstructive intent on yet another of the myriad texts describing social life—it yields a mighty insight: In modernity, people really did believe in the autonomy and last instance determination of the economic and in the irrelevance of the gender question, and they acted accordingly; but they were mistaken!

What is being argued here is that any (emancipatory) under-standing of the present requires us to position ourselves between voices (the *theoretical* and the *archaeological*, so to speak—the Althusserian, the Habermasian for that matter, and the Foucauldian!) and between languages (of *philosophy*, with its turn to the abstract and the privileging of human reason, and of *literature* and the unending, poetic searching of all that it is like to be human—the Aristotelian and the Derridean). There is, however, another level at which we need to place ourselves between languages, engaging both, privileging neither. For one of the lessons we get so clearly from Foucault (and increasingly though ever so obliquely, from Derrida) is that real events—the material subject of all philosophy and all literature—occur in real space, not abstracted and theorized, but laden with content:

> The space in which we live, which draws us out of ourselves, in which the erosion of our lives, our times and our history occurs, the space that claws and gnaws at us, is also, in itself, a heterogeneous space. In other words, we do not live in a kind of void, inside of

which we could place individuals and things . . . [but] inside a set of relations that delineates sites which are irreducible to one another and absolutely not superimposable on one another. (Foucault, 1986, p. 23)

These are the "heterotopias" that we encountered earlier; the "erosions" that occur there are of our prejudices, delusions, ideals but also of our disillusionments and negativities (so they are also the places of remotivation and Lenin's "striving of the most abstract kind for that which is new"); and they are specific *places*, "irreducible" and "absolutely not superimposable"—Paris is not Los Angeles, nor your habitat mine. There can be no emancipation without unmasking all linkages between space, knowledge, and power; and deconstructive "discourse" will have to be in both languages in which spatial relations can be represented—that of words and writing (which immediately fragments before our very eyes to those "further" languages of philosophy and of the poetic imagination) and that "second language" of architecture. And as the gender subtext runs through every significant linking role of power and authority that binds capitalist society together (worker, consumer, citizen, client) and through which knowledge and power are formed, so it permeates that spatial "erosion, clawing and gnawing" that underpins the favoring of a narrow, masculine experience—of human motivation, of what constitutes the moral, and of identity.

Now the problem is that the voices in which we speak, in both these languages, are masculine. So how are we to critique, in words and built (or at least buildable) images, a city of signs (Bataille) and of enclosure (Foucault) that is a men's world? It is surely not enough to proceed merely in the "first language," the excellent writing of Roslyn Deutsche, Doreen Massey, and a few others notwithstanding; the "other spaces," the counter image, the remotivating vision of a world rich for men *and* women must also be represented. But the voices of such "utterances" are silent.

| THE RETEMPORALIZING OF SPACE

Deceit is fundamental to the exercise, for emancipation from, and subjugation to, nature are inevitably contradictory.

—JAY APPLETON, *The Experience of Landscape*
(1975, p. 173)

Modernist reinvestment in the potential of human rationality has been the theme of one essay weaving through this chapter; a second has held out the idea of postmodernist defense of difference without hierarchy, and a diversity of worldviews held simultaneously—perhaps only a short step from grasping the nature of paradigm itself.[11] A third essay on possible emancipating paths now needs to be woven through these two.

In its cruder forms, elements of the human–nature dilemma have run through earlier chapters. The problem of how to regulate the exchange of society with external nature—the *learned* centrality of value, economic growth and the fetish of the commodity—is, in Habermas's (modernist) view, the distinguishing characteristic of the modern age: the "metanarrative" of history as learning! And postmodern society, in turn, is seen preeminently as having to face the new problem of how to regulate the exchange of society with our own internal nature—of how, with the collapse of that previously motivating myth of value, economic growth, and the commodity (the terrible recognition of Benjamin's Hell, the return of Nietzsche's abyss), we are to find motivation and meaning.

There is no shortage of answering voices. "Emancipation from nature," Paul Shepard has warned us, was always a chimera: It, rather than its mere symptom in the commodity, is the source of the postmodern emptiness, the palpable "presence of absence," Berman's (1989) "problem of otherness" that accounts for "why the modern world came to an end." Against modernity's appropriation of nature, the answering voices seem to pose three arguments, of which the least problematic must be "the ecological": We must "design *with* nature" (Ian McHarg's call of 1969), and all that will stand in our way are the prevailing interests of a global, capitalist economy and its legitimizing, mechanistic, Cartesian scientific vision and a narrowly constricted, allegedly Judeo-Christian privileging of the human! "The ecological" shades into "deep ecology": We must not just respect the natural world but must see ourselves as just another species occupying it, unprivileged and as expendable as any other.

The idea of landscape, says Denis Cosgrove (1984), is a way of seeing the world (p. 13)—a "cultural image, a pictorial way of representing, structuring or symbolising surroundings" (Cosgrove and Daniels, 1988, p. 1), Heidegger's "conquest of the world as picture." It is modern, a restrictive way of seeing that diminishes "alternative modes of experiencing our relations with nature" (Cosgrove, 1984, p. 269); if we are to be once more immersed in nature using all our senses and finding true humility (emancipation!), we must break free from "landscape," from present modes of representation.[12]

If the task for the "deep ecologist" is to break out of a whole (Enlightenment) way of seeing, experiencing, and appropriating nature, then this too has connotations of escaping from a gendered way of living in the world—to "see the eye" for what it is and, thereby, "to place ourselves between ways of seeing," as it were. But if the experience of nature is gendered, it is also certainly culturally differentiated. Though the minds of cultural "others" remain forever unknowable, *terra incognita*, their representations of nature in painting, poetry, and garden reveal a great deal about the differences. In the Taoist vision, on some voices, one retreats into nature in search of a revelation; the Chinese and the Japanese exhibit an animistic, mystical relationship with nature and would seem to strive for "interpretations of mood and spirit, rather than rendering of visual plastic effects sought in the West" (Rowland, 1965, p. 66).[13] This "mood," and the experience of unity with nature, can come as a flash of instantaneous recognition; and artistic technique would be developed to set it down similarly instantaneously before the vision faded (Rowlands, 1965, p. 100). These Eastern representations clearly reflect a more "immersed" experience of nature than that prevailing in the West, though all are "landscape"— garden, painting, or poetry, as pictorial ways of representing, structuring, or symbolizing surroundings. All are objectifications, though Western ways of objectifying nature are *different* from Eastern—the eye is also ethnocentric.

If the "ecological" is one answering voice to the postmodern void (the world must be remade, redesigned "with nature") and that of "deep ecology" is another (*we* must be remade, *remerged* with nature), then these glimpses of a different, Eastern vision can stand as deconstructive, countervoices against both, like Walter Benjamin's "dialectical images." This is the way in which they are commonly invoked. Yet the Eastern traditions are also suggestive of a third, Western answering voice: Emancipation lies not merely in remerging, but in reenchantment. In the disenchantment that culminated in the ("alleged") Enlightment—Berman's (1984) "division of psychic and material, mind and body, symbolic and literal" (p. 64), and in each duality the privileging of the latter—one-half of the potential of human experience was lost.[14]

LEARNING LANGUAGES, LEARNING VOICES

It is little short of astounding that two much-praised (and praiseworthy) summations at the end of the 1980s dealt so creatively and sensitively with the condition of the postmodern age and its emergence—the dissolution of old certainties, the compression of space and speeding up of time, substance (even the commodity) increasingly eroded by the sign, communication for communication's sake—yet seemed scarcely to notice the environmental question and the shift in the experience of nature. In David Harvey's *The Condition of Postmodernity* (1989) and Edward Soja's *Postmodern Geographies* (1989) there is a virtual blindness to the view of environmental Hell as effect of modernization—the domination of nature—or in turn as context accounting in part for the fall of that ultimate metanarrative, modernist material progress. There is, correspondingly, a blindness to the emergence of the new consciousness of nature of which various facets of the "environmental movement" are symptomatic. Simply, the "postmodern condition" and its experience are not unitary. For many, the void is palpably present, but there are also many for whom it has been filled with a rush, though perhaps more with an immanence (the glimpse of "new nature") than a presence as yet. We would seem indeed to be passing through a paradigm shift; and *anomie*, the normless void, is symptom of the passage.

The critics must also be criticized. Roslyn Deutsche's and Doreen Massey's (both 1991) rejections of Harvey's argument have already been referred to; Massey's also takes Soja to task. The gist is that individual viewpoints—specifically, of the white, male heterosexual—are taken by Harvey as universal (Massey) and that the clamoring of "other voices" and the "valorization of fragmentation and difference" are taken as merely concealing the "spatioeconomic relations that underlie the totality of late capitalist society" (Deutsche, 1991). We have seen how Massey's critique opens up the "other world" of women's experience of urban space; it is but a short further step to that other "difference," of women's and men's experience of nature, and thence to the "gender subtext" that lies beneath both differences: the unrecognized subtext of "the connnections between the twin oppressions of women and nature" (Warren, 1987, p. 6) and, for that matter, the further self-repression of men. This further step is not, however, taken by Deutsche or Massey.

The reductionist eye also seems to guide Habermas's view, though here the conceptual landscape is robust enough to stand reformulation, as we saw in the case of Nancy Fraser's feminist–theoretical onslaught on his conception of material and symbolic reproduction and the linking social roles through which, in modernity, the iron cage descends and emancipation might presumably be sought. But what of the theory of communicative action itself, the very center of Habermas's emancipatory enterprise? Does it survive the critical acid that we saw poured on it a few pages back—the realization, via the arguments of Gilligan and others, that the communicative securing of any consensus will depend on some dialogic correspondence of voices but that masculine and feminine voices are "different" in precisely that realm of the ethical justification of choices and actions? And does it survive the realization that there is no longer a shared, unitary view of the natural world and of our exchange with it? That science is representational and that ethical choice lurks behind every representation?

The question (and its answer) comes into focus with Habermas's preoccupation with the inner "logic of discourse" peculiar to each of the three (ultimately Kantian) spheres of cultural life: science, morality, and art. So when two or more speakers raise "intersubjective validity claims" that a statement is *true or false*, they are appealing to *scientific–theoretic rationality* (to do with regularities, probabilities, and laws); and the emancipatory endeavor might have something to do with the paradigmatic nature of our consciousness of the universe and of our place in it—ultimately, perhaps, with Bateson's learning of the nature of paradigm itself. If, however, the claims are that the statement is normatively *right or wrong*, then the appeal is to *moral–practical rationality* (the domain of norms and principles—worlds away from the laws of truth and falsehood); and emancipation will be attained by escaping from normative rigidity, toward the grounding of human behavior in communicatively secured principles—the end of unreflective, patriarchal oppression, for example. The argument is less clear in the sphere of *aesthetic–practical rationality*. Habermas (1985a) does suggest that "works of art raise claims with regard to their unity (harmony: *Stimmigkeit*), their authenticity, and the success of their expressions by which they can be measured and in terms of which they may fail" (p. 200). That "success of expression" may have much to do with whether the work is an *aesthetically sincere or otherwise expression of human experience*. And an emancipatory art is one that lifts us to new levels of consciousness of the human condition—of being.

Somewhat tentatively this argument is summarized in Table 11.1. The suggested links, from backing to conclusion, are from Habermas (1973) for the first two spheres; the addition for aesthetic–practical rationality is a present suggestion. Now there are two great problems with Habermas's endeavor. First, in each of these spheres of human rationality and action, it is the *warrant* that gets us through the impasse (the controversial validity claims) to the conclusion—it "does the work," as it were. But, as we have seen, in moral–practical rationality there are different ways in which humans handle claims of right and wrong: At the very least such claims are gender differentiated, there are different voices, and in the feminine the exploration of relationship may supplant Habermas's "norms and principles" altogether. Likewise in the area of aesthetic–practical rationality: If art is indeed about the

TABLE 11.1. Logic of Discourse: From Backing to Conclusion (after Habermas, 1973)

	Theoretic–cognitive (scientific) rationality	Moral–practical (political) rationality	Aesthetic–practical (artistic) rationality
Conclusion	Assertion	Prescription or evaluation	Representation
Controversial validity claim	Truth	Normative correctness	Sincere, revealing expression
Required from opponent	Explanation	Justification	Raised consciousness
Data	Causes, motives, etc.	Grounds	Images
Warrant	Uniformities, laws, etc.	Norms, principles, etc.	Visions
Backing	Observations, data, etc.	Interpretations of needs, etc.	Experiences

explication of human experience and the raising of consciousness, and if the experiences of men and women (and different tribes and nations) are as different as they now seem, then it is little wonder that, with warranting visions so different, the aesthetic judgment will be different. We must go still further: In the theoretic–cognitive rationality of science, there are, at the very least, the seemingly proliferating voices of different paradigms—one might get great agreement among scientists on many things but no longer on "uniformities and laws." Is one to appeal to the mechanistic, Cartesian view of the world—atomized, things that move other things—or to see it as organic, holistic, and ecological, Capra's "complicated tissue of events"? How is the natural world to be pictured? The present turmoil of science—the seeming end of the Newtonian age—might be "dismissed" as just the throwing away of one set of warranting rules and probabilities to make way for another, and so Habermas's theory might remain unscathed (even supported, if such a speeding up of paradigm shift is seen as evidence that we can indeed escape from set assumptions about the world and toward new forms of exchange with external nature!). However, the events of the present are more than that. For the turn to uncertainty, at the level of Habermas's "warrant," is positive rather than negative: It is not just because we might be "between paradigms," but rather the new emerging paradigm would seem to be *based on uncertainty*. With an acceptance of the social construction of knowledge is the positive acceptance of difference: Lorraine Code (1981) asks, "Is the sex of the knower epistemologically significant?"—or their race or class, one could add. An affirmative answer is suggested, for knowledge is "the product of a combination of objective and subjective factors." And while the objective factors *may* be invariant, the subjective certainly are not: We structure experience differently, linguistically define our place in the world through different voices (Lakoff, 1975; Miller and Swift, 1977), and—a problematic claim—female knowledge, on most evidence, is less objective, more subjective, than male knowledge. Concludes Code (1981),

> One might argue that women bring a richness of feeling and a depth of understanding to cognitive activity such that the final known *Gestalt* is richer, more multi-faceted, and better. Perhaps the admission of women to the kingdom of knowers, on an equal footing, will effect a shift in the standard evaluation of knowledge claims, granting greater respectability to the contribution made by the affective side of human nature. (p. 276)

It is a judgment of a kind with Capra's shift from "objective science" to "epistemic science," where the understanding of the process of knowledge is to be included explicitly in the description of natural phenomena (Capra and Steindl-Rast, 1991; also a variety of papers in Diamond and Orenstein, 1990).

The second problem with Habermas's model is that the spheres—autonomous science, morality, and art—tend no longer to hold solid (if they ever did!). It is the process that Walter Benjamin had observed, most clearly in dadaist montage, and already encountered in Chapter 10: the languages of argumentation "cross over," from one sphere to another. Susan Buck-Morss's (1989) summary is that "binary pairs of linguistic signs" are juxtaposed and, "in the process of applying these signs to material referents," the switches are crossed (p. 59). Certainly this slippage can be malign: Harvey (1989) refers to the "aestheticisation of politics" that seemingly characterizes all fascisms, and there is also the scientific–technological subversion of the political. Buck-Morss (1989) continues her summary of "crossing the switches":

> The critical power of this maneuver depends on both the code, wherein meaning arises from binaries of signifier/signifieds independent of the referents, and the referents, the materially existing

objects, which do not submit to language signs meekly, but have the semantic strength to set the signs into question. (pp. 59–60)

The juxtaposition triggers a switching of the warrant: No longer is the grounding aesthetic but moral–political, or scientific. We switch languages.

So where do these arguments leave us? Emancipation is escape from all forms of repression; more usefully expressed, as all repression seems to be manifested in or underlain by deafness to "other voices" and by unchallenged, paradigmatic viewpoints sanctioned in language (of real life, of the stultified stuff of philosophy and specializations, and of architecture—prisons of both Foucault and Bataille), it seems that emancipation must take the form of *learning—to position ourselves between voices*, thereby making accessible those human resources presently denied, and *critically crossing languages*, thus deconstructing the prisons.

The value of Habermas's theory of communicative action is that it offers a framework that focuses this task, even though the place of different voices in communicatively grounding validity claims is denied in the summary of Table 11.1, as is the interplay and the potential mutual erosion of languages. Benjamin, Derrida, and the theorists of feminism give us the viewpoints that can be brought to bear on this theory, to open it up—effectively a method to "compel" (emancipation no bed of roses!) the hearing of other voices, the reading of subtexts, and the recognition of all language as potential prison but also as penetrable. These latter critics also "compel" us to turn to *images*—the deconstructive images of Benjamin and Derrida, other representations of the natural world, the different perspectives and motivating visions of others. It is here that we find the task of architecture and urban design. It remains now to see how that task is to be pursued.

CHAPTER 12 | # Conclusion: New Architecture, New Urban Design

Deconstructing the artefact called architecture is perhaps to begin to think it as artefact, to rethink the artefacture from the starting point, and the technology, therefore, at the very point at which it remains uninhabitable.

—JACQUES DERRIDA, "Fifty-two Aphorisms for a Foreword" (aphorism 28) (1989a, p. 68)

A prefatory note: This is a book of stories, and the longest have been those interweaving through the chapters that would trace the waning of the modern—words that would try to reflect the extraordinary proliferation of representations of the space of present experience. It is the fragmentation that follows the breakdown of the previous, high modernist notion that there might be a *single* (or, at least, *best*) way of representing the space of human progress and universal good. The immediately preceding Chapter 11, in turn, has been the most important to the book's development (and, in the rereading, the least satisfying): It has had to "convey the argument" that underlay the original decision to write. But in the context of this argument, the long story of those earlier chapters must be judged virtually irrelevant. Where, in all the architectures and urban designs that seem to shine on the present, do we find representations of the feminine voice, of "new nature" (the now-possible relationships and responsibilities to external phenomena and technology that preoccupied Benjamin), of a world freed from repression, of new modes of communication and production—a recurrent theme?

Morris Berman (1984) states that "the problems with Descartes' view are perhaps obvious, but for now, it will suffice to note that real life operates dialectically, not critically. We love and hate the same thing simultaneously, we fear what we most need, we recognise ambivalence as a norm rather than an aberration" (p. 23). That the space of modern life is to be read dialectically—as Benjamin's "dialectical images"—has already been argued. If the built images of architecture and urban design (and those other texts of literature, painting, gardens, etc.) are in turn read as responses to the space of everyday life, standing against that space and either obfuscating, reinforcing, or unmasking its effect, so that it is seen "as if for the first time"—heightening, clarifying—then the result is the "new geography" foreseen in Chapter 10. It is directly to the purposive production of counterpointing images in architecture and urban design that we now turn. The argument is that any design practice supporting the human emancipatory endeavor will also have to proceed dialectically, in two senses: What is to be represented, "the message," always involves ambivalence (the problem of different voices); and the representation will itself work at a variety of levels, conveying more than one message.

We could, in a number of ways, cut through the conundrum of representing in words an inherently unstable enterprise of representing in dialectical images. The method chosen is close to the procedure of Chapter 10; it will present as four "essays." There is, first, the problem at its simplest: Every image stands against another (physically juxtaposed, resonating in the memory, triggering the imagination, or however), and this can be deconstructive—the revolutionary space of 1920s Russia against that of an opposed bourgeois world, the spatial expression of women's protest against the commodified cityscape of modern advertising. The dialectical images are those of hitherto unquestioned assumptions and their erosion. Second, there is that representation of the dilemma of self-identity—of "a self-regulated exchange of society with our own internal nature" that Habermas sees as the distinguishing characteristic of an emerging (postmodern) age. How is one to represent the coexisting, dialectically definable impulses to distancing versus immersion? What does not ring true is Habermas's speculation that the shift from modernity to postmodernity has been marked, most revealingly, by the shift from the centrality of the exchange of society with *external* nature (*value* as the thematically scarce resource) to that of the exchange of society with *internal* nature (*mean-*

ing, motivation as the focus). The exchange with broader, external nature surely remains central, just altered. So the third essay deals with the parallel problem of representing the new ambivalences of our place in broader nature: use (the ethos of modernity) versus mutual nurturing, or Heidegger's clearing, or perhaps reenchantment (the suppressed, other side of the relationship); the profane vision versus the resacralized, the masculine versus the feminine. The fourth way of viewing the representational task is through Benjamin's distinction between "new nature" and "old nature." How is the potential of new nature—newly possible relationships, responsibilities, and technologies—to be excavated from the layers of old nature in which we nostalgically dress the present?

So the representational task in "new architecture" and "new urban design" can be viewed as arising at a variety of levels (four in the present way of seeing it, though this is quite unprivileged); at each level there are ambivalences and dialectical oppositions, and between levels there are further reverberations.

1: THE DECONSTRUCTIVE IMAGE AS THE OBJECT OF REPRESENTATION (FLÂNEUR, FLÂNEUSE)

Underneath the surface of systemic rationalisation, on an unconscious "dream" level, the new urban–industrial world had become fully reenchanted. In the modern city, as in the ur-forests of another era, the "threatening and alluring face" of myth was alive and everywhere. It peered out of wall posters advertising "toothpaste for giants," and whispered its presence in the most rationalized urban plans that, with their uniform streets and endless rows of buildings, have realized the dreamed-of architecture of the ancients: the labyrinth.

—SUSAN BUCK-MORSS, *The Dialectics of Seeing*
(1989, p. 254, quoting Walter Benjamin)

So there was presented the world of advertisements, promising the allure of the commodity unbounded—the space of the bourgeois world (Benjamin's arcades constituted the first great efflorescence, when the bourgeois revolution of 1789 was itself a recent memory). The environment of the next great revolution—of 1917—is to stand against that of the bourgeois, the anticommodity against the commodity: "Cubism and Futurism have destroyed the old world of things [commodities, use values?] and we have emerged into non-objectivity, in other words the complete shedding of the old, so as to advance to the utilitarian and dynamically spiritual Suprematist world of things" (Malevich, quoted in Zhadova, 1982, p. 298).

The Agit-Prop stands, kiosks, and street art of Klucis and Gan, both Malevich acolytes, took a new, far more direct typography and technology of communication to reveal the decadence of the world of bourgeois advertising. Their oppositional violence would "decon-struct"—unmask—that bourgeois world as both the new enchantment (the Aladdin's cave, the promise) *and* "progress as fetish, modernity as Hell." This time it was not change for change's sake and new commodi-ties, but change for the sake of revolution.

A century and a half after Baudelaire, seventy years after Gan and Klucis, the world of images may not persist as reenchantment—the advertisements *may* have lost their magic if it is toothpaste that is paraded, and Baudrillard's world of abstracted communication may indeed be upon us. But it is not contentless to everyone (possibly to no one!). Dolores Hayden (1984) describes this world, under the banner "Advertisements, Pornography, and Public Space":

> The ways in which the public domain is misused for spatial dis-plays of gender stereotypes. . . . These appear in outdoor advertis-ing . . . commercial displays, architectural decoration, and public sculpture . . . giant females in various states of undress smiling and caressing products such as whiskey, food and records. Male models also sell goods, but they are usually active and clothed . . . men are most often shown doing active things, posed in the great outdoors; women are shown in reflective postures responding to male de-mands in interior spaces . . . billboards turn the public space of the city into a stage set for a drama starring enticing women and stern men . . . an urban landscape filled with images of men as sexual aggressors and women as submissive sexual objects. . . . Tawdry strip clubs, X-rated films, "adult" bookstores and sex shops. . . . Pornography is a bigger, more profitable industry in the United States than all legitimate film and record business combined. (pp. 217–221)

Baudrillard has simply missed the point (as has Venturi in the extolling of Vegas). Graffiti City, too, merely disguises Pornography City. The middle class can direct their rage against the spray can, while the planners, urban designers, and advertiser capital further the ob-scenity of a gendered, violent city legitimizing the male appropriation of the urban world.

Less satisfactory than Hayden's outraged description of the "rape culture" (Shapiro), "a world masculinity made unfit for women or men" (Rich), is her account of tentative steps to reappropriate the city. These come under the further banner of "Creating Innovative Institutions to Link Private Life and Public Space" (Hayden, 1984, p. 222): "cultural institutions that exist somewhere between the private domain and the public domain" and that "play a key role in initiating ideas, organizing financial support, and supplying the designers or administrators to make the whole more than the sum of the parts" (p. 222) (the Los Angeles Woman's Building, an arts workshop, is given as prototypical); counterposters for and about public places ("our voice and images in public places" [p. 223]); texts and images in public buses to tell of women's experiences in paid and household work, to be read by women and men; Suzanne Lacy's "Three Weeks in May," of 1977, regularly telecasting an up-to-the minute account of attempted and completed rapes on the streets of Los Angeles, to ferocious public indignation.

These sorts of actions aggregate to a mobilization of community art and performance, toward a counterimage to the present urban design of gendered violence, into which it would intrude as a new, disruptive, unwelcomed layer; but it lacks the broader commitment and appeal of the Proletkult and Agit-Prop onslaught on an earlier version of Hell. It would also seem to lack the sort of multiroled counteraction to correspond with Nancy Fraser's exposure of the gender subtext running through Habermas's description of the roles that we play in present society and that link the everyday life-world and the system-world of state and formal economy and that would presumably need to be unmasked in an emancipatory endeavor. The images would have to stand against the separation of public and private realms that enables the spaces of paid and unpaid work to be so clearly delineated and that reifies the male appropriation of the former; such images would likewise need to critique the overwhelmingly feminine world of the consumer role—the shopping malls, the soapie-simulated suburb—the space of female relegation. The role of citizen that links the life-world sphere of political participation to the sphere of the state—again masculine, exclusionary, and where violence finds its sanction in the celebration of soldiering—is in some way addressed in the sorts of actions that Hayden describes, though here too the reifying spatial separation of public and private realms would seem the first necessary focus of any counteraction. The fourth role—that of client—needs somehow to be represented as nonstigmatized, just another part of the life of the city, and to be accommodated in a far less differentiated urban space. We will come back to this task of the deconstructive image.

2: THE DILEMMA OF "INNER NATURE" AS THE OBJECT OF REPRESENTATION (DISTANCING, IMMERSING)

> *To what erotics of knowledge does the ecstasy of reading such a cosmos belong? Having taken a voluptuous pleasure in [the view of the city from on high], I wonder what is the source of this pleasure of "seeing the whole," of looking down on, totalizing the most immoderate of human texts. . . .*
>
> > *The ordinary practitioners of the city live "down below," below the thresholds at which visibility begins. They walk—an elementary form of this experience of the city; they are walkers, Wandersmänner, whose bodies follow the thicks and thins of an urban "text" they write without being able to read it.*
>
> > > —MICHEL DE CERTEAU, *The Practice of Everyday Life* (1984, pp. 92, 93)

Are we to be seen (do we see?) as "voyeurs or walkers," asks de Certeau? That the loss of identity, isolation, emptiness, the "presence of absence" is one part of the experience of postmodernity seems undeniable; so is something of its opposite: the sudden realization that we are not alone but inextricably bound with others (albeit unknowable—the recognition of difference, "otherness," and ease in its presence) and part of a broader, encompassing nature. Each aspect of that experience heightens the other—the definition of self proceeds dialectically. To represent that ambivalence becomes the second task of aesthetic production (whereas the first mode of representation was that of purposive opposition—the active, deconstructive insistence on opposites).

In explicating this task of representing the human condition as defined through difference, we could again turn to the dilemma of the masculine–feminine duality—to learning to see through two eyes and to represent through two voices, without hierarchy (whereas, again, the first mode insisted on hierarchy, to counteract a preexisting hierarchy).[1] Something that should also be viewed dialectically is the tension between the *universalizing* tendency of the economic sphere of society—toward global integration and a loss of local autonomy—and the narrowing, *localized* focus of regional culture and politics. It is a tension variously described as space versus place (Harvey, 1989, pp. 236–237) or as universal civilization versus local culture (Ricoeur, 1965). Berman (1984), for his part, refers to the dichotomy as that of "planetary versus globalist world views, or what has been termed ecosystem versus biospheric cultures"—lives that are tailored to an optimum relation-ship with nature at the level of the particular ecosystem versus lives founded on "the entire globe as one's province, drawing on vast net-works of trade and communication" (1984, p. 298; see also Dasmann, 1976a, 1976b). In the architecture of the present age, it is especially manifested in the still-advocated International Style program (univer-sal technology recelebrated) versus the postmodern search for regional vernaculars, local technology and the quality of place. Various of these oppositions are summarized in Table 12.1.

There is however another text that lies beneath all of these. It surfaces in de Certeau's question, Are we to define our way of being in the world as voyeurs or as walkers? In her critique of Harvey's *The Condition of Postmodernity*, Roslyn Deutsche (1991) also draws atten-tion to this distinction (as does Harvey): The voyeur, she suggests (also following ideas of Mulvey, 1989), "erects rigid boundaries between himself and the objects he views,"—the voyeur is distanced and emo-tionally uninvolved; "narcissistic looking," by contrast (but not to be equated with "walking" in the city), "sees an idealized reflection of the self in the world" (p. 11). According to Deutsche, "Separation from the surrounding world and an imaginary merger with it are, however, intimately linked aspects of the subject's paradoxical relation to im-ages. For the subject 'recognizes' an ideal self in its surroundings only through an image that is simultaneously alienating, a self-as-other" (p. 12).

There is a "defining separation of the subject" (Gilligan's source of male "true identity") that also, however, brings the "loss of immediacy and plenitude." But the individual can seek the compensation of the voyeuristic, totalizing view—the idea that the distanced, external world of objects can finally come together as a totality. Alienation becomes "the precondition for recuperating wholeness": "Severed from objects, that is, the sovereign subject also enjoys unmediated access to them" (Deutsche, 1991, p. 12).

Now something of the voyeuristic, distanced vision seems to run through the "fiction" of the universalizing, totalizing experience of space (the left-hand side of Table 12.1, so to speak): "Distancing, mastering, objectifying—the voyeuristic look exercises control through a visualization which merges with a victimization of its object" (Deutsche, 1991, p. 11, again following de Certeau). And, we might add, Deutsche's dialectically opposed way of looking and being—the narcissistic, seeming to get underneath the "real world," to "*close* the gap between the subject and the object of the representation" (p. 12)—would appear in turn to underlie the individuating, intensive, anchoring experience of *place* (the right-hand side of Table 12.1), the "imaginary merger."

At this level of analysis, one might conclude, consistently with Deutsche's insistence on the complementarity of the voyeuristic and the narcissistic, that both sides of the space–place tension are part of the human: We must "place ourselves between" these extremes if we

TABLE 12.1. Oppositions: Characteristics of Universal-Space and Particular-Place Orientations to Geographical Space

	Space	Place
The experience of space/place	Universalizing, extensive	Individuating, intensive
	Uprooting, underlying division and mobility of labor, leading to identity with class	Anchoring, reinforcing local community and "security of moorings," leading to identity with place and nation
	The myth of "Every Man"	Ease in the presence of difference, "otherness"
	The postmodern hyperspace	Locales
Context	Universal civilization	Local/national culture
Political practice	Domain of capitalist power	Domain of working class power
	Emphasis on universal technology and organization	Emphasis on vernacular culture, nationalism, geopolitics
Environmental program	Global responsibility	Local/national benefit
	International Style in architecture	Postmodern architecture

are to reestablish what it is to be human and to design accordingly; but modernity has tried to block off the right-hand side (and the narcissistic), and postmodernity to screen out the left side (and the voyeuristic). However, it would be a seriously partial conclusion. For both ways of looking are essentially masculine—the flâneur and the vicarious participant! The privileging of sight and the visual over other senses is widely argued to characterize the masculine; the turn to all the senses, the "real" immersion, marks the feminine—an experience of being that is based not "on the gaze which objectifies but on the touch which unites" (Suleiman, quoted in Garb, 1990, p. 268). To argue this way must not, however, lead us to slip back to that first mode of representation; this is not a call for the counteraction of the opposed "voice." Rather, both ways of experiencing space and place are part of being human: the masculine equivocation between distancing objectification and narcissistic imaginary merger, on the one hand, and the feminine touching, scenting, listening, reciprocating immersion, on the other.

The purposive, spatial representation of the feminine experience of space—a feminist architecture and urban design—is problematic, as we saw in the last chapter. But it does exist, and possibly ubiquitously. Throughout high modernity, women's making and unmaking of space has been the butt of jokes and fun—endlessly rearranging the furniture, selecting or else imagining new curtains or carpets, pruning the roses, crocheting doilies, doing flower arrangements, or other pretty things. What men do has been far more serious! Men's typical aesthetic production (in architecture, urban design, painting, sculpture, music composition) has been embraced in "serious," reflective, critical, "theoretical" discourse; the discourse has ensured that the voices will remain male. The same with a few areas shared by men and women (poetry, the novel, some musical interpretation). Not so those more typically female. And we have the false, ideological distinction between "art" and "craft"; most seriously, we get that denigration of the real genius of women's purposive spatial production—the achievement of habitability and the even more extraordinary quality of the variety and freshness that flows from subtle change, adaptability, textures, new smells and surfaces. The making of ground surfaces, walls, and ceilings is called architecture and is critically explored; the occupation and personalization of those surfaces is not. Yet both are representation.

A feminine spatial design will be very different from the male. It will break things down, make them accessible; remove the steps and the podia; break the facades with flowers and scented fruits; reduce the scale; reinstate the tactile, the sounds of water and birds, the places of children's play (Nietzsche's "play that calls new worlds to life"), the impermanent and the appropriable. It will also work to represent those welcome breakdowns of the modernist separation of public and private spheres—home-based work, shared childcare, localized art and craft workshops, the small gains of women's and children's places in the male-dominated world of the office district and the industrial plant. It may enter aesthetic–critical discourse not merely as direct representation (of women's experience of being and of space), but as something deconstructive, as Lenin's "that which is new," to be superimposed on the existing (male-centered) space and architecture of the city, the real "deconstruction," unmasking not just assumptions but those gendered subtexts themselves (Fraser). It is to "see" in discourse—to elevate to self-consciousness—the feminine side of spatial production, the making of habitable space in the broadest sense, so that it stands finally as Bataille's "architecture against [male] architecture," nonimprisoning, that "space from before the subject," or "an architecture that would not allow space for the time needed to become a subject" (Hollier, 1989, p. xi).

But more: Derrida's enterprise, suggests David Wood, is to *exemplify "without fully determining"* an "expanded space of reading"; its dimensions would accommodate something of a "deconstructive logic" (supplementarity, the effect of the preface, destabilizing the "trinitary horizon" of the dialectic) *and* the ethical "space of responsibility" (responsibility in the face of indecidability) that has increasingly preoccupied Derrida.[2] Such a reading is not to "undermine a finished text" but is to rise as a "responsiveness that re-engages with the conditions of a text's production"—with the originary passion of writing itself—with "a theatrical re-animation of the textual space of philosophy's passion" (Wood, 1992, p. 3). But (male) architecture of the present, like the texts that Derrida would assail, also awaits reanimation with the voice of passion to supplement that of cold reason. (Architecture, like the language of words, has its mixed origins—music and function.) Perhaps the passional voices of women, rooted in relationship rather than Habermasian justification, can release a similarly expanded "space of the reading of space"—a passional architecture.

All this amounts to the superimposition of fundamentally, paradigmatically different modes of perceiving and representing—and, thereby, making—space. If we can dehierarchize the male, compelling people to be self-consciously within two paradigmatic ways of seeing (being) simultaneously, we *may* have an environment ("second language") and a discourse ("first language") to trigger Bateson's learning about paradigm itself—an emancipatory step.

3: THE DILEMMA OF "EXTERNAL NATURE" AS THE OBJECT OF REPRESENTATION (MASTERING, NURTURING)

> Belief in progress, in endless perfectibility (—an unending
> moral task—) and the conception of eternal recurrence are
> complementary. They are ineluctable antinomies, in the
> face of which the dialectical conception of historical time
> needs to be developed. Against this dialectical conception,
> eternal recurrence emerges as precisely that "flat
> rationalism" of which the belief in progress is accused, and
> this latter belongs to the mythical mode of thinking just as
> much as does the conception of eternal recurrence.
>
> —Walter Benjamin, Gessamelte Schriften: Das
> Passagen-Werk (Vol. 5, 1982, p. 178; quoted
> in Buck-Morss, 1989, pp. 108–109)

In *Time Wars* (1987), Jeremy Rifkin locates the malaise of the times in time itself. That compression of time that has marked modernity—the experience of progress accompanying the accelerating tempo of modern life and its obverse in ephemerality and the loss of temporal orientations—now confronts a rediscovery of that much older experience of ecological time, governed by the "interlocking cycles of biological rhythms" (Young, 1988, p. 15). It is the problem of a linear versus a cyclical experience of time. The new oppositions permeate and transform the economic, political, and cultural–ideological levels of society:

> Advocates of the new time politics eschew the notion of exerting
> power over time. Their interest is in redirecting the human con-
> sciousness toward a more empathetic union with the rhythms of
> nature. They believe that if we are to "resacralize" life, we must
> "resacralize" time. It is by revaluing the time of each other and by
> understanding and accepting the inherent pace, tempo, and dura-
> tion of the natural world that we can offer our species the best hope
> for the future. (Rifkin, 1987, p. 12)

The very definition of the political is transformed. The spatial metaphors of partisan loyalty (left wing, right wing) lose their relevance, as many find difficulty in identifying with either "side." Spatial alignments are increasingly supplanted by temporal alignments, as the differing temporal underpinnings of opposed politicoeconomic directions for society come glaringly into focus (Rifkin, 1987, pp. 228–229).

The relations between these opposed poles of linear versus cyclical experiences of time are essentially dialectical, and we can attempt to summarize them in Table 12.2. There are differences in the experience of time itself (linear, accelerating, and predictable, vs. cyclical, ecological, and spontaneous) and in the broader politicoeconomic objectives that seem to be underlain by those differing experiences (an increasingly instrumentalized natural and social world to realize modernity's

TABLE 12.2. Oppositions: Characteristics of Linear–Artificial and Cyclical–Natural Conceptions of Time (after Rifkin)

	Linear time	Cyclical time
The experience of time	Quantifiable, fast-paced, efficient, predictable, accelerating	Empathy with the cycles and processes of nature, uncontrolled, continuing
	Rhythms accelerated, predictable, expedient	Rhythms slow paced, rhapsodic, spontaneous, vulnerable, ecological, participatory
Underlying objectives	A more efficient, simulated environment to secure the general well-being of society	"Resacralization" of life at every level of existence
Political practice	Emphasis on subsuming the natural biological and physical rhythms and creating an artificially controlled environment to ensure ever-increasing economic growth for present and future generations	Emphasis on reestablishing a temporal communion with natural biological and physical rhythms and a coexistence in harmony with the cycles, seasons, and periodicities of the larger earth organism
Environmental program	An environment regulated by sequences, durations, rhythms, etc., of computers, robotics, genetic engineering, space technologies	An economic and technological infrastructure compatible with sequences, durations, rhythms, etc., that punctuate the natural production and recycling activities of the earth's ecosystems
	High-technology, material progress vision of the future	Stewardship vision of the future

seeming promise of material progress, vs. ecological sustainability and our reintegration into the earth and its processes—resacralisation, or what Berman calls "reenchantment").[3] Differences similarly arise in consequent political practices—modernization, whether in capitalism or in state socialism, versus "green" politics and "sustainable development"—and in the environmental programs consistent with those broader programs and practices.

Where one must, however, disagree with Rifkin is in his consequent judgment that these conceptions of time are so opposed—contradictory, mutually exclusive—that one must prevail and the other fall (like the Russian Revolutionary landscape vs. the bourgeois—the purposive opposition, the objective of the first mode of representation): "While they may be able to coexist for a time in a political world that is comfortable with the notion of absorbing contradictions and negotiating compromises, in the end one of these two temporal orientations will ultimately prevail, providing a context for a new vision of the social order" (Rifkin, 1987, pp. 230–231).

Rather, as Berman observes in the quotation at the beginning of this chapter, life does proceed dialectically; what is learned cannot be unlearned, and *both* experiences of time are going to remain with us. But, as Walter Benjamin observes, both are permeated by mythic thinking: The idea of progress and that of eternal recurrence are dialetical opposites, but equally mythical. Thus Benjamin's approbation of Baudelaire: "It is above all the 'belief in progress' that he persecutes with hate, as heresy, a false doctrine, not merely a simple error" (quoted in Buck-Morss, 1989, p. 195)—the fetishization of change itself as "the eternity of Hell." Yet Baudelaire's "hellishly repetitive time" is equally false—nihilism, the myth of the eternal return, a false understanding of nature as unchanging—forever "old nature." If there is no change, there can be no purposive political response, no hope in any emancipatory endeavor—anathema to Benjamin.

This third representational task, then, is to press into consciousness and critical reflection a new understanding of being in linear time (indeed, an idea of progress, though it is certainly not material progress in the sense understood in modernity) and simultaneously in cyclical time (to embrace new technologies and responsibilities compatible with those natural production and recycling capacities of terrestrial ecosystems).[4] Again we have to position ourselves between experiences dialectically defined, but we also have to break open the masks of myth that presently distort them—to "break into this world and lay its harmonious structures in ruins," in Benjamin's words (quoted in Buck-Morss, 1989, p. 197)—"to interrupt the course of the world." The interruption is more the focus of the fourth task.

4: "NEW NATURE"
AS THE OBJECT OF REPRESENTATION

*To say that architecture must be withdrawn from the ends
that are assigned to it and first of all from the value of
habitation, is not to prescribe uninhabitable constructions,
but to take an interest in the genealogy of an ageless
contract between architecture and habitation. Is it possible
to undertake a work without fitting it out to be habitable?
Everything here must take into consideration those
"questions to Heidegger" on what he believed he could say
about what we translate in Latin by "inhabit" [habiter].*

—JACQUES DERRIDA, "Fifty-two Aphorisms for a
Foreword" (aphorism 29) (1989, p. 68)

Derrida's collaborator Eisenman and other deconstructionists indeed
question that contract between architecture and habitation; the questioning, however, remains contemplative more than revolutionary.
The absence of a political consciousness and program is extraordinary—at the least to unmask that further contract between architecture and repression (capital, gender, the state, dominant races, colonialism, domination of nature . . .) and at the most to present us with
architecture of different texts: an architecture of new internal nature
(between space and place and between distancing and immersion) and
of new external nature (between times).

We need to go back to those random notes-for-a-text of Walter
Benjamin concerning the entrapment in mythical thinking (classless,
Eisenmanian self-indulgence!). As a new means of production is, in the
beginning, immersed in the old one, so in the "collective consciousness" there are corresponding "wish images" where the new is intermingled with the old. Wish images emerge to throw light on "the
incompleteness of the social order of production," but also to transcend
it (Fourier's phalanstère, Wright's Broadacre City); they also exhibit "a
positive striving to set themselves off from the outdated—that means,
however, the most recent past" (Benjamin, quoted in Buck-Morss,
1989, p. 114). But an imagined, more distant, classless (i.e., politically
imaginary), mythic past is nowhere near so alien as that recent, still-
pressing memory: "In the dream in which every epoch sees in images
the epoch that follows, the latter appears wedded to elements of ur-history" (Benjamin, 1973, p. 159). Here architecture—the prison—seems
itself at present to lie imprisoned in an imaginary, classless, apolitical
utopia of the self-referential.

But "new nature"—the now-possible relationships and responsibilities to external nature and to technology (that thereby enable the

actualization of inner nature)—is itself held in a mythic state, its potential not yet realized. It is either idealized (itself seen as utopian— Scheerbart's *Glasarchitektur*, Sant'Elia's futurism) or cloaked in archaic forms. It is the intersection of mythic nature and mythic past—the dreams of technology, with the apolitical memory of unfulfilled dreams—that yields these wish images that can propel us to the revolutionary rupture (as was argued in Chapter 10). We are again compelled to dialectical thinking: "Utopian imagination . . . cuts across the continuum of technology's historical development as the possibility of revolutionary rupture. . . . This means that each of the 'corresponding' elements—mythic nature and mythic consciousness—works to liberate the other *from* myth" (Buck-Morss, 1989, p. 116).

A specific instance begins to illustrate what this might mean. In Broadacre City, of Frank Lloyd Wright, a different sort of society was envisioned, agricultural and industrial production (*and* cultural production) mixed, dwellings dispersed and disappearing into the landscape, each household nurturing its productive acre (see Figure 12.1). As Lionel March observed in 1970, "the existing city is mostly the shell of historic urban life," but Broadacre City breaks that down, escapes from it, though *we* still "fail to see the new patterns of urbanization as positive forms in their own right because we attempt to construe them in terms of our habitual assumptions derived from the past" (reprinted in Brooks, 1981, pp. 202–203). It indeed comes close to the ruptural break, the remotivating "wish image": Utopia is extolled.[5] But it is then eroded by that image of new technology: radio, helicopters, the car, and so forth. But March is sadly right in his further observation that in his later career Wright effectively realized the elements of Broadacre City—the houses, the university, the "democratic" institutions—but that without the unifying political program these are without meaning or content (signifiers without signifieds) and thus fail to erode that space of the existing city. Only the imagery, ultimately, is overlain.[6]

The vision of a reconciled world emerged from the mutual erosion of "mythic nature and mythic past," but it was always apolitical in a world where class was salient (it is an accusation that could never be leveled at Le Corbusier, the Bauhaus, or the Russians; but then their work failed to address the time of human progress and the time of nature as Wright's did). So Wright, in turn, is mythic past, awaiting the moment of its erosion and liberation; the acid, presumably, will be "new nature" of a new era—the reality of "now-possible relationships and responsibilities."

Mythic nature and mythic consciousness also collide in the far more recent representations of James Wines and Alison Sky's SITE group (Sculpture in the Environment). In their most interesting work,

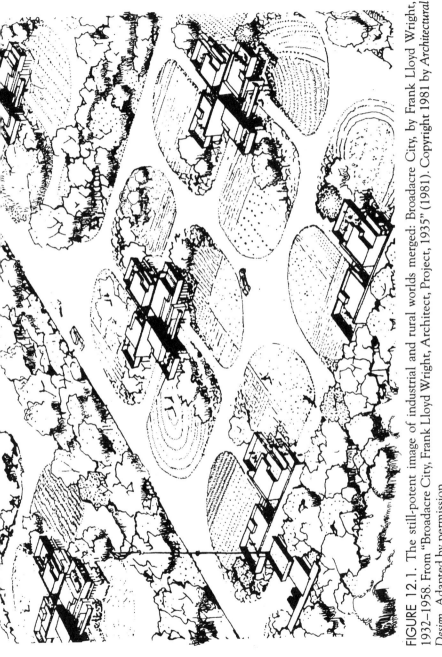

FIGURE 12.1. The still-potent image of industrial and rural worlds merged: Broadacre City, by Frank Lloyd Wright, 1932–1958. From "Broadacre City, Frank Lloyd Wright, Architect, Project, 1935" (1981). Copyright 1981 by *Architectural Design*. Adapted by permission.

buildings are literally broken apart, incomplete; the woodland and forest invade them, and one marvels at the havoc as the trees get bigger and the buildings come asunder.[7] The architectural representations (of institutions and the memory of them) are often loaded with historical references but are far from historicist; the representations of nature are *not* those of the garden as we conventionally understand it but are more ecological, changing and chaotic (almost the melancholic entropy of the baroque), botanical, and destructive of assumptions. But we look in vain for a political consciousness—for the new ways of production and consumption, even more for the representation of roles, in the Habermas–Fraser sense, that would constitute "new nature."

The real impact of these images, of real life and external nature reconciled, whether by Wright or more recently, is potentially critical rather than remotivating—consciousness raising rather than redemptive critique, in Benjamin's sense. Critical artists, observes Roslyn Deutsche (1991), "expose the repressed constructions that produce illusions of coherence"; however,

> whether or not [those artists] address such issues of subjectivity . . . [they] call attention to the constructed character of their images and thus reflect critically and openly on their own activities in meaning production instead of perpetuating beliefs that, as vanguard figures, they transmit superior perceptions of preexisting aesthetic or political realities to others who cannot see them. (p. 22)

Representation itself is problematized, but so is "reality": for "reality"—meanings, relations, values—is constituted for us in representations. So, "precisely by acknowledging the image as a social relation, it chooses to be openly in the world, intervening in diverse political activities" (Deutsche, 1991, p. 22). The deconstructionist SITE group tend to do this; the high modernist Wright no longer does. (It is this form of political intervention, incidentally, that Deutsche tellingly cites against Harvey's claim that a preoccupation with images causes postmodern art forms to turn inward to apolitical self-referentiality.)

Wright's images are redemptive; overwhelmingly, SITE's images are critical: We are shown that the relationship between the self and institutions, on the one hand, and external nature, on the other, is constituted in a complex of representations. This realization prompts a return to Eisenman (and to Derrida's aphorism 29 that began this essay). Here too the constitution of reality in representation is deconstructed: "Dwelling," the contract between architecture and habitation, is questioned in the houses series; the place of architecture in the production of memory and identity (the self) is to be laid open in the larger designs; something of the space–place dialectic is similarly exposed in the Berlin housing. However, the central question of the emancipatory endeavor—the gender subtext; the redefinition of human motivation; the relations (constituted in representation) between self, others, and nature; or the realization of our being alone (Nietzsche's abyss)—is not addressed in Eisenman's work.

It is hard to find explicit attempts to represent these redefinitions and relationships (in effect, new nature!). There is some insight from Rem Koolhaas's entry for the La Villette competition, encountered earlier (see Figure 12.2). The lateral strips of different plantings and activities and the various superimpositions would yield the sort of multilayered, discontinuous, indeterminate space that could stand as a representation of the space of the present city. It is also a model of how the city must now be designed: The new landscape of a sustainable economy and renewing ecology will indeed be "grafted in," in Derrida's terms, to an existing city that it will radically interrupt and call to account.

In the model and paintings made of the scheme, however, it is far more chaotic than this, even messy. It is as if it has already been occupied (by a horde of ungrateful women, unable to appreciate the purity of the conception) and made habitable. The contract between architecture and habitation is finally revealed for what it is: one between architecture and men, *against* habitation! It is close to the chaotic, democratic space of long-occupied suburbia, but even more of community gardens that, when extended to colonize the land abandoned in the economic disasters and decays of the late modern city, begin to transform relationships with space and nature and the way in which society is integrated ("new nature"). Witness Rachel Bagby's Philadelphia Community Rehabilitation Corporation that has reappropriated the decaying city for gardening, housing, local employment—all linked to community education, literacy, and reempowerment programs. Something of the story is told by Bagby's daughter (Bagby, 1990); a fair judgment would be that a new text is being written on the city—new gender relationships, new nature—that may come close, in some part, to eroding the already gendered text that Fraser sees underlying the Habermasian account of modern life. There is the hint that some small aspect of an "other" space is here presented, stripped of the myth that still distorts the images of SITE ("the past haunts the present," observes Buck-Morss [1989, p. 293]—new nature held back in conventional imagination); but whether it can indeed erode the "mythic consciousness" of our nostalgia (be it for modernity's decaying city of progress and patriarchy or for a romantic vision of

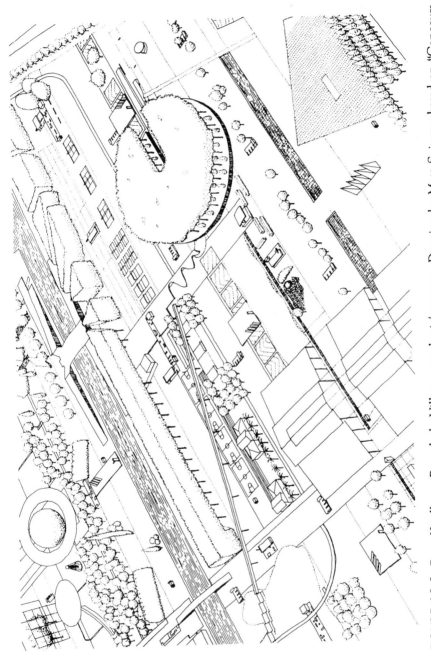

FIGURE 12.2. Rem Koolhaas: Parc de la Villette, synthesis/montage. Drawing by Matt Spinaze, based on "Concours International pour le Parc de la Villette" (1983, June).

reconciliation with "old nature"), and itself be eroded by such dreams reactivated, is still to become clear to us.

|FINALLY

There have been two conclusions to the present text. The first had to do with how to read space; the second has been about its design—more specifically, about its design in the context of the enterprise of human emancipation and fulfillment.

Clearly, given the ability of dominant interests to appropriate all architectural forms, there can be no such thing as "an emancipatory design"; only *the activity of design* has any such potential. Le Corbusier, the Bauhaus, and the Russians, in their actions, furthered aspects of the emancipatory endeavor of their time: Bourgeois smugness and repression in everyday life were countered. The later Le Corbusier similarly stood against the totalizing vision of the high modernists (including himself, now nostalgically held, as classless and apolitical memory, in "mythic consciousness"—Lenin's vision of the old); Tschumi, Eisenman, and colleagues stand against the assumed roles of architecture and designed space (perhaps potentially against the contract between architecture and habitation, but not yet against that between architecture, language, and power—the prison of both Bataille and Foucault). Nowhere, however, do we find a stand against the coercive subtexts permeating the social roles linking everyday life and the instrumentalizing "systems" of economy and polity (and, seen otherwise, linking public and private spheres whose fracturing marks modernity), even though architectural space is profoundly implicated in the constitution of those texts and reproduction of the roles. The gender subtext is not addressed, nor those of race and clan—nor, it must be admitted, have they received appropriate attention in these pages.

To repeat, the fact that every counteraction will soon be either derided or appropriated (by "that which is old") is merely a distraction from the real lesson that derives from the history of design in the modern age. For there is no evidence that *the process* of mounting the unmasking, deconstructive, counterimage will meet the same fate. There is thus the imperative for a savage, furious, Foucauldian architecture, as if to match that of the 1920s—to attack the institutions, appropriate space, make habitable, green the city, soften, break the townscape of presently unquestioned meanings and relationships of power. The representational means for this task are already hinted at, in the layered, superimposed architectures and urban designs of Eisenman, Tschumi, Koolhaas, and the like. But a truly deconstructive

architecture must be one of *nonarbitrary layerings* rather than the superimpositions for superimposition's sake of the present designers—street
corners appropriated, pompous courthouses, city halls and other public
buildings appropriated for women's and children's uses, fruit trees in the
shopping mall, hanging baskets of flowers in the office foyer, appropria-
tions of the monuments for community arts (see Figure 12.3). The
layerings will *not* be devoid of content.

It is this lesson that is thematic of the first way of seeing design,
outlined above. The second has to do with the ambivalence of being
itself and of its representation, seeing through different eyes and utter-
ing through different voices: the male and the female, the rational and
the living voice, universal space and the proliferation of heterotopias,
the profane and the sacred, the instrumentally useful and the poetic,
the viewed and the felt—difference without hierarchy, seeing ourselves
without cutting off one part of what it is to be human. The most urgent
change is in the way in which architects, urban designers, and urban
planners are to be taught: We need to abandon "the view," the primacy
of seeing, the totalizing vision of "the plan," and the vantage points
from which to gaze in admiration at our designs. Rather, we want
spaces that are also fine to touch, smell, and hear and to change with
the passing whim, a richer and more complex space that lends itself to
the vastest array of relationships between people, establishing identity
through relationship as much as through separation, for play, "to bring
new worlds into existence." It will be through such heterogeneous,
chaotic space, for new forms of play and self-identity, that we will
escape a present urban space where work is the focus but where increasing numbers of people will not have work. We might learn what is
learning—Berman's Learning III.

The third way of seeing the design task is about the ambivalence
of being in a multiplicity of times—simultaneously in the times of
human progress (redefined, no longer fetishized as in Baudelaire's
Hell), of almost indiscernible ecological change (Braudel), and of the
rhythms of daily life and its destruction (Fox). There must be an
architecture that addresses the complexities and ambiguities of the
environmental movement and that forces ecological responsibility into
consciousness—and with it the realization that ecological and economic sustainability is inescapable. It may be an architecture of solar
panels, windmills, recycled buildings, and low-energy materials—"design with nature" but also design with the internet, the computer, the
virtual university, and new technologies still hidden in mythic thinking (Benjamin's "mythic nature"). Certainly the architecture and urban design of the present play with ambivalences, and much is to be
learned from these exciting endeavors; but their focus is overwhelm-

FIGURE 12.3. Other superimpositions (clockwise from top left): Tilted planes, excavation, interrupted space, montages of media and images (SITE)/A "garden of succession" as the world of nature erodes the world of built forms (Weller and England)/The mutual invasion of architecture and landscape (SITE)/Technologies of sustainable development (various sources). Author's drawing, based on SITE (1980) and Weller (1989).

ingly self-indulgence rather than a fundamental repositioning of human experience (between eyes, voices, languages, spaces, and times).

The fourth way of seeing design parallels the first: Not only must the counterimages erode those ideas and images presently prevailing (masked in the nostalgically recalled past—"mythic consciousness"), but they must also enable us to break out of a blindness to newly possible relationships and responsibilities (the mythic forms distorting new nature and ultimately hiding from us the new ways of occupying time in a world where the old centrality of work is shrinking). A new architecture will not be what we expect. What this means is that, in one sense, we await the new crucible, as the Bauhaus and possibly Russia were in the 1920s. However, one thing does seem certain: The crucible will be one of powerful images *and* of powerful discourse—Eisenman's first and second languages, Derrida's two voices. New geography and new architecture and urban design will collide.

Notes

1. The reference is to Habermas's (1976) argument that in late capitalism economic crises are increasingly displaced into the administrative system, which in turn is unable to produce the requisite rational decisions (hence, rationality crises), thence into the legitimation system, which is unable to produce the requisite generalized motivations (legitimation crisis), and finally and most catastrophically into the broader cultural realm of socially reproduced meanings, values, and practices, which are no longer able to match the motivations that the state and education systems declare to be necessary (motivation crisis). The question of motivation crisis and the "postmodern condition" (Lyotard, 1984), as opposed explanations of the present, weaves throughout the present text.

2. The "end of philosophy" has a long genealogy: In the Derridean deconstruction of metaphysics, it is traced back to Nietzsche through Levinas, Freud, and especially Heidegger (Haar, 1992, p. 53); only Nietzsche, however, is seen to have possibly broken free (Derrida, 1976, p. 19).

3. For a further pursuit of these themes, see the later Berman (1989).

4. Bateson (1973) argued that learning is to be understood as operating at three levels. Learning I, also called "proto-learning," is the simple solving

of a problem in a specific context; Learning II, or "deutero-learning," occurs with the discovery of the context itself: One "learns to learn" by figuring out the context of knowledge and action. One's individual character and one's conception of reality—and they are two sides of the same coin—have their origin in Learning II, which is equivalent to paradigm formation. Learning III, by contrast, is learning about one's own character and worldview, which is about the very nature of paradigm itself—about Learning II.

5. Habermas's distinction between theoretic–cognitive ("scientific"), moral–practical ("political"), and aesthetic–practical modes of rationality has its parallel—and certainly its genealogy—in the interweaving arguments of Kant's great critiques: of pure reason, of practical reason, and of judgement. The interweaving (Makkreel, 1990) is not so subtly reflected in Habermas however.

| CHAPTER 2

1. The notions of utterance, the specialized social language in which it is expressed, the carrying voice with its intonations in which "value" is revealed, and the dialogicality or "double logics" of speaker and receiver are from Bakhtin (1981, 1986); but see especially Wertsch (1991). They will run through much of the argument that follows, but will be explicitly addressed in Chapter 5.

2. This can be seen in relation to Foucault's ambivalent denial of philosophy, recounted in Megill (1985, p. 187). In the structuralist arguments of *The Order of Things* (Foucault, 1966/1970), both subject and object dissolve, and it is only in language that the world is constituted. By the time we get to *The Archaeology of Knowledge* (1969/1972), language disappears and is replaced by its incompatible mirror image, discourse: The world is constituted not of facts, but of interpretations. And divination is as one with other modes of interpretation.

3. Although Foucault repeatedly represents his enterprise as "archaeology," he also implies a negative judgment: Archaeology transforms "documents" into "monuments," destroying the transparency of the text (through which we can view something else) and giving it instead its own solidarity and importance (1972, pp. 138–139).

4. By contrast, there is no *visionary* utopian promise in Foucault's reading: As Megill (1985) observes (contrasting Foucault with the late-Enlightenment Fourier), there is "no vision of happiness or liberation" (p. 197).

5. Baudrillard (1987) takes the Foucauldian architecture/geography further, speaking of a space shattered like a windshield but still holding together, of power distributed in mathematically "uncertain" space, and of dispersed, interstitial power (see also Philo, 1992, pp. 151–152).

|CHAPTER 3

1. Berman (1984), following Freud, argues that it is only with modernity that there arises that "quality of ego strength" by which we now seem to define the mentally healthy individual. It is "a mode of being-in-the-world which is fully 'natural' only since the Renaissance . . . a tool necessary for functioning in a manipulative and reifying (i.e., life-denying) society" (p. 152). It is "maximizing" rather than "optimizing" behavior. But all ecological systems, whether in the biological or the social realm, are "homoeostatic"; that is, they tend to a steady state, and so to optimize rather than maximize certain variables. If any part of a system seeks to maximize something, like wealth, or power, or gratification, then "the system will go into runaway, destroying itself and its immediate environment in the process" (Berman, 1984, p. 267; see also Bateson, 1973). With modernity, suggest both Bateson and Berman, the contradiction always immanent in a mode of production becomes especially destabilizing.

2. Contradiction, argues Giddens (1984), "is [increasingly] concentrated upon the tension between the internationalizing of capital (and of capitalistic mechanisms as a whole) and the internal consolidation of nation-states" (pp. 197–198). In the extreme version of this contradiction, the state was trapped in the imperatives (imperialisms) of foreign colonization in the period to 1914 to secure both raw materials and expanding markets for capitalist interests that could still project the signs of *national* identity. A result was one of the largest urban design projects in history: to represent globally the idea of "empire," yet somehow to obfuscate the contradiction of racism implicit in that idea. The efforts of Lutyens to invent an Anglo-Indian style for New Delhi, between 1913 and 1938, are illustrative: To appear to welcome home rule yet preserve the economic benefits of colonialism required the capital to be shifted and represented in an architecture that could be both "British" and "native" (referring to the Moghul city of Fatehpur Sikri) (Frampton, 1985a, p. 211). For other stories of new architectures to represent the state, whether colonial or suddenly decolonized, see Vale (1992).

3. Zarathustra (Zoroaster) was the reputed founder of the Persian religion and, to Nietzsche, "the first to see in the struggle between good and evil [light and dark as its metaphor] the essential wheel in the working of things. The translation of morality into the realm of metaphysics, as force, cause, end-in-itself, is his work." Zarathustra must therefore take responsibility for leading us *beyond* good and evil if, as Nietzsche alleges, the old religions and their mandated morality have collapsed (Nietzsche, 1969; quoted in Hollingdale, 1961, p. 26).

4. Luce Irigaray's *Amante marine de Friedrich Nietzsche* of 1980 (*Marine Lover of Friedrich Nietzsche*, 1991) is a feminist, philosophical engagement with Nietzsche's *Thus Spoke Zarathustra*. Irigaray immerses herself in the erotic

flood of Nietzsche's language, in what is effectively an intertextual love affair. A sympathetic account is Oppel (1993); see also Ansell-Pearson (1993, pp. 39–42).

5. It is an unfortunate term, much loved by the Nazis who misappropriated it and much else from Nietzsche. We find other, more felicitous translations: "the higher man" (variously in Nietzsche, 1961), "the overman" (in Haar, 1992; Vasseleu, 1993).

| CHAPTER 4

1. The utopian socialists' reactions to nineteenth-century urban conditions are well summarized in Frampton (1985a) and Tafuri and Dal Co (1986); the classic critique is that of Mumford (1961). Relevant is Engels's comment, from his 1872 essay "The Housing Question" (Engels, 1969): That while the relations of production remain untransformed, any economic utopianism to improve the lot of labor (by the new towns or by the new gimmick of building societies to enable homeownership) would merely create a new avenue for bourgeois mortgage investment, while subduing labor with the joys of debt. A useful summary and critique of the arts-and-crafts movement, and of William Morris's attempted transformation of capitalist production and industrial society, is also to be found in Frampton (1985a).

2. This unresolved tension found philosophical expression in the twentieth-century debate from beyond the tomb between Nietzsche and Marx. Both Bataille and Benjamin viewed Nietzsche and Marx as the preeminent (but opposed) thinkers of "revolutionary excess"; see Bataille's "Nietzsche and the fascists" (1985) and Benjamin's "The Work of Art in an Age of Mechanical Reproduction" (1977b). The debate is summarized in Caygill (1993).

3. Reyner Banham (1960) dates this break, and Le Corbusier's "second career," from the Villa Cook of 1926, "the first full, programmatic manifestation of Le Style Corbu" (p. 238).

4. The debate concerns different texts, as well as intertextuality. The Foundation Manifesto of Futurism, of 1909, was a savage rejection of feminism and the past and an ecstatic extolling of new technology, speed, the motor car, and "the era of the great mechanised individuals"; it was also autobiographical of its writer, Fillipo Marinetti, as was Nietzsche's Thus Spoke Zarathustra, whose voice it clearly echoes. And like Nietzsche's text, it is anchored in real space: a room in Marinetti's house. Sant'Elia's Messaggio on the problems of modern architecture, of 1914, was more abstracted, but similarly abjured the past and extolled new technology: "We must invent and rebuild ex novo our Modern city like an immense and tumultuous shipyard, active, mobile and everywhere dynamic." But it did not mention futurism, despite Sant'Elia's contact with Marinetti's group. Thus

the debate: Can a textual difference signify an ideological difference and a distancing from protofascism? (The debate is reported in Banham, 1960, pp. 127–136.)

5. Another form of synthesis was to occur in the Maison Domino from 1914 to 1915: standardized units of six columns supporting floor slabs (each like a six-dot domino), assemblable in any variety of combinations (again like dominoes), including, in one illustration, the Versailles-like plan of Fourier's *phalanstère*. Two further synthesizing ideas emerged at this time: the Villes Pilotis, elevated on columns, or *pilotis*, to permit the ground plane to flow uninterrupted beneath the buildings, and the Maison Citrohan of 1920, a double-height living space, main bedroom suspended over it on a gallery, open at one end, and clearly evoking the *megaron* of the ancient Mediterranean civilizations (though avowedly transformed from a truck drivers' restaurant in Paris, frequented by Le Corbusier) (*Le Corbusier 1910–1960*, 1960, p. 25).

6. The following summary is in some measure derivative from Manfredo Tafuri's account in *Modern Architecture* (Vol. 1, Tafuri and Dal Co, 1986, pp. 175–190) and from Kenneth Frampton's account in *Modern Architecture* (1985a, pp. 167–177).

7. Marx's views on aesthetics are pertinent. Artistic production, argues Margaret Rose (1984), was seen by Marx as an instance of human labor: It is part of social production and accordingly subject to technological, social, and cultural forces. Under capitalism, artistic labor and its products are also subject to alienation by being valued simply as commodity. So, in such a context, what are the chances of art's contributing to human emancipation? The first answer is to invoke a "reflectionist aesthetic"— the socialist realism of Georg Lukács, attributed to Marx's ideas, and based largely on the aesthetics of nineteenth-century fiction (Ulmer, 1985, p. 86). Art is a reflection of reality; but a politically committed art can reflect the *ideal* reality of an emancipated workers' state. Rose argues, however, that there is a second, "productivist aesthetic," which is closer to the real spirit of Marx's thought. It is traceable to Saint-Simon and has been expounded in more recent times by Brecht, Althusser, and especially Adorno. The last, it should be noted, studied with Arnold Schönberg, of whom Buck-Morss (1977) comments: "Schönberg rejected the notion of artist-as-genius and replaced it with the artist as craftsman; he saw music not as the expression of subjectivity, but as a search for knowledge which lay outside the artist, as potential within the object, the material. For him, composing was discovery and invention through the practice of music-making" (p. 123).

8. Frampton's designation of the Agit-Prop program as "architecture" would somewhat redefine that term. Its use here would have to embrace informational banners and kiosks rather than buildings and their spaces, as well as street theater and all the other available means for layering proletarian ideas, values, and meanings over the bourgeois ones that prevailed in the

urban space of Russian cities and towns (Malevich: "We will give them other names"); see King (1988). The term would also have to extend to the demountable furniture and other paraphernalia of everyday life addressed by Proletkult. Such a redefinition will arise again in Chapter 12, in relation to the question of a "feminist architectural space."

9. Arturo Soria y Mata devised his linear garden city in the early 1880s: It would be five hundred meters wide, while its extremities might be "Cadiz or St. Petersburg or Peking or Brussels." It would be indeterminate, connecting local "places" in a potentially international, even global, space. It was also the antithesis of the Ebenezer Howard radial city plan. Only some twenty-two kilometers of it, skirting Madrid, were ever built. See Frampton (1985a, pp. 27–28).

10. *Proun* ("object") would be the seminal object with which to reject the nonobjectivity of Malevich (to whom Lissitzky was in fact indebted). It begins as painting, proceeds to the construction of three-dimensional models, and thence to the construction of all the objects of everyday life. "Thus *Proun* supersedes painting and its artists on the one hand, the machine and its engineers on the other; proceeds to the construction of space, organises its dimensions by means of its elements, and creates a new, manifold yet unified, image of our nature" (Lissitzky, quoted in Banham, 1960, p. 194). Giving the artistic construction of space priority over technology is somewhat startling for that era.

11. Signs were also involved in the eventual undermining of the Russian Revolution as, again, Castoriadis (1987) observes: Though Lenin had argued *theoretically* against the idea of a government and administration cut off from the organized masses, nothing was more appealing to him than just that. So a conventional bureaucratic state had to be disguised with new rhetoric—Soviets, People's Commissariats—"the same old things with new words" (p. 122). Signs are also central to the *first* term in Lenin's tripartite contradiction triggering revolution.

| CHAPTER 5

1. For other perspectives on intertextuality, observe Quoniam (1988); Duncan and Duncan (1988).

2. This comment derives from Benjamin's (1979) insistence on translation as historical–materialist practice, where "powerful forces that lie bound in the 'once-upon-a-time' of historicism are set free. . . . It has recourse to a consciousness of the present that shatters the continuum of history" (p. 352).

3. The account of the Bauhaus and its antecedents is especially indebted to Greenberg (1979) and Willett (1978); see also Frampton (1985a) and Sharp (1966).

4. The translation in this instance was not from the Mazdaism claimed by Itten (i.e., from the original Zarathustra prior to Nietzsche's double reading) but from the Viennese, antiseccessionist avant-garde. Itten had established an art school in Vienna in 1916, influenced by educationist Franz Cisek (and more remotely Froebel and Montessori), painter Oskar Kokoschka, and architect Adolf Loos (Frampton, 1985a, p. 124). Torn from the context of end-of-Empire Vienna and translated to that of socialist ideals in corrupted, bourgeois–republican Weimar, these ideas— and especially their modes of representation—then collided with Itten's Mazdaznan proclivities more recently acquired (in 1921) from a Mazdaznan center near Zurich.

5. Giddens's (1979) description is apposite: "A direct, primary, literal meaning designates, in addition, another meaning which is indirect, secondary and figurative and which can be apprehended only through the first" (p. 107, referring to Ricoeur, 1974).

6. Klee's most spatial drawings present another model of emancipation: "Man's ability to measure the spiritual, earthbound and cosmic, set against his physical helplessness; that is his fundamental tragedy. The tragedy of spirituality. The consequence of this simultaneous helplessness of the body and mobility of the spirit is the dichotomy of human existence. Man is half a prisoner, half borne on wings. Each of the two halves perceives the tragedy of its halfness by awareness of its counterpart" (Klee, 1961, p. 407). His emancipation was, through drawing and painting, to comment on that human condition and in the artist's haven of ambiguity to choose the contours of his own world. He was *free to choose*; the drawings would depict a world of spaces that were "not merely illusory, but wavered between reality and ideality, between playfulness and significance" (Greenberg, 1979, p. 62).

7. Far clearer, more uncompromising projects of Le Corbusier predated the Dessau Bauhaus (Maison Domino, 1915; Ville contemporaine, 1922); the same is true of the projects of the constructivists (Tatlin's tower, 1919–1920; schemes by Lissitzky and Melnikov of 1922–1925) and Mies van der Rohe (the expressionist-influenced Berlin Friedrichstrasse office building, 1921). However these were unbuilt. The Bauhaus, by contrast, could be visited and experienced.

8. In *Of Grammatology* (1976), Derrida distinguishes between the terms "what Rousseau wants to say" and "what Rousseau says" to introduce the idea of double readings and the importance of their juxtaposition. For an account of the ensuing debate between Derrida and de Man (e.g., de Man, 1983; Derrida, 1986c), see Bernasconi (1992). A similarly double reading of images would also seem always to be inevitable, as the continuing rereading of constructivist images demonstrates.

9. "The word in language is half someone else's. It becomes 'one's own' only when the speaker populates it with his own intention, his own accent, when he appropriates the word, adapting it to his own semantic and

expressive intention. Prior to this moment of appropriation, the word does not exist in a neutral and impersonal language (it is not, after all, out of a dictionary that the speaker gets his words!), but rather it exists in other people's mouths, in other people's concrete contexts, serving other people's intentions: it is from there that one must take the word, and make it one's own" (Bakhtin, 1981, pp. 293–293; quoted in Wertsch, 1991, p. 59).

CHAPTER 6

1. These paraphrasings are from Dreyfus (1993, p. 305).

2. The "collective voice" of CIAM echoes an Enlightenment–Werkbund–Sachlichkeit instrumentalism. For example: "Rationalization and standardization . . . expect from the consumer (that is to say, the customer who orders the house in which he will live) a revision of his demands in the direction of a readjustment to the new conditions of social life. Such a revision will be manifested in the reduction of certain individual needs henceforth devoid of real justification; the benefits of this reduction will foster the maximum satisfaction of the needs of the greatest number, which are at present restricted" (La Sarraz Declaration, 1928; quoted in Frampton, 1985a, p. 269). Le Corbusier's more complex voice, by contrast, reflects almost a Newtonian vision of technology: "Not in pursuit of an architectural idea, but simply guided by the results of calculation (derived from the principles which govern our universe) and the conception of a living organism, the engineers of today make use of primary elements and, by co-ordinating them in accordance with the rules, provoke in us architectural emotions, and thus make the work of man ring in unison with universal order" (Vers une architecture, 1923; Le Corbusier, 1959, p. 33).

3. If a mode of architectural representation is analogous with a Bakhtinian "social language," then these types parallel "speech genres": the particular forms of utterance corresponding to specific "situations of speech communication, typical themes, and, consequently, also to particular contacts between the meanings of words and actual concrete reality under certain typical circumstances" (Bakhtin, 1986, p. 87).

4. Buck-Morss (1989) comments: "Yet [Benjamin] has always understood these dream images as ambivalent." While Fourier's phalanstère may have anticipated public housing, it also privatized the public space of the arcades, a "reactionary transformation" (p. 469, n. 54).

5. This description is largely derivative from Guignon (1993) and from the collection that it introduces.

6. Taylor's attribution is contestible, and I would rather give priority to Nietzsche, from whose work much of Heidegger's derives (though not as

much as from his teacher, Husserl). But note Heidegger's judgment that Nietzsche still proceeded within the systems of binary opposites opened by Plato and is merely "the most unbridled Platonist" (Heidegger, 1967, p. 133; quoted in Guignon, 1993, p. 18).

7. The academic debates on Heidegger's links with Nazism have boomed since the mid-1980s, most notably since the publication of *Heidegger and Nazism* (Farías, 1989). Among the less hysterical, less journalistic analyses are those of Bourdieu (1991) and Sheehan (1993); the most reflective analysis is Derrida's (1989c), which is also among the more significant and accessible of Derrida's later work.

8. Buck-Morss (1989, p. 471, n. 97) draws attention to the argument that Nazi urban design stressed monumentality with the goal of "awakening" the soul of the German *volk* (see also Taylor, 1974, p. 30). Further, for Hitler, " 'community' architecture never meant building to meet the needs of the community" (Taylor, 1974, p. 28); the state architecture of ancient Rome was favored over the Weimar Republic's preoccupation with "hotels and department stores."

9. This amounted to resolving the issue of Marx's "two aesthetics" in favor of the "reflectionist" (a politically committed art can reflect the ideal reality of an emancipated workers' state) over the "productivist" (of Bogdanov, Brecht, and Adorno). See Rose (1984); see also Chapter 4, n. 7.

10. Frampton (1985a, pp. 211–212) cites another example of stripped-down neoclassicism enmeshed in a conveniently refound vernacular, all to legitimize a political lie, in Lutyens's New Delhi. See also Chapter 3, n. 2.

11. The main exemplars were the visionary projects rejected in the 1930s in favor of the neoclassical and the moderne: Mies van der Rohe's Reichsbank of 1933, the tower blocks of Le Corbusier's Ville radieuse of 1935 and his Quartier de la Marine in Algiers of 1938–1942, etc. Other exemplars were the few executed modern movement projects of that era, preeminently Mies's first buildings for the Illinois Institute of Technology (arguably the purest of all suprematist-oriented urban designs), Le Corbusier's Salvation Army Refuge in Paris of 1929 and his Pavillon Suisse for Paris's Cité universitaire of 1930–1932, and indirectly the 1930s work of Frank Lloyd Wright. The most influential text on this transition—itself catalyzing the transition—was Sigfried Giedion's Charles Eliot Norton lectures delivered at Harvard University in 1938–1939, published as *Space, Time and Architecture* in 1941 and variously revised and augmented (Giedion, 1954).

12. In Bakhtin's theory, a *social language* characterizes the discourse peculiar to a specific social stratum (profession, age group, etc.) in a specific social system and time; in turn, the typical forms of utterance peculiar to specific situations (prayers, chants, or political exhortations) are *speech genres* (Bakhtin, 1986, p. 78; Wertsch, 1991, p. 61). See n. 3 above.

13. The soubriquet "International Style" is usually attributed to Henry-

Russell Hitchcock and Philip Johnson's 1932 catalog title for an exhibition at New York's Museum of Modern Art.

14. It is difficult to believe that Heidegger would not have been aware of Le Corbusier's 1923 description, in very similar terms, of the Parthenon and the Athens Acropolis in *Vers une architecture* (see, e.g., Le Corbusier, 1959, p. 188). And note Jencks (1987a) on the alleged links between Le Corbusier and Nietzsche (see, e.g., pp. 25, 187, n. 11).

15. For an extended exploration of these themes, see also Zimmerman (1990). Zimmerman (1993) summarizes the late Heidegger as combining antiessentialism (anti-Platonism) with three claims: "(1) that the ontological event of *appearing* is acausal and, hence, incapable of being explained by any narrative (mythical, religious, metaphysical, scientific) regarding how things may have been *produced*, (2) that being and appearing are in effect the same, and (3) that things manifest themselves in a mutually appropriative dance" (pp. 260–261).

16. Though a brilliant polemicist for the Bauhaus, Sigfried Giedion had come upon its debates only in 1925 and thus had missed the real complexity of its aesthetic turmoil. His seminal *Bauen in Frankreich; Eisen, Eisenbeton* (1928) was intended to bring the earlier technological preoccupations (even determinism) of Muthesius and Meyer up to date by "internationalizing" the modern movement's antecedents. Its effect, like that of *Space, Time and Architecture*, originally published in 1941, was however to significantly construct the age's perceptions of its own history—as precisely the world that Heidegger was rebelling against. The 1943 convergence of the two is thus remarkable.

17. The Unité was in fact repeated: at Nantes-Rezé (1952–1957), Berlin (1956–1958), Meaux (1957–1959), Briey-en-Forêt (1957–1960) and Firminy-Vert (1962–1968). Each, however, seems more place specific than universally applicable.

18. Both are akin to what Bellah et al. (1985, p. 334) would call, in the realm of moral discourse, *first language*—the *dominant* vocabularies and characteristic patterns of moral reasoning among the many that the individual typically employs.

19. Tafuri argues similarly, that "the edifice is a complete and closed entity only because practical considerations have obliged it to be such. It thus speaks of the objective it cannot attain: to dilate itself . . . so as to give shape to the entire landscape, both urban and natural" (Tafuri and Dal Co, 1986, p. 314).

20. The "old guard" of CIAM saw this issue as one of "the space of public appearance" and the monumentality of institutions mutually constituting each other, with Giedion's 1943 manifesto as a starting point for the debate. The younger affiliates rejected such denials of complexity. See, for example, Frampton (1985a, p. 271).

21. We will find an explanation for these in a later chapter, with Walter Benjamin's (1982) insistence (following Jules Michelet) that "every ep-

och dreams the one that follows it," but in that dream "the latter appears wedded to elements of ur-history, that is, of a classless society" (p. 47). These are "ur-images."

22. The issues pursued by Kahn in this period include the following: What is the city and urban life (unsatisfactorily sought in his Gargantuan studies for Philadelphia)? What is worship (a Philadelphia synagogue of 1961–1970; a Dominican priory for Media, Pennsylvania, of 1965–1968)? What is the state (most notably in the Dacca government center)? What is science, knowledge, and uncertainty (the A. N. Richards Laboratories at the University of Pennsylvania of 1957–1961, the Salk Institute at La Jolla of 1959–1965)? What is collective life?

23. For example, McDonald's became franchised in 1955 (Kroc, with Anderson, 1977); for its place in the broader context of the development of signature architecture, see Rubin (1979).

24. The interest in residential differentiation during the 1950s and 1960s is symptomatic. Something of a seminal account, though marred by the pattern fetish, is by Timms (1971).

25. Heidegger saw Nietzsche as still a metaphysical philosopher, caught in classical dualisms. A more specific departure was Heidegger's different response to "nihilism": If we accept that we must *choose* our values (Nietzsche), we quickly realize that we can *unchoose* them; instead, the only emancipation is to be gripped by shared concerns and commitment, and the task is to make such a world and, in turn, the task of the work of art is "to bring worlds into existence" (Dreyfus, 1993, pp. 290–204; Megill, 1985, p. 3; both refer specifically to the 1936 essay "The Origin of the Work of Art," in Heidegger, 1971a).

26. The most notable avenue for this reinterpretation has been the pages of the journal *Environment and Planning D: Society and Space*. Note in particular D. Rose (1984), Pratt and Hanson (1988), Winchester and White (1988), Warde (1991), and Geltmaker (1992).

CHAPTER 7

1. The linking of the disintegration of planning (from plans to projects) to the idea of postmodernism-as-process is first made in Dear (1986). Where Dear illustrates with Los Angeles, Harvey (1989) focuses on Baltimore, and Knox (1991) on Washington.

2. Subsequent writers have found substantial difficulty with Harvey's arguments, most specifically with his persistent and even uncritical privileging of the economic "infrastructure" in historical explanation, his apparently consequent dismissal of the shifts in the experience of space, time, nature, "self" and "otherness" (the postmodern experience!) as mere changes in surface appearance as capitalist economic practices go through yet another innovative wave, and his (again consequent) indifference to heterogeneities of experience. See, for example, Deutsche (1991), Massey (1991).

3. The nearest to a definition of flexible accumulation might be that it "rests on flexibility with respect to labour processes, labour markets, products, and patterns of consumption. It is characterized by the emergence of entirely new sectors of production, new ways of providing financial services, new markets, and, above all, greatly intensified rates of commercial, technological, and organizational innovation" (Harvey, 1989, p. 147).

4. This is the spatial fragmentation and differentiation of experience confronted in the preceding chapter, of which see n. 26.

5. Pertinent here is Giddens's (1979) argument on the mutually constituting effects of structures of *signification*, *domination*, and *legitimation* in social systems and their reproduction. See also Giddens (1984, pp. 29–34).

6. It is Habermas's voice that sounds through this second formulation of the contradiction. In "Toward a Reconstruction of Historical Materialism," Habermas (1979a, pp. 130–177) attempts to distinguish shifts over time in the forms of social integration. He sees this integration effected by (1) normal structures of everyday interaction (where there is no conflict to be resolved), (2) structures of consensual worldviews insofar as they determine issues of morality and law, and (3) structures of institutionalized law and binding moral codes. In the modern age, there is a domain of strategic action regulated on universalistic principles (capitalist enterprise, bourgeois civil law) differentiated from a domain of political decision-making similarly grounded (formal democracy). At the level of worldviews (2, above), unity can no longer be secured "objectively" through a unifying principle such as God or Nature (Nietzsche), but only reflectively, through the "unity" of reason (Habermas's central assertion). My point is that, in the present moment, the props of universalistic principles (the reign of reason) are ceasing to hold: The edifice of modernity is unstable; reason is not characterized by unity.

7. This reading of modernity's radicals does not define "the aesthetic" as a "realm of aesthetic objects and sensations" but as "an attempt to expand the aesthetic to embrace the whole of reality." Art (Nietzsche) or language (Heidegger) or discourse (Foucault) or the text (Derrida) is seen as the primary realm of human experience, in which reality is constituted (Megill, 1985, p. 2).

8. The "antiartist" term is invoked to underscore the dadaist resonances in Derrida: Compare, for example, Richter (1965). What distinguishes Derrida from the dadaists, including Walter Benjamin, is that he is antirepresentational: He would attack the "ocular metaphor" of understanding (Megill, 1985, p. 306).

9. Derrida scrutinizes Rousseau's proposition that language is originally metaphorical but shifts with the "natural" progress of writing toward literalness—hence, representation and nonmetaphoricity. This is both progress and regress (a "pro-regress"). As the text comes to exist only for itself, it ceases to be representational. For the progress of this debate, see Derrida (1976), de Man (1983), then Derrida (1986c).

10. This point is closer to Philo's reading of Foucault than to Soja's. Philo (1992) argues that Foucault's attack on totalizing history compels a geographical eye that sees only "spaces of dispersion": "spaces where things proliferate in a jumbled-up manner on the same 'level' as one another," where "there simply is no 'essential' to be sighted." There are no different experiences of space unfolding in different epochs, only the imagined differences of the present (p. 139).

11. Ulmer (1985, p. 88) attributes this argument to Lacan in structuralist psychoanalysis and to Althusser in ideological criticism.

12. The following account will largely follow the argumentation of Jameson (1985), and much will effectively paraphrase it.

13. For a contrary argument, see Rose (1991, p. 95).

14. An earlier voice: Walter Benjamin, in "The Author as Producer" (1934), observed the potential for "new literary technologies" to destroy the myth of artistic genius and the completed, self-contained work and to replace the Great Work with the idea of writing as "intervention," "interruption"—a political practice in breaking down the distinction between author and audience and democratizing information and communication.

15. In a very restricted sense, superimprinting of texts yields the "double coding" that Jencks (1987b) sees as the identifying characteristic of postmodernism in architecture.

16. The precursor of this montage-allegory was Walter Benjamin: "Montage became for him the modern, constructive, active, unmelancholy form of allegory, namely the ability to connect dissimilars in such a way as to 'shock' people into new recognitions and understandings" (Mitchell, 1977, p. xiii).

17. This could well be a program for postmodern architecture: Collage/montage, grafting and disrupting, the pastiche and the equivocal can especially describe the work of Michael Graves, Charles Moore, and the "mainstream"; deconstruction and destabilizing parasitism characterize the work of Peter Eisenman and the architectural deconstructionists. See, for example, Jencks (1988a, 1988b).

CHAPTER 8

1. The distinction between moral–practical rationality and theoretic–cognitive rationality is originally Kantian (the focuses of the *Critique of Practical Reason* and the *Critique of Pure Reason*, respectively). The present reference however is to its development in Habermas (e.g., 1973). The artificiality of the distinction will subsequently need to be unmasked (in Chapter 11 following; see also Megill, 1985, pp. 332–336).

2. An extension of this emphasis on representation (expression) arises in the somewhat antimodernist interweaving of aesthetic (representational)

and class critiques, in the journal *Environment and Planning D: Society and Space*, that began with Rose (1984). See Chapter 6, n. 26 above.

3. *De la grammatologie* was published in 1967; see Derrida (1976). His first publication would seem to be 1962 (Leventure, 1992).

4. For an exploration of these arguments, see Hillier and Hanson (1984).

5. Meier's Smith House, at Darien, Connecticut (1965–1967), had caused critical confusion: It was faultlessly detailed, yet its clean volumes, surfaces, and lines were more an abstract composition (a postmodernist "play") than a logical, "modern" outgrowth of architectural program, site characteristics, and constructional techniques chosen. It was seen as 1920s Le Corbusier reduced to mere style or decoration. His Douglas House of Harbor Springs, Michigan (1971–1973), went further, reducing Le Corbusier's "method" to a vertical and horizontal layering of lines and surfaces. Graves's houses were, similarly, virtually plays with Corbusian or constructivist elements to no immediately ostensible program.

6. Various of these themes, of Venturi's work of the early 1960s, also emerge with a number of other North American designers in the late 1960s: most notably the parodying eclecticism and the oddly angled walls with Charles Moore (the Santa Barbara Faculty Club of 1968, Kresge College of 1972–1974), and an elegant play with applied decoration and a mannerist awkwardness with Robert Stern (Lang House of 1973–1974, then the many-leveled eclecticism of the Westchester Residence from 1974–1976). See Arnell and Bickford (1981).

7. The most notable interweaving comes in the mid-1970s, in the house designs of Michael Graves: The Corbusian references shifted to a far more eclectic (and "Venturian") set—broken pediment, string course, and latticework in his 1974 Claghorn House in Princeton; a sophisticated play with high-modernist grids and rustic clapboard vernacular in the 1976–1978 Schulman House, also in Princeton.

8. A further significant social language to emerge in North America over this era was that of a "neo–art deco" running through Jahn's expressionist Houston tower and especially the work of Kohn Pedersen Fox (KPF) Associates (their Procter and Gamble Headquarters in Cincinnati, e.g., of 1982–1986).

9. The city as an aggregation of "products of different régimes" runs through Dear's (1986) notion of planning in the context of "postmodernism as process."

10. A self-referential mocking of audiences is identified by Lash and Urry (1987) in (postmodernist) "pop" music from the late 1970s and 1980s, vis-à-vis the (modernist) "rock," dominant until the 1970s. Some aspects of their comparison of these rival "critiques of consumer society," which in turn derive from arguments of Simon Frith, also reflect the shift in architectural production. Rock presented a "modernist aesthetics of

beauty" and an auratic intent; pop (or punk) propounded "an anti-aes-
thetic of discordant and intentionally nerve-jangling cacophony," mocking the auratic tradition of individuality and originality, thematizing
repetition. Rock was to be listened to carefully (as the modern movement
building was to be carefully explored); pop/punk was "a matter of the
visual, the image"; it was to be seen (as the postmodern building was to be
merely background spectacle). And "to listen to a punk recording for the
first time was like already having listened to it before" (as déjà vu can
characterize the experience of a postmodernist building). Finally, the
pop/punk artists "expressed contempt for the mass audience they intended
to shock, and self-referentially mocked their own popularity" (Lash and
Urry, 1987, p. 291).

11. Tafuri and Dal Co (1986) even suggest that Aymonino's Gallaratese
exhausts that particular high-modernist tradition in Europe—whatever
follows will have to be *post*-high-modernist or else boring and sterile (p.
372).

12. It is in this context that Anthony Vidler writes of a "third typology":
Where the first typology, or elemental architectural language, related to
the return of architecture to its natural origins (e.g., through reference to
the primitive hut) and the second to modern technology, this third is to
reinstate an autonomous language of architecture and urban design independent of social context, using "the clarity of the eighteenth century city
to rebuke the fragmentation, decentralization, and formal disintegration"
of the modern (Krier et al., 1978, p. 32).

13. Frampton (1985a, p. 294) makes the connections between this program
and the rationalist architecture of Piranesi, Ledoux, and Boullée from the
eighteenth century, Pugin's *Contrasts* of 1843; and Michel Foucault's
preoccupation with regulatory, quasi-punitive institutions in *Surveiller et
punir* of 1975 (Foucault, 1977). More broadly, there are clear links to
Foucault's idea of heterotopias—Rossi would reestablish the architectural
representation of heterotopias in city and countryside, thereby finding
once more the *content*, meaning, of the space of everyday life.

| CHAPTER 9

1. Though Derrida (1989a) makes it clear in the aphorisms that it is the
architecture of logocentric language and thought that will be deestab-
lished in deconstruction, yet in aphorism 48 this equation itself is (typically) interrupted (an example of the method): "Contrary to appearances
'deconstruction' is not an architectural metaphor" (p. 69).

2. A good introduction to this story of Eisenman's transformations is Jencks
(1988a), reproduced in Papadakis et al. (1989).

3. From Chapter 2 previously: "To articulate the past historically does not
mean to recognise it 'the way it really was.' . . . It means to seize hold of a

memory as it flashes up in a moment of danger" (Benjamin, 1969, p. 255).
There is also Eisenman's statement in relation to Cannaregio (1994): "All
three memories—future, present, past—have their shadows, the loss of
memory. Perhaps we must now learn how to forget" (p. 50).

4. The Russian language, observes Cooke (1989), has two words for "construction" (another way of saying it lacks the ambiguity of the English):
There is *stroitel'stvo*, which is what you do on building sites; and there is
konstruktsiia, which has to do with "the structure of ideas, with the
construction of arguments through assembling sequences of ideas" (p. 11).
Constructivism derives from the second word.

5. Jencks (1988a) continues: "This non-place could be the flatscape of a
parking lot, or a suburban sprawl littered with supermarkets, parkways,
little houses and garden plots. In this sense it's an abstraction of social
reality, an attempt to make high art from the heterogeneous fragmenta-
tions that surround any major city" (p. 3).

6. Film is claimed by Ulmer to be "the primary vehicle for modern allegory":
"It composes narrative out of a succession of concrete images, which make
it particularly suited to allegory's essential pictogrammatism" (Craig
Owens, quoted in Ulmer, 1985, p. 96).

7. Jameson (1984) speaks of space and time being "stretched" to become the
content for the new global capitalism; see also Dear (1986).

8. The question of "two languages" of spatial representation is approached
from a different direction in Folch-Serra (1990): As landscape as a "way of
seeing the world" is spawned in conversation, it becomes "not only
'graphically visible' in space but also 'narratively visible' in time, in a field
of discourses all attempting to account for human experience" (p. 258).
All readings of space become intertextual and interlinguistic.

9. There are also elements of this "two language" intertextuality in Bernard
Tschumi's *Joyce's Garden* (1976–1977) and *The Manhattan Transcripts*
(1976–1981).

10. The pun/"deconstruction" refers to Nietzsche's essay title: "Why I
Write Such Good Books" (in Nietzsche, 1969). One reading of the pun
would invoke the myth-making claim seemingly expressed in the
Nietzschean text, reflected upon in Megill (1985, p. 99). Where
Nietzsche would resurrect the myth-making role of "first language"
(narratives in time), Eisenman might do the same for "second language"
(narratives in space).

11. In Bernasconi's (1992) paraphrasing, "What is added to take the place of
a lack or default is itself a lack," for the "logic of supplementarity" is driven
by a "desire to recapture a presence which never existed" (p. 145).

12. Adds Megill (1985), the horizontality (pure surface) of the labyrinth
parallels much of "postmodern" art, including the arts of Foucault and
Derrida. "And this art, which does not return to a beginning and which
has neither subject nor object, goes by the name of writing" (p. 319).

| CHAPTER 10

1. Goethe's synthesis of essence and appearance would apply to the sphere of nature and was interpreted thus by Simmel. Benjamin would translate it to the sphere of the cultural. Despite the enterprise's phenomenological overtones (Heidegger's rejection of the Platonist distinction between enduring essence and ephemeral properties [1962, original 1927]), Benjamin was in fact dismissive of both Husserl and Heidegger, as his colleague Scholem has recounted (1982, p. 22).

2. The museum (and park) is linked to the abbatoir through another necessity of modernity: "to appropriate and discipline proletarian expenditure, to acknowledge but also to reabsorb nonwork time, particularly Sundays and holidays among the working and dangerous classes" (Hollier, 1989, p. xiv). Emile Zola's concern: Where is idleness to go? Out on the town (the Folies, the dens, the fallen nature of the arcades) or out of town (the healthy countryside, or the mental health of the museums)? Interior or exterior? asks Hollier (pp. xv–xx).

3. Hollier also invokes Zola's (1867) condemnation of "the absurdity of urban landscaping, where lawns try to recall nature for consumptive city dwellers. 'It looks like a bit of nature that did something wrong and was put in prison' " (Zola, 1976, p. 321; quoted in Hollier, 1989, p. xv).

4. Benjamin makes a great deal of Blanqui's critique of modernist progress, even more than of Nietzsche's, whose voice is ultimately that of the embittered bourgeois, disdainful of the masses. Auguste Blanqui, socialist-anarchist, lifelong champion of proletarian causes, opponent of Marx's theories (and optimism), at the end of his life sees endless repetition as most clearly revealed in capitalist mass production and sees the only future as one of endless catastrophe. Blanqui is thereby the better bearer of Benjamin's lesson of the Hell of modernity (see Buck-Morss, 1989, pp. 106–107, 107n.).

5. Buck-Morss (1989) quotes *Konvolut* F, "Iron Construction": While Marx argued that new means of production are fettered by still-existing archaic (capitalist) relations of production, Benjamin saw these fetters as constituted in the "collective imagination"—in representation—and he believed that Marx meant this as well (p. 115). The conclusion to such an idea: Last-instance determinacy rests in the aesthetic. Megill (1985) argues similarly for the ideas of Nietzsche, Heidegger, Foucault, and Derrida.

6. See especially Jencks (1987b).

7. Contra Bataille, we can see, in every monument, the ruin that is to come. The 1931 prize-winning design to remodel the Rond Point de la Defense in Paris featured a giant, neoclassical "angel of victory," confidently facing the future, dwarfing the crowd still cowering in the shadows of the past. Klee's painting (of 1920) seems to reduce this already to ruin. See Buck-Morss (1989, p. 93).

8. Note again (from Chapter 7) Ulmer's (1985) distinction between traditional (baroque) allegory (meaning under the guise of other meaning) and
   "narrative allegory" (the material of the signifier favored over the meaning of the signified). The latter is attributed to Benjamin by Mitchell
   (1977, p. xiii).

9. The "text" that Benjamin would use for this "deconstruction" would be
   virtually the whole of Baudelaire's ouevre, though *Les Fleurs du mal* would
   take a special part of the burden (Baudelaire, 1962).

|CHAPTER 11

1. Heidegger would express this openness differently: We are to "submit
   resolutely" to what the mood of human anxiety would reveal to us,
   thereby assuming "responsibility for being the mortal openness that we
   already are" and becoming "authentic." We break out of our constricted
   existences (rather than "fleeing from anxiety into everyday practices and
   distractions"), let this openness expand, and allow things and other humans to manifest themselves in all the richness and complexity of their
   being. This is the Heideggerian sense of emancipation (Zimmerman,
   1993, p. 245).

2. The core argument of *Dialectic of Enlightenment* is that "with each conquest over external nature the internal nature of those who gain ever new
   triumphs is more deeply enslaved" (Habermas, 1985d, p. 74). The only
   possible path to emancipation (Habermas quotes Marcuse) might be to
   "rely on a subjectivity which is still sensitive to a utopian horizon" (p. 74),
   though Habermas would ultimately return to the project of rationality
   rather than the Marcusian aesthetic. According to Bernstein (1985),
   "One might epitomize Habermas's entire intellectual project . . . as writing a *new* Dialectic of Enlightenment—one which does full justice to the
   dark side of the Enlightenment legacy, explains its causes but nevertheless
   redeems and justifies the hope of freedom, justice, and happiness which
   still stubbornly speaks to us" (p. 31).

3. Wellmer's (1985) summary here is that "the *paradox* of rationalization
   would be that a rationalization of the life-world was the *precondition* and
   the *starting point* for a process of systemic rationalization and differentiation, which then has become more and more autonomous vis-à-vis the
   normative constraints embodied in the life-world, until in the end the
   systemic imperatives begin to instrumentalize the life-world and threaten
   to destroy it" (p. 56).

4. The spatialization of this differentiation was a focus of Lefebvre's (1976)
   project: the centralization of control over material reproduction but the
   dispersal of symbolic reproduction (p. 18). See Chapter 7 preceding.

5. This is the sense in which Luce Irigaray juxtaposes her "fairy tale" *Marine
   Lover of Friedrich Nietzsche* (1991) with Nietzsche's own in *Thus Spoke*

Zarathustra (1961). It is a collision that illuminates its opposite—distancing; and Nietzsche is the philosopher of unbridgeable difference.

6. But observe the argument of Foucault (1978) that it is the progressive shift from *the erotic* to *sexuality* that marks modernity.

7. And see Zimmerman (1993, p. 245); n. 1 above.

8. Foucault (1982) views this as a shift from "total history" to "general history"—"nothing is fundamental: this is what is interesting in the analysis of society" (p. 18).

9. Lyotard, Vattimo, and various other postmodernists expressly reject the metanarrative of unfolding rationality underlying Habermas's argument. See Bellamy (1987, pp. 728–729).

10. But note Thomas McCarthy's (1990) countervoice: that Derrida's enterprise is utterly apolitical.

11. This is Bateson's (1973) distinction of Learning III. See Chapter 1, n. 4, preceding.

12. In Heidegger's emancipatory path, *we* become the landscape, as the clearing where "things" are allowed "to reveal themselves primordially." We finally comprehend our own "radical groundlessness and nothingness" (Zen) (Zimmerman, 1993, p. 245).

13. Zimmerman draws attention to Heidegger's interest in Buddhism and Taoism. Heidegger had especially explored the resonances between the Chinese *tao* and his own idea of *Ereignis* or "event of appropriation," claiming humanity as the site of the self-manifesting of entities (Nature). This would change human history by freeing us from our compulsion to see entities instrumentally, as mere resources for actions without ultimate purpose beyond mistaken notions of human gratification (Heidegger, 1971b, p. 92).

14. From a vast literature on the search for this other side of the human, two contrasting voices only will be noted. Fox (1988) turns eclectically to the mystical traditions, though mainly to those of the European Middle Ages; Derrida (1989c) turns to Heidegger.

| CHAPTER 12

1. This is not to suggest that such learning is ever attainable—the conclusion that must emerge from any careful reading of Nietzsche (1961) and Irigaray (1991). See Oppel (1993).

2. That Derrida is concerned with responsibility and an "ethical space" is sometimes contested (e.g., McCarthy, 1990); however, see Llewelyn (1992) and the long debate collected in Wood (1993).

3. And again observe Fox (1983, 1988) on nature traditions in both Western and non-Western mysticism.

4. One reading of Nietzsche would be that unreflective faith in a given morality died with modernity ("the death of God"), to be replaced by our clutching at progress (the world of the commodity) as our new god and source of ethical certainty. The danger is that with the collapse of our guiding belief in material progress, we will grasp for a new god, say "sustainable development" and ecological responsibility, rather than finally face Nietzsche's abyss—the need to "make oneself" and to face the responsibility for the giving of space and time.

5. Its genealogy is commonly traced from Thorstein Veblen, La Follette, and the Wisconsin Progressive Era, but much earlier from "Rousseau by way of Goethe, Carlyle, Emerson, Thoreau and Whitman" (Smith, 1981, p. 191). It is also closest, as Frampton (1985a, p. 187) observes, to the world promised by Marx and Engels in 1848 in *The Communist Manifesto*, abolishing the distinction between town and country.

6. A countercomment, however, from Lewis Mumford, in 1929: "His architecture is not in the current of the present regime any more than Walt Whitman's writings were in the current of the Gilded Age: Hence his value is not that he has dominated the scene and made it over in his image, but that he has kept the way open for a type of architecture which can come into existence only in a much more humanized and socially adept generation than our own" (quoted in Brooks, 1981, p. v).

7. A relatively complete though uncritical review of SITE's work is in SITE (1980). Another fine collection of images of architecture and the garden mutually invading is Solomon (1988).

References

Adorno, T. W. (1970). *Aesthetic Theory* (G. Adorno and R. Tiedemann, Eds.; C. Lenhardt, Trans.). Andover, UK: Routledge and Kegan Paul.

Alexander, C. (1979). *The Timeless Way of Building*. New York: Oxford University Press.

Alexander, C., Ishikawa, S., and Silverstein, M. (with Jacobson, M., Fiksdahi-King, I., and Angel, S.). (1977). *A Pattern Language*. New York: Oxford University Press.

Alexander, C., Neis, H., Anninou, A., and King, I. (1987). *A New Theory of Urban Design*. New York: Oxford University Press.

Althusser, L. (1969). *For Marx*. London: Allen Lane.

Althusser, L. (1971). *Lenin and Philosophy and Other Essays*. London: New Left Books.

Ansell-Pearson, K. (1993). "Nietzsche, woman and political theory." In P. Patton (Ed.), *Nietzsche, Feminism and Political Theory* (pp. 27–48). London: Routledge.

Appleton, J. (1975). *The Experience of Landscape*. London and New York: Wiley.

Architectural Drawings of the Russian Avant-Garde. (1990). With essay by C. Cooke. New York: Museum of Modern Art.

Architecture de C.-N. Ledoux (1983). Reprint. Princeton NJ: Princeton University Press. (Original edition, Paris: Lenoir, 1847)

Arnell, P., and Bickford, T. (1981). *Robert A. M. Stern 1965–1980: Toward a Modern Architecture After Modernism.* New York: Rizzoli.

Arnell, P., and Bickford, T. (Eds.). (1985). *Frank Gehry: Buildings and Projects.* New York: Rizzoli.

Bagby, R. L. (1990). "Daughters of growing things." In I. Diamond and C. F. Orenstein (Eds.), *Reweaving the World: The Emergence of Ecofeminism* (pp. 231–248). San Francisco: Sierra Club Books.

Bakhtin, M. M. (1981). *The Dialogic Imagination: Four Essays by M. M. Bakhtin* (M. Holquist, Ed.; C. Emerson and M. Holquist, Trans.). Austin: University of Texas Press.

Bakhtin, M. M. (1986). *Speech Genres and Other Late Essays* (C. Emerson and M. Holquist, Eds.; V. W. McGee, Trans.). Austin: University of Texas Press.

Banham, R. (1960). *Theory and Design in the First Machine Age.* London: Architectural Press.

Bann, S. (1990). "From Captain Cook to Neil Armstrong: Colonial exploration and the structure of landscape." In S. Pugh (Ed.), *Reading Landscape: Country-City-Capital* (pp. 214–230). Manchester and New York: Manchester University Press.

Baran, P. A., and Sweezy, P. M. (1966). *Monopoly Capital: An Essay on the American Economic and Social Order.* New York: Monthly Review Press.

Barthes, R. (1976). *Sade, Fourier, Loyola* (R. Howard, Trans.). New York: Hill and Wang.

Bataille, G. (1971). *Oeuvres complètes* (Vol. 1). Paris: Gallimard.

Bataille, G. (1985). *Visions of Excess: Selected Writings, 1927–1939* (A. Stockl, Ed.). Minneapolis: University of Minnesota Press.

Bateson, G. (1973). *Steps to an Ecology of Mind.* London: Paladin.

Baudelaire, C. (1962). *The Flowers of Evil [Les Fleurs du mal]* (rev. ed.) (M. Mathews and J. Mathews, Eds.). New York: New Directions.

Baudelaire, C. (1978). *The Painter of Modern Life and Other Essays.* New York: Garland Publications.

Baudrillard, J. (1981). *For a Critique of the Political Economy of the Sign.* St. Louis, MO: Telos Press.

Baudrillard, J. (1983). *In the Shadow of Silent Majorities, or The End of the Social.* New York: Semiotexte.

Baudrillard, J. (1985). "The ecstasy of communication." In H. Foster (Ed.), *Postmodern Culture* (pp. 126–136). London and Sydney: Pluto Press.

Baudrillard, J. (1987). "Forget Foucault." In J. Baudrillard (Ed.), *Forget Foucault* (pp. 7–64). New York: Columbia University Press.

Baudrillard, J. (1988). *America* (C. Turner, Trans.). London: Verso.

Bédard, J.-F. (Ed.). (1994). *Cities of Artificial Excavation: The Work of Peter Eisenman, 1978–1988.* New York: Rizzoli.

Bell, D. (1973). *The Coming of Postindustrial Society.* New York: Basic Books.

Bell, D. (1976). *The Cultural Contradictions of Capitalism.* New York: Basic Books.

Bellah, R. N., Madsen, R., Sullivan, W. M., Swidler, A., and Tipton, S. M. (1985). *Habits of the Heart: Individualism and Commitment in American Life.* Berkeley and Los Angeles: University of California Press.

Bellamy, R. (1987). "Post-modernism and the end of history." *Theory, Culture and Society, 4*, 727–733.

Benjamin, A. (1988). "Derrida, architecture and philosophy." *Architectural Design, 58*(3/4), 8–11.

Benjamin, W. (1969). "Theses on the philosophy of history." In H. Arendt (Ed.), *Illuminations* (H. Zohn, Trans.). New York: Schocken Books.

Benjamin, W. (1972). *Gessamelte Schriften* (Vol. I) (R. Tiedemann and H. Schweppenhäuser, Eds., with T. W. Adorno and G. Scholem). Frankfurt: Suhrkamp Verlag.

Benjamin, W. (1973). "Paris: The capital of the nineteenth century." In *Charles Baudelaire: A Lyric Poet in the Era of High Capitalism* (H. Zohn, Trans.). London: New Left Books.

Benjamin, W. (1977a). *The Origin of German Tragic Drama* (J. Osborne, Trans.). Introduction by G. Steiner. London: New Left Books.

Benjamin, W. (1977b). *Illuminations*. (H. Zohn, Trans.). London: Fontana.

Benjamin, W. (1978). *Reflections: Essays, Aphorisms, Autobiographical Writings* (P. Demetz, Ed.; E. Jephcott, Trans.). New York: Schocken Books.

Benjamin, W. (1979). "Edward Fuchs, collector and historian." In *One-Way Street and Other Writings* (E. Jephcott and K. Shorter, Trans.) (pp. 349–386). London: New Left Books.

Benjamin, W. (1982). *Gessamelte Schriften: Das Passagen-Werk* (Vol. 5). (R. Tiedemann and H. Schweppenhuser, Eds., with T. W. Adorno and G. Scholem). Frankfurt: Suhrkamp Verlag.

Benjamin, W. (1992). "The task of the translator: An introduction to the translation of Baudelaire's *Tableaux Parisiens*." In H. Arendt (Ed.), *Illuminations* (H. Zohn, Trans.) (pp. 70–82). London: Fontana.

Berman, M. (1984). *The Reenchantment of the World*. New York: Bantam Books.

Berman, M. (1989). *Coming to Our Senses*. New York: Simon and Schuster.

Bernasconi, R. (1992). "No more stories, good or bad: De Man's criticisms of Derrida on Rousseau." In D. Wood (Ed.), *Derrida: A Critical Reader* (pp. 137–166). Oxford: Blackwell.

Bernstein, R. J. (1985). "Introduction." In R. J. Bernstein (Ed.), *Habermas and Modernity* (pp. 1–32). Cambridge: Polity Press.

Bondi, L., and Domosh, M. (1992). "Other figures in other places: On feminism, postmodernism and geography." *Environment and Planning D: Society and Space, 10*, 199–213.

Bourdieu, P. (1984). *Distinction: A Social Critique of the Judgement of Taste*. Andover, UK: Routledge and Kegan Paul.

Bourdieu, P. (1991). *The Political Ontology of Martin Heidegger* (P. Collier, Trans.). Stanford, CA: Stanford University Press.

Bradbury, M., and McFarlane, J. (1976). *Modernism, 1890–1930*. Harmondsworth, England: Penguin.

"Broadacre City, Frank Lloyd Wright, architect, project, 1935." (1981). *Architectural Design, 51*(10/11), 86.

Broadbent, G. (1990). *Emerging Concepts in Urban Space Design*. London and New York: Van Nostrand Reinhold.

Brooks, H. A. (Ed.). (1981). *Writings on Wright: Selected Comment on Frank Lloyd Wright*. Cambridge, MA: MIT Press.

Brownlee, D. B., and DeJong, D. G. (1992). *Louis I. Kahn: In the Realm of Architecture*. New York: Rizzoli.

Buck-Morss, S. (1977). *The Origin of Negative Dialectics: Theordor W. Adorno, Walter Benjamin and the Frankfurt Institute*. London: Macmillan.

Buck-Morss, S. (1989). *The Dialectics of Seeing: Walter Benjamin and The Arcades Project*. Cambridge, MA: MIT Press.

Bürger, P. (1981). "Avant-garde and contemporary aesthetics: A reply to Jürgen Habermas." *New German Critique*, 22 (Winter).

Bürger, P. (1984). *Theory of the Avant-garde* (M. Shaw, Trans.). Minneapolis: University of Minnesota Press.

Calvino, I. (1979). *Invisible Cities* (W. Weaver, Trans). London: Pan Books.

Capra, F. (1983). *The Turning Point: Science, Society and the Rising Culture*. London: Fontana Paperbacks.

Capra, F., and Steindl-Rast, D. (1991). *Belonging to the Universe: Explorations on the Frontiers of Science and Spirituality*. San Francisco: Harper.

Caramel, L., and Longatti, A. (1987). *Antonio Sant'Elia: The Complete Work*. New York: Rizzoli.

Carson, R. (1962). *Silent Spring*. Boston: Houghton Mifflin.

Castells, M. (1977). *The Urban Question*. London: Edward Arnold.

Castillejo, D. (1981). *The Expanding Force in Newton's Cosmos*. Madrid: Ediciones de Arte y Bibliofilia.

Castoriadis, C. (1987). *The Imaginary Institution of Society* (K. Blamey, Trans.). Cambridge: Polity Press.

Caygill, H. (1993). "The return of Nietzsche and Marx." In P. Patton (Ed.), *Nietzsche, Feminism and Political Theory* (pp. 189–203). London: Routledge.

Châo, S. R. and Abramson, T. D. (Eds.). (1987). *Kohn Pedersen Fox: Buildings and Projects 1976–1986*. New York: Rizzoli.

Chernikhov, I. (1931). *The Construction of Architectural and Machine Forms*. Leningrad: The Leningrad Society of Architects. (Reprinted [1984] in *Architectural Design*, 54[9/10], 41–88)

Chodorow, N. (1978). *The Reproduction of Mothering*. Berkeley: University of California Press.

Clark, K., and Holquist, M. (1984). *Mikhail Bakhtin*. Cambridge, MA: Harvard University Press.

Code, L. B. (1981). "Is the sex of the knower epistemologically significant?" *Metaphilosophy*, 12(3/4), 267–276.

"Concours International pour le Parc de la Villette." (1983, February). *Architecture d'Aujourd'hui*, 225, 72–83; 227(June), 90–99.

Cooke, C. (1988a). "The lessons of the Russian avant-garde." *Architectural Design*, 58(3/4), 13–15.

Cooke, C. (1988b). "Russian Constructivism and the city." *UIA Journal*, 1(1), 16–25.

Cooke, C. (1989). "Russian precursors." In A. Papadakis, C. Cooke, and A.

Banjamin (Eds.), *Deconstruction Omnibus Volume* (pp. 11–19). New York: Rizzoli.

Cosgrove, D. (1984). *Social Formation and Symbolic Landscape*. London: Croom Helm.

Cosgrove, D., and Daniels, S. (1988). *The Iconography of Landscape*. Cambridge: Cambridge University Press.

Crimp, D. (1985). "On the museum's ruins." In H. Foster (Ed.), *Postmodern Culture* (pp. 43–56). London and Sydney: Pluto Press.

Dasmann, R. E. (1976a). "Toward a dynamic balance of man and nature." *The Ecologist*, 6, 2–5.

Dasmann, R. E. (1976b). "National parks, nature conservation and 'future primitive.' " *The Ecologist*, 6, 164–167.

Dear, M. J. (1986). "Postmodernism and planning." *Environment and Planning D: Society and Space*, 4, 367–384.

de Certeau, M. (1984). *The Practice of Everyday Life* (S. F. Rendall, Trans.). Berkeley and Los Angeles: University of California Press.

De Feo, V. (1963). *URSS Architettura 1917–1936*. Rome: Editori Riuniti.

Deleuze, G. (1983). *Nietzsche and Philosophy* (H. Tomlinson, Trans.). London: Athlone Press.

de Man, P. (1983). *Blindness and Insight*. London: Methuen.

Derrida, J. (1976). *Of Grammatology* (G. Spivak, Trans.). Baltimore: Johns Hopkins University Press.

Derrida, J. (1977). "Signature event context." *Glyph, 1*.

Derrida, J. (1978). *Writing and Difference* (A. Bass, Trans.). Chicago: University of Chicago Press.

Derrida, J. (1979). *Spurs: Nietzsche's Styles* (B. Harlow, Trans.). Chicago: University of Chicago Press.

Derrida, J. (1981a). *Dissemination* (B. Johnson, Trans.). Chicago: University of Chicago Press.

Derrida, J. (1981b). *Positions* (A. Bass, Trans.). Chicago: University of Chicago Press.

Derrida, J. (1982). *Margins of Philosophy* (A. Bass, Trans.). Chicago: University of Chicago Press.

Derrida, J. (1986a). *Glas*. (J. P. Leavey Jr. and R. Rand, Trans.). Lincoln, NE: University of Nebraska Press.

Derrida, J. (1986b). "Point de folie-maintenant l'architecture." *AA files, 12*, 65–75.

Derrida, J. (1986c). *Memoires for Paul de Man*. New York: Columbia University Press.

Derrida, J. (1988). "Why Peter Eisenman writes such good books." *Architecture and Urbanism* [Extra Edition: Peter Eisenman], August, 113–124.

Derrida, J. (1989a) "Fifty-two aphorisms for a foreword." In A. Papadakis, C. Cooke, and A. Benjamin (Eds.), *Deconstruction Omnibus Volume* (pp. 67–69). New York: Rizzoli.

Derrida, J. (1989b). "Jacques Derrida in discussion with Christopher Norris."

In A. Papadakis, C. Cooke, and A. Benjamin (Eds.), *Deconstruction Omnibus Volume* (pp. 71–75). New York: Rizzoli.

Derrida, J. (1989c). *Of Spirit: Heidegger and the Question.* (G. Bennington and R. Bowlby, Trans.). Chicago: Chicago University Press.

de Saussure, F. (1960). *Course in General Linguistics.* London: Peter Owen.

Deutsche, R. (1991). "Boys town." *Environment and Planning D: Society and Space, 9,* 5–30.

Diamond, I., and Orenstein, G. F. (Eds.). (1990). *Reweaving the World: The Emergence of Ecofeminism.* San Francisco: Sierra Club Books.

Dickens, P. G. (1979). "Marxism and architectural theory: A critique of recent work." *Environment and Planning B, 6,* 105–116.

Diprose, R. (1993). "Nietzsche and the pathos of distance." In P. Patton (Ed.), *Nietzsche, Feminism and Political Theory* (pp. 1–26). London: Routledge.

Dobbs, B. J. T. (1975). *The Foundations of Newton's Alchemy.* Cambridge: Cambridge University Press.

Doel, M. A. (1992). "In stalling deconstruction: Striking out the postmodern." *Environment and Planning D: Society and Space, 10,* 163–179.

Dreyfus, H. L. (1993). "Heidegger on the connection between nihilism, art, technology and politics." In C. Guignon (Ed.), *The Cambridge Companion to Heidegger* (pp. 289–316). Cambridge: Cambridge University Press.

Duncan, J., and Duncan, N. (1988). "(Re)reading the landscape." *Environment and Planning D: Society and Space, 6,* 117–126.

Economakis, R. (Ed.). (1992). *Leon Krier: Architecture and Urban Design 1967–1992.* London: Academy Editions.

Eisenman, P. (1971). "Meier's Smith House." *Architectural Design, 41*(8), 524.

Eisenman, P. (1981). "A poetics of the model: Eisenman's doubt." Interview with Peter Eisenman by David Shapiro and Lindsay Stamm. In *Idea as Model* (pp. 121–125). New York: Rizzoli.

Eisenman, P. (1986). *Moving Arrows, Eros and Other Errors: An Architecture of Absence.* London: The Architectural Association.

Eisenman, P. (1989). "An *Architectural Design* interview by Charles Jencks." In A. Papadakis, C. Cooke, and A. Benjamin (Eds.), *Deconstruction Omnibus Volume* (pp. 141–149). New York: Rizzoli.

Eisenman, P. (1994). "Three texts for Venice" and "The city of artificial excavation." In J.-F. Bédard (Ed.), *Cities of Artificial Excavation: The Work of Peter Eisenman, 1978–1988* (pp. 46–53, 72–81). New York: Rizzoli.

Eisenman, P., and Robertson, J. (1983). "Koch-Friedrichstrasse, Block 5." *Architectural Design, 53*(1/2), 91–93.

Engels, F. (1969). "The housing question." In *Selected Works* (Vol. 2). Moscow: Progress Publishers.

Farías, V. (1989). *Heidegger and Nazism* (J. Margolis and T. Rockmore, Eds., P. Burrell, Trans.). Philadelphia: Temple University Press.

Folch-Serra, M. (1990). "Place, voice, space: Mikhail Bakhtin's dialogical landscape." *Environment and Planning D: Society and Space, 8,* 255–274.

Forster, K. (1981). "Residues of a dream world." *Architectural Design, 51*(6/7), 69–72.

Foster, H. (1985). "Postmodernism: A preface." In H. Foster (Ed.), *Postmodern Culture* (pp. ix–xvi). London and Sydney: Pluto Press.

Foster, H. (1990). "Some uses and abuses of Russian Constructivism." In *Art into Life: Russian Constructivism, 1914–1932* (pp. 241–253). New York: Rizzoli.

Foucault, M. (1967). *Madness and Civilization: A History of Insanity in the Age of Reason.* Andover, UK: Tavistock.

Foucault, M. (1970). *The Order of Things: An Archaeology of the Human Sciences.* New York: Pantheon Books. (Original work published 1966)

Foucault, M. (1972). *The Archaeology of Knowledge* (A. M. Sheridan-Smith, Trans.). Andover, UK: Tavistock. (Original work published 1969)

Foucault, M. (1977). *Discipline and Punish: The Birth of the Prison* (A. Sheridan, Trans.). London: Allen Lane.

Foucault, M. (1978). *History of Sexuality: Vol 1. An Introduction* (R. Hurley, Trans.). New York: Pantheon Books.

Foucault, M. (1982). "Interview with Michel Foucault on space, knowledge and power." *Skyline*(March), 17–20.

Foucault, M. (1986). "Of other spaces" (J. Miskowiec, Trans.). *Diacritics, 16,* 22–27.

Fourier, C. (1822). *Traité de l'Association Domestique Agricole.* Paris.

Fourier, C. (1828). *Le Nouveau monde industriel.* Paris.

Fox, M. (1983). *Original Blessing: A Primer in Creation Spirituality.* Santa Fe: Bear and Company.

Fox, M. (1988). *The Coming of the Cosmic Christ.* New York: Harper and Row.

Frampton, K. (1982). "The isms of contemporary architecture." *Architectural Design, 52*(7/8), 60–84.

Frampton, K. (1985a). *Modern Architecture: A Critical History.* London: Thames and Hudson.

Frampton, K. (1985b). "Towards a critical regionalism: Six points for an architecture of resistance." In H. Foster (Ed.), *Postmodern Culture* (pp. 16–30). London and Sydney: Pluto Press.

Fraser, N. (1991). "What's critical about critical theory? The case of Habermas and gender." In M. L. Shanley and C. Pateman (Eds.), *Feminist Interpretations and Critical Theory* (pp. 254–276). Cambridge: Polity Press.

Fry, E. (1966). *Cubism.* London: Thames and Hudson.

Futagawa, Y. (Ed.). (1985). *Ricardo Bofill: Taller de Arquitectura* (Introduction by C. Norberg-Schulz). Tokyo: A.D.A. Edita.

Gallet, M. (1980). *Claude-Nicolas Ledoux 1736–1806.* Paris: Picard.

Garb, Y. J. (1990). "Perspective or escape? Ecofeminist musings on contemporary earth imagery." In I. Diamond and G. F. Orenstein (Eds.), *Reweaving the World: The Emergence of Ecofeminism* (pp. 264–278). San Francisco: Sierra Club Books.

Garnier, T. (1932). *Une cité industrielle: Etude pour la construction des villes* (2nd ed.). Paris: Editions Vincent, Fréal et Cie. (Original work published 1917)

Geltmaker, T. (1992). "The queer nation acts up: Health care, politics, and sexual diversity in the County of Angels." *Environment and Planning D: Society and Space, 10*, 609–650.

Giddens, A. (1979). *Central Problems in Social Theory: Action, Structure and Contradiction in Social Analysis*. London: Macmillan.

Giddens, A. (1981). *A Contemporary Critique of Historical Materialism: Volume 1. Power, Property and the State*. London: Macmillan.

Giddens, A. (1984). *The Constitution of Society: Outline of the Theory of Structuration*. Cambridge: Polity Press.

Giedion, S. (1928). *Bauen in Frankreich; Eisen, Eisenbeton*. Leipzig and Berlin: Klinkhardt and Biermann.

Giedion, S. (1954). *Space, Time and Architecture* (3rd ed.). Cambridge, MA: Harvard University Press. (Original work published 1941)

Gilligan, C. (1982). *In a Different Voice: Psychological Theory and Women's Development*. Cambridge, MA: Harvard University Press.

Gramsci, A. (1971). "Americanism and Fordism." In Q. Hoare and G. N. Smith (Ed. and Trans.), *Selections from the Prison Notebooks* (pp. 227–320). London: Lawrence and Wishart.

Grassi, G. (1967). *La Costruzione logica dell'architettura*. Padua.

Graves, R. (1779). *Columella, or the Distresed Anchoret* (Vols. 1 and 2). London.

Greenberg, A. C. (1979). *Artists and Revolution: Dada and the Bauhaus, 1917–1925*. Ann Arbor, MI: UMI Press.

Griffiths, J. (1989). "Deconstruction deconstructed." In A. Papadakis, C. Cooke, and A. Benjamin (Eds.), *Deconstruction Omnibus Volume* (pp. 93–97). New York: Rizzoli.

Grosz, E. (1989). *Sexual Subversions*. Sydney: Allen and Unwin.

Guignon, C. (1993). "Introduction." In C. Guignon (Ed.), *The Cambridge Companion to Heidegger* (pp. 1–41). Cambridge: Cambridge University Press.

Haar, M. (1992). "The play of Nietzsche in Derrida." In D. Wood (Ed.), *Derrida: A Critical Reader* (pp. 52–71). Oxford: Blackwell.

Habermas, J. (1971). *Toward a Rational Society: Student Protest, Science and Politics* (J. J. Shapiro, Trans.). London: Heinemann Educational Books.

Habermas, J. (1973). "Wahrheitstheorien." In H. Fahrenbach (Ed.), *Wirklichkeit und Reflexion: Walter Schulz zum 60. Geburtstag*. Pfullingen: Neske.

Habermas, J. (1976). *Legitimation Crisis* (T. McCarthy, Trans.). London: Heinemann Educational Books.

Habermas, J. (1979a). *Communication and the Evolution of Society* (T. McCarthy, Trans.). London: Heinemann Educational Books.

Habermas, J. (1979b). "Consciousness-raising or redemptive criticism: The contemporaneity of Walter Benjamin." *New German Critique, 17*(Spring).

Habermas, J. (1981). *Theorie des kommunikativen Handelns, II*. Frankfurt. [English version published 1987. *The Theory of Communicative Action: Lifeworld and System: A Critique of Functionalist Reason* (Vol. 2). (T. McCarthy, Trans.). Boston: Beacon Press.]

Habermas, J. (1984). *The Theory of Communicative Action: Volume 1. Reason* and the Rationalization of Society (T. McCarthy, Trans.). Cambridge: Polity Press.

Habermas, J. (1985a). "Questions and counterquestions." In R. J. Bernstein (Ed.), Habermas and Modernity (pp. 192–216). Cambridge: Polity Press.

Habermas, J. (1985b). "Modernity: An incomplete project." In H. Foster (Ed.), Postmodern Culture (pp. 3–15). London and Sydney: Pluto Press.

Habermas, J. (1985c). "Moderne und postmoderne Architektur." In Die Neue Unübersichtlichkeit. Frankfurt: Suhrkamp.

Habermas, J. (1985d). "Psychic thermidor and the rebirth of rebellious subjectivity." In R. J. Bernstein (Ed.), Habermas and Modernity (pp. 67–77). Cambridge: Polity Press.

Habermas, J. (1987). The Philosophical Discourse of Modernity: Twelve Lectures (F. Lawrence, Trans.). Cambridge: Polity Press.

Hartsock, N. (1987). "Rethinking modernism: Minority vs. majority theories." Cultural Critique, 7, 187–206.

Harvey, D. (1973). Social Justice and the City. London: Edward Arnold.

Harvey, D. (1978). "The urban process under capitalism: A framework for analysis." International Journal of Urban and Regional Research, 2, 101–131.

Harvey, D. (1979). "Monument and myth." Annals of the Association of American Geographers, 69, 362–381.

Harvey, D. (1989). The Condition of Postmodernity: An Enquiry into the Origins of Cultural Change. Oxford: Basil Blackwell.

Hayden, D. (1984). Redesigning the American Dream. Ontario: General Publishing.

Heller, A., and Fehér, F. (Eds.). (1986). Reconstructing Aesthetics: Writings of the Budapest School. Oxford: Basil Blackwell.

Hillier, B., and Hanson, J. (1984). The Social Logic of Space. Cambridge: Cambridge University Press.

Heidegger, M. (1959). An Introduction to Metaphysics (R. Manheim, Trans.). New Haven, CT: Yale University Press.

Heidegger, M. (1962). Being and Time (J. Macquarrie and E. Robinson, Trans.). New York: Harper and Row.

Heidegger, M. (1966). Discourse on Thinking (J. M. Anderson and E. H. Freund, Trans.). New York: Harper and Row. (Original work published 1959)

Heidegger, M. (1967). Wegmarken. Frankfurt: Klostermann.

Heidegger, M. (1971a). Poetry, Language, Thought (A. Hofstadter, Trans.). New York: Harper and Row.

Heidegger, M. (1971b). On the Way to Language (P. D. Hertz, Trans.). New York: Harper and Row.

Heidegger, M. (1977). "The age of the world picture." In The Question Concerning Technology (W. Lovitt, Trans.). New York: Harper and Row.

Heidegger, M. (1989). Gesamtausgabe: Vol. 65. Beitrge zur Philosophie (Vom Ereignis) (1936–1938) (F.-W. von Herrmann, Ed.). Frankfurt: Klostermann.

Hollier, D. (1989). Against Architecture: The Writings of Georges Bataille (B. Wing, Trans.). Cambridge, MA: MIT Press.

Hollingdale, R. J. (1961). "Introduction." In F. Nietzsche, *Thus Spoke Zarathustra* (R. J. Hollingdale, Trans.) (pp. 9–36). Harmondsworth, England: Penguin.

Holquist, M., and Emerson, C. (1981). "Glossary." In M. Holquist (Ed.), *The Dialogic Imagination: Four Essays by M. M. Bakhtin* (C. Emerson and M. Holquist, Trans.). Austin: University of Texas Press.

Horkheimer, M., and Adorno, T. (1972). *Dialectic of Enlightenment* (J. Cumming, Trans.). New York: Herder and Herder.

Huyghe, R. (1962). *Art and the Spirit of Man*. London: Thames and Hudson.

Irigaray, L. (1991). *Marine Lover of Friedrich Nietzsche* (G. C. Gill, Trans.). New York: Columbia University Press.

Ivanov, V. V. (1974). "The significance of M. M. Bakhtin's ideas on sign, utterance, and dialogue for modern semiotics." In H. Baran (Ed.), *Semiotics and Structuralism: Readings from the Soviet Union*. White Plains, NY: International Arts and Sciences Press.

Jacobs, J. (1964). *The Death and Life of Great American Cities*. Harmondsworth, England: Penguin. (Original work published 1961)

Jameson, F. (1984). "Postmodernism, or the cultural logic of late capitalism." *New Left Review, 146*, 53–92.

Jameson, F. (1985). "Postmodernism and consumer society." In H. Foster (Ed.), *Postmodern Culture* (pp. 111–125). Sydney and London: Pluto Press.

Jay, M. (1985). "Habermas and modernism." In R. J. Bernstein (Ed.), *Habermas and Modernity* (pp. 125–139). Cambridge: Polity Press.

Jencks, C. (1983). "The perennial architectural debate." *Architectural Design, 53*(7/8), 4–22.

Jencks, C. (1985). *Towards a Symbolic Architecture: The Thematic House*. London: Academy Editions.

Jencks, C. (1987a). *Le Corbusier and the Tragic View of Architecture*. Harmondsworth, England: Penguin.

Jencks, C. (1987b). *The Language of Post-Modern Architecture* (5th ed.). London: Academy Editions. (Original work published 1977)

Jencks, C. (1988a). "Deconstruction: The pleasures of absence." *Architectural Design, 58*(3/4), 17–31.

Jencks, C. (1988b). *Architecture Today*. London: Academy Editions.

Johnson, E. J. (Ed). (1986). *Charles Moore: Buildings and Projects 1949–1986*. New York: Rizzoli.

Kant, I. (1956). *Critique of Practical Reason* (L. W. Beck, Trans.). Indianapolis: Bobbs-Merrill.

Kant, I. (1965). *Critique of Pure Reason* (N. K. Smith, Trans.). New York: St Martin's Press.

Kant, I. (1974). *Critique of Judgement* (J. H. Bernard, Trans.). New York: Hafner.

Khan-Magomedov, S. O. (1983). *Pioneers of Soviet Architecture: the Search for New Solutions in the 1920s and 1930s*. New York: Rizzoli.

Khan-Magomedov, S. O. (1986). *Rodchenko: The Complete Work*. London: Thames and Hudson.

King, R. J. (1987). "Monopoly rent, residential differentiation and the second global crisis of capitalism: The case of Melbourne." *Progress in Planning*, 28(3), 195–298.

King, R. J. (1988). "Urban design in capitalist society." *Environment and Planning D: Society and Space*, 6, 445–474.

Klee, P. (1961). *The Thinking Eye: The Notebooks of Paul Klee* (J. Spiller, Ed.; R. Mannheim, Trans.). London.

Knesl, J. A. (1984). "The powers of architecture." *Environment and Planning D: Society and Space*, 2, 3–22.

Knoespel, K. (1989). "The mythological transformations of Renaissance science: Physical allegory and the crisis of alchemical narrative." In F. Amrine (Ed.), *Literature and Science as Modes of Expression* (pp. 99–112). Dordrecht: Kluwer Academic Publishers.

Knox, P. (1991). "The restless urban landscape: Economic and sociocultural change and the transformation of Metropolitan Washington, D.C." *Annals of the Association of American Geographers*, 8(12), 181–209.

Kopp, A. (1970). *Town and Revolution: Soviet Architecture and City Planning 1917–1935* (T. E. Burton, Trans.). London: Thames and Hudson.

Kopp, A. (1985). *Constructivist Architecture in the USSR* (S. de Vallée, Trans.). London: Academy Editions.

Kostelanetz, R. (Ed.). (1978). *Esthetics Contemporary*. Buffalo, NY: Prometheus.

Koukoutsi, V. E. (1989). *Residences Secondaires: How Eisenman Houses Fictive Structures of History*. Unpublished master's thesis, Department of Architecture, Massachusetts Institute of Technology, Cambridge, MA.

Krier, L. (1979). "The cities within a city: Luxembourg." *Architectural Design*, 49(1), 19–32.

Krier, L. (1984). "Urban components." *Architectural Design*, 54(7/8), 42–49.

Krier, L. (1988). "Atlantis, Tenerife." *Architectural Design*, 58(1/2), 57–64.

Krier, L., and Vidler, A. (1978). *Rational Architecture: The Reconstruction of the European City*. Brussels: Archives d'Architecture Moderne.

Krier, R. (1979). *Urban Space*. London: Academy Editions.

Kroc, R. (with Anderson, R.) (1977). *Grinding it Out: The Making of McDonald's*. Chicago: Henry Regnery Co.

Lakoff, R. (1975). *Language and Women's Place*. New York: Harper and Row.

Lampugnani, V. M. (Ed.). (1986). *The Thames and Hudson Encyclopaedia of 20th Century Architecture* (B. Bergdoll, Trans.). London: Thames and Hudson. (Original work published 1963)

Lane, B. (1985). *Architecture and Politics in Germany, 1918–1945*. Cambridge, MA: Harvard University Press.

Lash, S., and Urry, J. (1987). *The End of Organized Capitalism*. Cambridge: Polity Press.

Le Corbusier (1925). *Urbanisme*. Paris: Crès.

Le Corbusier (1933). *La Ville radieuse*. Paris: Editions Vincent, Fréal et Cie.

Le Corbusier (1959). *Towards a New Architecture* (F. Etchells, Trans.). London: The Architectural Press. (Original French edition, 1923; original English edition, 1927)

Le Corbusier, 1910–1960. (1960). Zurich: Editions Girsberger.

Le Corbusier et Pierre Jeanneret: Oeuvre complète 1910–1929. (1935). Zurich: W. Boesiger et O. Stonorov.

Ledoux, C.-N. (1804). *L'Architecture considérée sous le rapport de l'art, des moeurs et de la législation*. Paris. (Reprinted in *Architecture de C.-N. Ledoux*, London: Architectural Press, 1983)

Lefebvre, H. (1970). *La Révolution urbaine*. Paris: Gallimard.

Lefebvre, H. (1974). *La Production de l'espace*. Paris.

Lefebvre, H. (1976). *The Survival of Capitalism*. London: Allison and Busby.

Lenin, V. I. (1982). "Better less, but better." In L. A. Zhadova (Ed.), *Malevich: Suprematism and Revolution in Russian Art, 1910–1930* (p. 89). London: Thames and Hudson.

Leventure, A. (with T. Keenan). (1992). "A bibliography of the works of Jacques Derrida." In D. Wood (Ed.), *Derrida: A Critical Reader* (pp. 247–289). Oxford: Blackwell.

Lipietz, A. (1982, March–April). "Towards a global Fordism." *New Left Review, 132*, 33–47.

Lissitzky, L. M. (1930). *Russland: die Rekonstruktion der Architektur in der Sowjetunion*. Vienna: Schroll.

Lissitzky-Kuppers, S. (1967). *El Lissitzky: Life. Letters. Texts* (H. Aldwinckle, Trans.). London: Thames and Hudson.

Llewelyn, J. (1992). "Responsibility with indecidability." In D. Wood (Ed.), *Derrida: A Critical Reader* (pp. 72–96). Oxford: Blackwell.

Lodder, C. (1983a). *Russian Constructivism*. New Haven and London: Yale University Press.

Lodder, C. (1983b). "The Costakis collection: New Insights into the Russian avante-garde." *Architectural Design, 53*(5/6), 14–33.

Lotman, Y. M. (1988). "Text within a text." *Soviet Psychology, 26*(3), 32–51.

Lukács, G. (1971). *History and Class Consciousness*. London: Merlin Press.

"Luxembourg, the new European quarters, 1978." *Architectural Design, 54*(7/8), 81–85.

Lyotard, J.-F. (1978). "One of the things at stake in women's struggles." *Substance, 20*.

Lyotard, J.-F. (1984). *The Postmodern Condition: A Report on Knowledge* (G. Bennington and B. Massumi, Trans.). Manchester: Manchester University Press.

Macleod, R. (1971). *Style and Society: Architectural Ideology in Britain, 1835–1914*. London: RIBA.

Makkreel, R. A. (1990). "Kant and the interpretation of nature and history." In M. Kelly (Ed.), *Hermeneutics and Critical Theory in Ethics and Politics* (pp. 169–181). Cambridge, MA: MIT Press.

Malevich, K. (1928). In *Sovremannaia Arkhitectura, 5*.

Malevich, K. (1982). "UNOVIS—The champions of the new art." In L. A. Zhadova, *Malevich: Suprematism and Revolution in Russian Art, 1910–1930* (p. 297). London: Thames and Hudson. (Original work published 1920)

March, L. (1981). "An architect in search of democracy: Broadacre City." In H. A. Brooks (Ed.), *Writings on Wright: Selected Comment on Frank Lloyd Wright* (pp. 195–206). Cambridge MA: MIT Press.

Marx, K. (1970). *A Contribution to the Critique of Political Economy* (M. Dobb, Ed.). New York: International Publishers.

Marx, K. (1976). *Capital* (Vol. 1). Harmondsworth, England: Penguin.

Marx, K., and Engels, F. (1952). *The Communist Manifesto*. Moscow: Progress Publishers.

Marx, K., and Engels, F. (1965). *The German Ideology*. London: Lawrence and Wishart.

Massey, D. (1991). "Flexible sexism." *Environment and Planning D: Society and Space, 9*, 31–57.

McCarthy, T. (1985). "Reflections on rationalization in *The Theory of Communicative Action.*" In R. J. Bernstein (Ed.), *Habermas and Modernity* (pp. 176–199). Cambridge: Polity Press.

McCarthy, T. (1990). "The politics of the ineffable: Derrida's Deconstruction." In M. Kelly (Ed.), *Hermenentics and Critical Theory in Ethics and Politics* (pp. 146–168). Cambridge, MA: MIT Press.

McHarg, I. (1969). *Design with Nature*. Garden City, NY: Doubleday.

McLuhan, M. (1967). *The Medium is the Massage: An Inventory of Effects*. New York: Bantam Books.

Megill, A. (1985). *Prophets of Extremity: Nietzsche, Heidegger, Foucault, Derrida*. Berkeley and Los Angeles: University of California Press.

Michell, J., and Rhone, C. (1991). *Twelve-tribe Nations and the Science of Enchanting the Landscape*. London: Thames and Hudson.

Miller, C., and Swift, K. (1977). *Words and Women*. Garden City, NY: Doubleday Anchor Books.

Miller, J. H. (1977). "The critic as host." *Critical Inquiry, 3*.

Mitchell, S. (1977). "Introduction." In W. Benjamin, *Understanding Brecht* (A. Bostock, Trans.). London: New Left Books.

Moore, C., and Allen, G. (1976). *Dimensions: Space, Shape and Scale in Architecture*. New York: Architectural Record Books.

Mulvey, L. (1989). "Visual pleasure and narrative cinema." In *Visual and Other Pleasures*. Bloomington: Indiana University Press.

Mumford, L. (1961). *The City in History: Its Origins, Its Transformations, and Its Prospects*. London: Secker and Warburg.

Nietzsche, F. (1961). *Thus Spoke Zarathustra* (R. J. Hollingdale, Trans.). Harmondsworth, England: Penguin.

Nietzsche, F. (1968a). *The Will to Power* (W. Kaufmann, Trans.). New York: Vintage.

Nietzsche, F. (1968b). *Twilight of the Idols* and *The Anti-Christ* (R. J. Hollingdale, Trans.). Harmondsworth, England: Penguin.

Nietzsche, F. (1969). *Ecce Homo* (W. Kaufmann, Trans.). New York: Vintage.

Nietzsche, F. (1972). *Beyond Good and Evil* (R. J. Hollingdale, Trans.). Harmondsworth, England: Penguin.

Nietzsche, F. (1974). *The Gay Science* (W. Kaufmann, Trans.). New York: Vintage.

Norris, C. (1991). "Editor's foreword." In R. C. Holub, *Jürgen Habermas: Critic in the Public Sphere* (pp. vii–x). London: Routledge.

Norris, C. (1992). "Deconstruction, postmodernism and philosophy: Habermas on Derrida." In D. Wood (Ed.), *Derrida: A Critical Reader* (pp. 167–192). Oxford: Blackwell.

Offe, C. (1985). *Disorganized Capitalism: Contemporary Transformations of Work and Politics.* (J. Keane, Ed. and Trans.). Cambridge: Polity Press.

Okhitovich, M. (1929). "K probleme goroda" [On the problem of the city]. *Sovremennaia Arkhitektura, 4,* 130–134.

Oppel, F. (1993). " 'Speaking of immemorial waters': Irigaray with Nietzsche." In P. Patton (Ed.), *Nietzsche, Feminism and Political Theory* (pp. 88–109). London: Routledge.

"The OSU Center for the Visual Arts, Columbus, Ohio, 1985." *Architectural Design, 55*(1/2), 44–47.

Owens, C. (1985). "The discourse of others: Feminism and postmodernism." In H. Foster (Ed.), *Postmodern Culture* (pp. 57–82). London and Sydney: Pluto Press.

Papadakis, A., Cooke, C., and Benjamin, A. (Eds.). (1989). *Deconstruction Omnibus Volume.* New York: Rizzoli.

Papademetriou, P. (1971). "Le Corbusier à la mode." *Architectural Design, 41*(1), 24.

Peter Eisenman Houses of Cards. (1987). [With critical essays by P. Eisenman, R. Krauss, and M. Tafuri.] New York and Oxford: Oxford University Press.

Pevsner, N. (1963). *An Outline of European Architecture.* Harmondsworth, England: Penguin.

Philo, C. (1992). "Foucault's geography." *Environment and Planning D: Society and Space, 10,* 137–161.

Pia, P. (1961). *Baudelaire* (P. Gregory, Trans). London: Evergreen Books.

Poggioli, R. (1968). *The Theory of the Avant-Garde* (G. Fitzgerald, Trans.). Cambridge, MA: Belknap Press.

Pollock, G. (1988). *Vision and Difference: Femininity, Feminism and Histories of Art.* Andover, UK: Routledge, Chapman and Hall.

Porphyrios, D. (1982). "Classicism is not a style." *Architectural Design, 52*(5/6), 51–57.

Pratt, G., and Hanson, S. (1988) "Gender, class and space." *Environment and Planning D: Society and Space, 6,* 15–35.

Pugh, S. (1990). "Loitering with intent: From Arcadia to the arcades." In S. Pugh (Ed.), *Reading Landscape: Country-City-Capital* (pp. 145–159). Manchester and New York: Manchester University Press.

Quonian, S. (1988). "A painter, geographer of Arizona." *Environment and Planning D: Society and Space,6,* 3–14.

Raban, J. (1974). *Soft City.* London: Hamish Hamilton.

Relph, E. (1976). *Place and Placelessness.* London: Pion.

Richter, H. (1965). *Dada: Art and Anti-art.* London: Thames and Hudson.

Ricoeur, P. (1965). "Universal civilization and national cultures." In *History and Truth.* Evanston IL: Northwestern University Press.

Ricoeur, P. (1974). "Existence and hermeneutics." In *The Conflict of Interpretations.* Evanston IL: Northwestern University Press.

Rifkin, J. (1987). *Time Wars: The Primary Conflict of Human History.* New York: Simon and Schuster.

Ronner, H., and Jhaveri, S. (Eds.). (1987). *Louis I. Kahn: Complete Works 1935–1974*. Basel and Boston: Birkhäuser.

Rorty, R. (1985). "Habermas and Lyotard on Postmodernity." In R. J. Bernstein (Ed.), *Habermas and Modernity* (pp. 161–175). Cambridge: Polity Press.

Rorty, R. (1986, July 24). "The contingency of community." *London Review of Books*, 10–14.

Rose, D. (1984). "Rethinking gentrification: Beyond the uneven development of Marxist urban theory." *Environment and Planning D: Society and Space*, 2, 47–54.

Rose, M. (1984). *Marx's Lost Aesthetic: Karl Marx and the Visual Arts*. Cambridge: Cambridge University Press.

Rose, M. (1986). "Habermas and Postmodern Architecture." *Australian Journal of Art*, 5, 113–119.

Rose, M. (1991). *The Post-Modern and the Post-Industrial: A Critical Analysis*. Cambridge: Cambridge University Press.

Rosenau, H. (1976). *Boullée and Visionary Architecture*. London: Academy Editions.

Rossi, A. (1982). *The Architecture of the City* (D. Ghirardo and J. Ockman, Trans.). Cambridge MA: MIT Press. (Italian edition published 1966)

Rowe, C., and Koetter, F. (1978). *Collage City*. Cambridge, MA: MIT Press.

Rowland, B. Jr. (1965). *Art in East and West*. Cambridge, MA: Harvard University Press.

Rubin, B. (1979). "Aesthetic ideology and urban design." *Annals of the Association of American Geographers*, 69(3), 339–361.

Said, E. W. (1985). "Opponents, audiences, constituencies and community." In H. Foster (Ed.), *Postmodern Culture* (pp. 135–159). London and Sydney: Pluto Press.

Sassen, G. (1980). "Success anxiety in women: A constructivist interpretation of its sources and its significance." *Harvard Educational Review*, 50, 13–25.

Scheerbart, P. (1914). *Glasarchitektur*. Berlin.

Scholem, G. (1982). *Water Benjamin: The Story of a Friendship* (K. Ready and G. Smith, Eds.). London: Faber and Faber.

Schutte, O. (1984). *Beyond Nihilism: Nietzsche without Masks*. Chicago: University of Chicago Press.

Sculpture in the Environment. (1980). *SITE: Architecture as Art*. London: Academy Editions.

Sharp, D. (1966). *Modern Architecture and Expressionism*. London: Longman Green.

Sheehan, T. (1993). "Reading a life: Heidegger and hard times." In C. Guignon (Ed.), *The Cambridge Companion to Heidegger* (pp. 70–96). Cambridge: Cambridge University Press.

Shepard, P. (1967). *Man in the Landscape*. New York: Ballantine Books.

Shepard, P. (1973). *The Tender Carnivore and the Sacred Game*. New York: Scribner.

Smith, N. K. (1981). "The domestic architecture of Frank Lloyd Wright." In

H. A. Brooks (Ed.), Writings on Wright: Selected Comment on Frank Lloyd Wright (pp. 189–193). Cambridge, MA: MIT Press.

Solomon, B. S. (1988). Green Architecture and the Agrarian Garden. New York: Rizzoli.

Soja, E. (1989). Postmodern Geographies. New York: Verso.

Speer, A. (1970). Inside the Third Reich. New York: Avon Books.

Suleiman, S. R. (Ed.). (1986). The Female Body in Western Culture: Contemporary Perspectives. Cambridge, MA: Harvard University Press.

Tafuri, M. (1976). Architecture and Utopia: Design and Capitalist Development. Cambridge, MA: MIT Press.

Tafuri, M. (1987). The Sphere and the Labyrinth: Avant-Gardes and Architecture from Piranesi to the 1970s (P. d'Acierno and R. Connolly, Trans.). Cambridge, MA: MIT Press.

Tafuri, M., and Dal Co, F. (1986). Modern Architecture (Vols. 1 and 2) (R. E. Wolf, Trans.). London: Faber and Faber.

Taut, B. (1919). Die Stadtkrne. Jena: Diederichs.

Taylor, C. (1985). Human Agency and Language: Philosophical Papers 1. New York: Cambridge University Press.

Taylor, C. (1989). Sources of the Self: The Making of the Modern Identity. Cambridge, MA: Harvard University Press.

Taylor, C. (1993). "Engaged agency and background in Heidegger." In C. Guignon (Ed.), The Cambridge Companion to Heidegger (pp. 317–336). Cambridge: Cambridge University Press.

Taylor, R. R. (1974). The Word in Stone: The Role of Architecture in National Socialist Ideology. Berkeley: University of California Press.

Thompson, J. B. (1981). Critical Hermeneutics: A Study of the Thought of Paul Ricoeur and Jürgen Habermas. Cambridge: Cambridge University Press.

Timms, D. W. G. (1971). The Urban Mosaic: Towards a Theory of Residential Differentiation. Cambridge: Cambridge University Press.

Touraine, A. (1974). The Post-Industrial Society: Tomorrow's Social History— Classes, Conflicts and Culture in the Programmed Society (L. Mayhew, Trans.). London: Wildwood House. (French edition published 1969).

Tschumi, B. (1981). "The Manhattan Transcripts." Architectural Design [Special Profile]. London: Academy Editions.

Tschumi, B. (1986). "La case vide." AA Folio, 8.

Tschumi, B. (1988). "Parc de la Villette, Paris." Architectural Design, 58(3/4), 33–39.

Ulmer, G. L. (1985). "The object of post-criticism." In H. Foster (Ed.), Postmodern Culture (pp. 83–110). London and Sydney: Pluto Press.

Vale, L. J. (1992). Architecture, Power and National Identity. New Haven: Yale University Press.

Vasseleu, C. (1993). "Not drowning, sailing: Women and the artist's craft in Nietzsche." In P. Patton (Ed.), Nietzsche, Feminism and Political Theory (pp. 71–87). London: Routledge.

Vattimo, G. (1985). La fine della modernita: Nichilismo ed ermeneutica nella cultura post-moderna. Milan: Aldo Garzanti.

Venturi, R. (1966). *Complexity and Contradiction in Architecture*. New York: The Museum of Modern Art.

Venturi, R., Scott-Brown, D., and Izenour, S. (1972). *Learning from Las Vegas*. Cambridge, MA: MIT Press.

Vidler, A. (1987). *The Writing of the Walls: Architectural Theory in the Late Enlightenment*. Princeton, NJ: Princeton Architectural Press.

Voloshinov, V. N. (1973). *Marxism and the Philosophy of Language* (L. Matejka and I. R. Titunik, Trans.). New York: Seminar Press. (Original work published 1929)

Walker, R. A. (1981). "A theory of suburbanization: Capitalism and the construction of urban space in the United States." In M. J. Dear and A. J. Scott (Eds.), *Urbanization and Urban Planning in Capitalist Society* (pp. 383–429). New York: Methuen.

Warde, A. (1991). "Gentrification as consumption: Issues of class and gender." *Environment and Planning D: Society and Space*, 9, 223–232.

Warren, K. J. (1987). "Feminism and ecology: Making connections." *Environmental Ethics*, 9, 3–20.

Waugh, P. (1989). *Feminine Fictions*. Andover, UK: Routledge, Chapman and Hall.

Weber, M. (1958). *The City* (D. Martindale and G. Neuwirth, Trans.). New York: The Free Press.

Weller, R. (1989). "Is it landscape architecture? A review of some recent international design competitions." *Landscape Australia*, 11(4), 358–363.

Wellmer, A. (1985). "Reason, utopia, and the *Dialectic of Enlightenment*." In R. J. Bernstein (Ed.), *Habermas and Modernity* (pp. 35–66). Cambridge: Polity Press.

Wertsch, J. V. (1985). *Vygotsky and the Social Formation of Mind*. Cambridge, MA: Harvard University Press.

Wertsch, J. V. (1991). *Voices of the Mind: A Sociocultural Approach to Mediated Action*. Cambridge, MA: Harvard University Press.

Westfall, R. (1984). "Newton and alchemy." In B. Vickers (Ed.), *Occult and Scientific Mentalities in the Renaissance* (pp. 315–335). Cambridge: Cambridge University Press.

Wheeler, K. V., Arnell, P., and Bickford, T. (Eds.). (1983). *Michael Graves Buildings and Projects 1966–1981*. London: The Architectural Press.

Whiteman, J. (1986). "Site unseen: Notes on architecture and the concept of fiction" (Review of P. Eisenman, *Moving Arrows, Eros and other Errors*). *AA files*, 12(Summer), 76–84.

Wiebenson, D. (1969). *Tony Garnier: The Cité Industrielle*. London: Studio Vista.

Willett, J. (1978). *The New Sobriety, 1917–1933: Art and Politics in the Weimar Period*. London: Thames and Hudson.

Wilson, P. (1983). "The park and the peak—Two international competitions." *AA Files*, 4(July), 76–87.

Winchester, H. P. M., and White, P. E. (1988). "The location of marginalised groups in the inner city." *Environment and Planning D: Society and Space*, 6, 37–54.

Wittgenstein, L. (1972). *Philosophical Investigations* (G. E. M. Anscombe, Trans.). Oxford: Basil Blackwell and Mott.

Wood, D. (1992). "Reading Derrida: An Introduction." In D. Wood (Ed.), *Derrida: A Critical Reader* (pp. 1–4). Oxford: Blackwell.

Wood, D. (Ed.). (1993). *Of Derrida, Heidegger, and Spirit.* Evanston, IL: Northwestern University Press.

Wright, F. L. (1910). *Frank Lloyd Wright, ausgefuhrte Bauten und Entwurfe.* Berlin: Ernst Wasmuth.

Wright, F. L. (1911). *Frank Lloyd Wright (Chicago).* Berlin: Ernst Wasmuth.

Young, M. (1988). *The Metronomic Society.* London: Thames and Hudson.

Zhadova, L. A. (1982). *Malevich: Suprematism and Revolution in Russian Art 1910–1930.* London: Thames and Hudson.

Zimmerman, M. E. (1990). *Heidegger's Confrontation with Modernity: Technology, Politics and Art.* Bloomington: Indiana University Press.

Zimmerman, M. E. (1993). "Heidegger, Buddhism, and deep ecology." In *The Cambridge Companion to Heidegger* (pp. 240–269). Cambridge: Cambridge University Press.

Zola, E. (1976). "Les Squares." In R. Ripoll (Ed.), *Contes et nouvelles.* Paris: Gallimard.

Zucker, P. (Ed.). (1945). *New Architecture and City Planning.* Salem, NH: Arno.

Zucker, P. (1959). *Town and Square: From the Agora to the Village Green.* New York: Columbia University Press.

Zukowsky, J. (Ed.). (1986). *Mies Reconsidered: His Career, Legacy and Disciples.* Chicago: The Art Institute of Chicago.

Zygas, K. P. (1981). *Form Follows Form: Source Imagery of Constructivist Architecture 1917–1925.* Ann Arbor, MI: UMI Research Press.

Index